TREATING ADOLESCENT SUBSTANCE ABUSE USING FAMILY BEHAVIOR THERAPY

A STEP-BY-STEP APPROACH

BRAD DONOHUE
NATHAN AZRIN

WILEY

John Wiley & Sons. Inc.

This book is printed on acid-free paper. ∞

Library of Congress Cataloging-in-Publication Data:
Donohue, Brad.
    Treating adolescent substance abuse using family behavior therapy : A step-by-step approach / Brad Donohue, Nathan Azrin.
      p. ; cm.
    Includes bibliographical references and index.
     ISBN 978-0-470-62192-9 (alk. paper : paper/cd-rom); 978-1-118-16395-5 (eMobi); 978-1-118-16394-8 (ePub); 978-1-118-16393-1 (ePDF)
      1. Teenagers—Substance use—Treatment.   2. Substance abuse—Treatment.   3. Family psychotherapy.   4. Behavior therapy.   I. Azrin, Nathan H., 1930- II. Title.
    [DNLM: 1. Adolescent. 2. Substance-Related Disorders—therapy. 3. Behavior Therapy. 4. Family Therapy. WM 270]
    RJ506.D78D66 2012
    362.29'18—dc23
                                              2011025465

Printed in the United States of America

10 9 8 7 6 5 4 3 2 1

Contents

Foreword

This comprehensive clinical specification of Family Behavior Therapy (FBT) for substance-abusing adolescents has the potential to make a substantive contribution to the public health and has been long awaited. Adolescent substance abuse leads to many serious short- and long-term deleterious outcomes for the youths, their families, and society. Although federal entities such as the National Institute on Drug Abuse have devoted considerable resources to the development and validation of effective treatments for adolescent substance abuse, the gap between science and practice remains very wide.

The most promising treatments for adolescent substance abuse have not been widely transported among substance abuse treatment providers, and the vast majority of substance abuse treatment services provided in community settings have not demonstrated effectiveness. Thus, a clear need exists for greater availability of effective substance abuse treatments to community providers.

FBT is as an efficient option for treating adolescent substance abuse. In part, this prospective is based on the promising results from FBT clinical trials and the demonstrated effectiveness of the adult counterpart on which FBT is derived (i.e., the Community Reinforcement Approach). The potential, however, is also based on the intensive emphasis that FBT devotes to engaging caregivers in the treatment of their adolescents. Decades of correlational, longitudinal, and experimental (i.e., clinical trials) research have shown the central roles that caregivers play in the development, maintenance, and attenuation of serious antisocial behavior in adolescents; and FBT leverages this knowledge throughout its intervention protocols.

Perhaps the clearest way to substantiate my very favorable view of FBT is to enumerate the many strengths of the model as presented in this book:

> The authors intentionally specified FBT in ways that should make it relatively easy to learn and implement. For example, session guidelines, therapist checklists, and useful forms are provided to guide implementation.

> Multiple options are available for training in FBT, including self-instruction, workshops provided by FBT experts, and ongoing clinical consultation.

> The intervention protocols draw on the long and successful traditions of the behavioral therapies (e.g., contingency management) and cognitive behavioral therapies (e.g., problem-solving skill training, communication training).

> Research has shown that high treatment fidelity is often essential to achieving favorable clinical outcomes in the implementation of evidence-based treatments. This book provides session checklists that enable therapists to assess their fidelity to FBT implementation standards after every session.

> The authors encourage and provide methods for assessing consumer satisfaction, a rarity in even the evidence-based practice community.

> The authors also encourage the assessment of key clinical outcomes, using validated self-report and biological (i.e., urine drug screens) measures. Such outcome monitoring can verify the direction of treatment or suggest that other strategies used in FBT be considered.

> The clinical style of FBT is extremely positive and strength focused, with a clear emphasis on engaging youths and caregivers in treatment. For example, strategies are provided for changing in-session conflict into constructive problem solving, and each session is structured to positive aspects of family relations and treatment progress.

> Therapists are given pragmatic, easy-to-understand tools to address treatment noncompliance, in-session conflict, and lack of productivity. Such problems emerge in almost every clinical case and can derail treatment gains if not addressed satisfactorily.

> The proscribed interventions are direct and efficient, yet very positive. Moreover, motivational interviewing-like strategies are specified to address issues that might not respond to more directive efforts. In short, the book provides an engaging balance of approaches that provide the

flexibility needed to address a range of presenting problems, challenges, and family contexts.

➤ The contingency management intervention described in the book is especially well conceived—evidence of the extensive experience that the authors have in implementing this approach with families and teaching the model to clinicians.

➤ Importantly, to promote sustainability and ecological validity, the family generates and provides the contingencies for the adolescent in the FBT contingency management intervention. This approach contrasts favorably with many other contingency management interventions in the field where contingencies (e.g., vouchers) are provided by the treatment program.

➤ The structure of the FBT program is logical and flexible. Certain universal interventions are provided to all youths and families (e.g., motivational interventions), but the sequence of subsequent interventions is determined by family members. Such flexibility is consistent with family empowerment.

➤ It bears repeating: FBT promotes positive interactions among family members and between the clinician and family members from beginning (e.g., every session starts by reviewing positive outcomes) to end (e.g., the final session celebrates clinical progress).

In conclusion, Drs. Donohue and Azrin have done an outstanding job of putting onto paper the intricacies of their exemplary FBT approach. As noted earlier, this is an extremely positive and strength-focused text that provides therapists with a structure and the tools to implement interventions that have a long history of promoting the types of clinical changes desired by family members and community stakeholders.

SCOTT W. HENGGELER, PhD
Professor, Department of Psychiatry and Behavioral Sciences
Director, Family Services Research Center
Medical University of South Carolina
April 29, 2011

Preface

In 2006, the Program Review Manager for the Substance Abuse and Mental Health Services Administration's (SAMHSA's) National Registry of Evidence-Based Programs and Practices (NREPP), Stephen Gardner, invited Nate and me to complete an application to have FBT listed as an evidence-based treatment (EBT) in their newly formulated National Registry of Evidence-Based Programs and Practices (NREPP). Stephen explained that community agencies were experiencing difficulties adopting EBTs, and NREPP was being developed to assist in identifying best programs and practices. After our application was successfully reviewed, we were immediately inundated with calls and emails from mental health administrators who were interested in FBT training. Many queried if we had developed self-study methods to assist them in affordably learning the nuts and bolts of FBT. At that time we didn't have much in the way of dissemination materials such as books, videos depicting FBT implementation, interactive web sites, and so on. We did, however, have carefully developed prompting checklists depicting the step-by-step procedures involved in conducting FBT (i.e., "cheat sheets"). Our treatment providers (TPs) had used these checklists during therapy sessions in our clinical trials to prompt specific intervention procedures. We were initially hesitant to introduce them to TPs in the community because our research team hadn't tested our checklists in these settings. However, we were ultimately encouraged to do so after Scott Henggeler and his colleagues scientifically demonstrated the utility of this approach in TPs who had learned to implement contingency management within multisytemic therapy (MST). In disseminating FBT, we experienced overwhelming positive feedback from TPs about the prompting checklists. However, our checklists lacked appropriate context (e.g., sufficient rationales, implementation examples, cultural adaptations), which led TPs to be overly dependent on FBT trainers.

One of the persons who helped us initially disseminate FBT into community settings was a coinvestigator on a clinical trial involving FBT, Dan Allen. With Nate's support, Dan agreed to assist in writing the first book about FBT based on the aforementioned prompting checklists (i.e., *Treating Adult Substance Abuse Using Family Behavior Therapy*). Now, several months later, we are excited to have completed *Treating Adolescent Substance Abuse Using Family Behavior Therapy*. Similar to the first book, this treatment manual was developed to flexibly and effectively address substance abuse utilizing a straightforward and theoretically sound behavioral intervention that is family based. Importantly, the intervention includes multiple components that are each capable of treating a wide range of problem behaviors in youth, such as illicit drug and alcohol abuse, family discord, school/work attendance, and conduct and mood disorders. Each component is organized into a series of therapeutic instructions, with each instruction building upon the next. TPs are free to exercise their own positive style when implementing each step, and they often integrate information between steps to assist in clarification, engagement, and so on. Other innovative features of FBT include its tight integration of (a) standardized and time-efficient goal-setting procedures that are tied to specific drug use triggers and competing rewards; (b) pragmatic methods to assist TPs in assessing their own estimates of treatment integrity; (c) ongoing standardized methods of assessing the extent to which clients participate and are satisfied in therapy; (d) standardized client record-keeping procedures and accompanying quality assurance system; and (e) strong evidence base in treating drug abuse and other associated problem behaviors. Each of these factors is very important to treatment delivery, although very few programs do so reliably.

This book, therefore, reviews procedures involved in the implementation of FBT as applied to the very distinctive and difficult-to-treat adolescent substance abuse population. FBT for adolescents involves the administration of validated assessment methods and well-established behavioral intervention components (i.e., Consequence Review, Level System, Treatment Planning, Reciprocity Awareness, Positive Request, Environmental/Stimulus Control, Self-Control, Job-Getting Skills Training). Each intervention component is systematically described in Chapters 5 through 12. Each intervention component includes an overview of the intervention approach, rationale for the intervention, required materials, and detailed description of the intervention procedures (including implementation dialogue between TP and client/family). Within each chapter, case examples and completed worksheets assist in bringing the interventions to life. This systematic organization permits readers to quickly identify and skim through parts of each chapter that may be particularly relevant. For instance, if a TP is about to implement the Self-Control intervention, and is not confident in how to initiate a practice trial, the TP can quickly review dialogue in the respective section where these instructions are detailed within the text. All necessary materials that will be required to implement FBT are listed in the back of each chapter, including the prompting checklists, handouts, and worksheets. At the back of the book there is a quiz that may be completed after the book is read to assist in gaining continuing education units (CEUs) that are required by most major TP licensing boards.

This book is primarily intended for TPs and instructors who teach substance abuse treatment in their courses. Indeed, there is ample information available to suggest that students who go on to become TPs need intensive training in evidence-based therapies, such as FBT, and that these interventions should be integrated within their class curriculums. Along these lines, we have developed a course format that is consistent with this book and freely available to instructors who are interested in teaching FBT. Relevant to this FBT class curriculum, each chapter represents an intervention component (e.g., Self-Control) that may be taught during an academic week. We hope you find the book rewarding and the interventions exciting to implement.

BRAD DONOHUE
NATHAN AZRIN

Acknowledgments

We would like to acknowledge our families for their encouragement in writing this book, as well as our colleagues and students for their assistance in developing this Family Behavior Therapy approach. We are especially grateful for the continued support of the National Institute on Drug Abuse, as well as the National Institute of Mental Health in permitting us to evaluate the efficacy of FBT in randomized controlled trials. We are indebted to the folks at John Wiley & Sons, particularly Rachel Livsey, Amanda Orenstein, and Kim Nir for their professional perspective, unrivaled assistance, and aptitude throughout the publication process. We also would like to thank the following colleagues who reviewed this book and provided valuable feedback: C. Aaron McNeece, Professor Emeritus, Florida State University; Ken Winters, Professor, University of Minnesota; Lin Fang, Assistant Professor, University of Toronto; Eric Wagner, Professor, Florida International University; and David Springer, Professor, University of Texas, Austin.

CHAPTER 1

Introduction to Family Behavior Therapy

Overview

This chapter provides an overview of the application of Family Behavior Therapy (FBT) as applied to adolescents. First, the historical, theoretical, and empirical underpinnings of FBT are reviewed to assist in understanding its conceptualization and development during the past 20 years. We then describe youth and their families who are most likely to benefit from FBT, and offer recommendations in determining a method of assessment to assist in treatment planning. Although content of each of the FBT intervention components is extensively reviewed in Chapters 4 through 13, a summary of each intervention component is provided in this chapter. The method of using our relatively novel prompting checklists to guide treatment providers (TPs) in intervention implementation is reviewed, and procedures involved in the assessment of treatment integrity are underscored.

Chapter at a Glance

> Historical, theoretical, and empirical background of FBT

> Clinical populations and therapeutic contexts appropriate for FBT

> General structure of FBT

> Maintenance and assessment of FBT intervention integrity

Historical and Theoretical Background

The FBT that is reviewed in this book was initiated in 1989 by the authors and their colleagues with support from the National Institute on Drug

Abuse. During the time of FBT's initial development, very few evidence-supported interventions were available to treat adolescent drug abuse. Behavioral treatment programs for preadolescent conduct disorders were comparatively advanced due to the pioneering work of Sidney Bijou, Don Baer, Todd Risley, Mont Wolf, and others. Two behavioral programs that stood out to us in their emphasis on positive reinforcement, standardized method, and effectiveness included Constance Hanf's parent training program for noncompliant preadolescent children that was empirically validated in studies by Rex Forehand and his colleagues at the University of Georgia (see Forehand & McMahon, 1981); and Gerald Patterson's social learning approach to family therapy (e.g., Patterson, Reid, Jones, & Conger, 1975) that continues to be enhanced by his colleagues at the Oregon Social Learning Center. The scientific work of these esteemed investigators validated our desire to enhance drug-incompatible skills in youth through family-based reinforcement, while rejecting punishment-based interventions that were shown to result in numerous negative side effects.

Consistent with behavioral theory, we conceptualized substance use to be a strong inherent reinforcer (i.e., pleasurable sensations, peer support, elimination of aversive emotions). Although negative consequences occur as a result of substance use, the severity of these consequences is often minimized or suppressed, or the full impact is not realized until well after the habitual processes of drug use has begun. To assist youth in gaining long-term abstinence from illicit drugs, we hypothesized that FBT would need to (a) reinforce the development of skills that are incompatible with drug use (e.g., recognizing antecedents or "triggers" to drug use, controlling drug cravings, utilizing communication skills to decrease arguments and other stressful antecedents to drug use), (b) modify the environment to facilitate reinforcement for time spent in drug-incompatible activities (e.g., enrollment in school or work, changing driving routes to avoid drug use triggers, creating a social network of nonaddicted friends), and (c) reward actions that are incompatible with drug use.

We decided to base the development of FBT on the Community Reinforcement Approach (CRA) due to its consistency with the aforementioned model and because CRA had been shown to successfully treat the related problem of alcohol abuse in adults (e.g., Azrin, Sisson, Meyers, & Godley, 1982; Hunt & Azrin, 1973; Sisson & Azrin, 1989). Communication skills training, a critical component in behavioral marital therapy (Stuart, 1969), had been successfully incorporated into Gerald Patterson's program with parents of conduct-disordered youth when marital problems were evidenced. Therefore, it made good sense to incorporate methods of facilitating family activities and communication skills training into FBT that were similar to CRA. As can be seen in Chapters 8 and 9, we made very few changes to the original CRA communication skills therapy protocols other than to emphasize youth/parent relationships.

To assist in managing youth who refused to go to school we modified another CRA component, the Job Club intervention for adults (Azrin, Flores, & Kaplan, 1975), to be developmentally appropriate in youth (see Chapter 12). For instance, shortly after we initiated our first controlled trial, it became apparent to us that, relative to adults, we needed to spend additional time motivating youth to wear appropriate clothing to job interviews, arranging transportation for them to attend interviews, and teaching them to speak respectfully during their job interviews. They also demonstrated relatively greater difficulties responding to questions that are commonly asked in job interviews. Therefore, the Job Club intervention was modified to train youth in these important areas.

It was initially anticipated that many adolescents would be unmotivated to desire abstinence from illicit drugs, and likely evidence frequent lapses in drug use throughout treatment. Therefore, relapse prevention strategies similar to those of Alan Marlatt (1985), and concepts of motivational interviewing methods similar to those formalized by William Miller (1983), were utilized to shape clinical style and general approach to therapy (see Chapters 3 and 5). The youth who were treated in our clinical trials were extremely responsive to these supportive methods, and our TPs found them to be consistent with their conceptualization to the addictions and enjoyable to implement. Relapse prevention strategies were also embedded within a newly developed stimulus control method in which youth learned to identify antecedents ("triggers") to drug use and non–drug use, and to implement skills to assist in managing these antecedent stimuli (see Chapters 10 and 11). We theorized that youth and parent motivation would be enhanced with external reinforcement through contingency contracting. We decided to establish a point system in which youth would be rewarded for behaviors that were incompatible with substance use. About the time we were developing this contracting procedure, Stephen Higgins and his colleagues (1991) had demonstrated the efficacy of CRA and voucher-based contingency management in reducing drug abuse. The latter study demonstrated the importance of using objective methods of assessing drug abuse (i.e., urinalysis testing) in contingency management. Similar to their work, we made all rewards contingent on no signs of drug use through urinalysis and reports from others. The developed system included standardized methods of quickly determining target responses, and rewards from the participants' social ecology. The point system appeared to be relatively effective in our first randomized controlled trial with youth (Azrin, Donohue, Besalel, Kogan, & Acierno, 1994). However, some parents evidenced difficulties managing earned points, and it seemed more complicated than necessary. Therefore, in a subsequent trial (Azrin et al., 2001), this point system was replaced with a much easier to implement level system (Chapter 6). The developed level system was similar to those that are often utilized in state-of-the-art residential youth programs. However, the contingencies were managed by parents rather than staff.

One of the interventions we developed in our first trial of FBT was an Urge Control (Self-Control) intervention (see Chapter 11) to reduce drug cravings/urges. This intervention was based on Joseph Cautela's (1967) Covert Sensitization therapy. In Covert Sensitization, the person with the addiction is instructed to think of aversive stimuli just as alcohol use is about to occur during imagery trials. After repeated pairings of aversive and alcohol-related thoughts, desire for alcohol use diminishes. However, in our earlier pilot trials, youth were often resistant to extended imagination of aversive thoughts. Moreover, Covert Sensitization does not teach skills relevant to managing substance use. Therefore, we developed an Urge Control (or Self-Control) intervention to assist youth in identifying the earliest thought of drug use and very briefly imagining aversive stimuli when the urge is relatively low. This change permitted cravings and desires for drug use to be overshadowed easily and quickly by aversive thoughts and images. Once the urge was terminated in the imagined trial, youth were taught to engage in a series of skill sets culminating in a brief problem-solving exercise to identify drug-incompatible behaviors, and imagine escape from the drug use situation. The latter skill-based modifications were unique to the previous Covert Sensitization procedure. Because youth reported that they had a difficult time imagining themselves doing the non-drug-associated actions that were brainstormed, we had them verbally describe themselves doing responses that were incompatible with problem behavior. That is, they were prompted to complete "practice" trials by describing themselves doing the desired behavioral sets aloud, and were subsequently praised for their efforts. Adolescents reported great satisfaction with these trials, probably because of the abundant encouragement and praise they received throughout.

Thus, FBT is consistent with the CRA and other behavioral therapies, but does differ in meaningful ways. Since our initial trial 2 decades ago, FBT has undergone continued enhancement. Standardized quality assurance programs specific to FBT have been originated to assist in managing infrastructural and administrative needs (see Donohue et al., 2009; Chapter 2), and the method of assessing treatment integrity that is described later in this chapter has been favorably evaluated in a community setting (Sheidow, Donohue, Hill, Henggeler, & Ford, 2008). Easy-to-follow prompting checklists that are described at the end of this chapter have been developed to guide TPs in efficient and effective administration of therapies during sessions (included at the end of each of Chapters 4 through 13), and standardized telephone therapies aimed at improving session attendance have been favorably examined in controlled trials involving youth to complement FBT (Donohue et al., 1998). Standardized agendas have also been developed to assist TPs in transitioning between treatment sessions (see Chapter 4), interventions have been tied directly to standardized treatment plans (see Chapter 7), and the treatment termination process is now clear and specific to future goal preparation (see Chapter 13). Relevant to dissemination, other standardized procedures have been developed to assist in determining readiness for FBT adoption in community agencies, and prompting checklists have been developed to guide trainers when implementing FBT workshops and ongoing training sessions (freely available from the first author).

Empirical Background

Relevant to outcome support, FBT is one of the few evidence-based treatments to demonstrate efficacy in controlled clinical trials involving both adults and adolescents who have been identified to abuse illicit drugs (see reviews, for example, by Bukstein & Horner, 2010; Carroll & Onken, 2005; Dutra et al., 2008; Macgowan & Engle, 2010). In the first randomized controlled trial of FBT (Azrin, McMahon, et al., 1994), adolescents and adults were randomly assigned to receive FBT (referred to as behavior therapy at that time) or a nondirective control group after completion of baseline data. Results indicated that, as compared with control group participants, the participants assigned to FBT demonstrated significantly greater improvements throughout the year following baseline in drug and alcohol use frequency, conduct problems, family functioning/satisfaction, work/school attendance, depression, and parental satisfaction with the youth. The results were maintained at 9 months' follow-up (Azrin et al., 1996), with adolescents in FBT showing better outcomes than adults in FBT and adolescents and adults in the control group. Other randomized controlled trials that have explicitly examined dually diagnosed substance abusing adolescents and their parents (Azrin, Donohue, et al., 1994; Azrin et al., 2001) have shown similar positive effects. The studies of FBT have generally indicated favorable results regardless of gender, ethnicity, or type of substance used (i.e., alcohol, marijuana, hard drugs). Based on a meta-analysis of outcome studies conducted by an independent review group (Bender, Springer, & Kim, 2006), it was concluded that FBT was one of only two treatments to show large treatment effect sizes for dually diagnosed adolescents across substance use, and internalizing and externalizing behavior problems. Favorable substance abuse outcomes have also been indicated in the very similar Adolescent Community Reinforcement Approach (ACRA; Dennis et al., 2004; Godley, Godley, Dennis, Funk, & Passetti, 2007) and Community Reinforcement Approach in homeless adolescents (Slesnick, Prestopnik, Meyers, & Glassman, 2007). The dissemination of ACRA in 33 sites is particularly impressive (Godley, Garner, Smith, Meyers, & Godley, 2011). Relevant to family participation in FBT, we developed a brief telephone intervention that was shown to improve initial session attendance of youth and their parents by 29% in an outpatient setting (Donohue et al., 1998). More intensive CRA-like engagement programs, such as CRA Family Training (CRAFT) have been empirically developed by Bob Meyers and his colleagues (see review by Smith & Meyers, 2004). These programs have significantly enhanced family involvement in CRA (e.g., Meyers, Miller, Smith, & Tonigan, 2002; Miller, Meyers, & Tonigan, 1999).

These findings offer support for FBT in the treatment of adolescent substance abuse within community settings that are charged with the implementation of evidence-supported "best practices." For instance, FBT is now listed in national clearinghouses as an evidence-based therapy (e.g., Substance Abuse and Mental Health Service Administration's National Registry of Evidence-Based Practices, California Evidence-Based Clearinghouse for Child Welfare), and this treatment was one of the first behavioral programs reviewed in the National Institute on Drug Abuse's Principles of Drug Addiction Treatment

(National Institute on Drug Abuse, 1998). In Module 10, published by the National Institutes of Alcoholism and Alcohol Abuse (2005), this behavioral approach was said to be an "emerging developmentally sensitive approach" for drug use problems.

Appropriate Intervention Settings and Referrals

Settings

Evidence-based treatments (EBTs) are experimentally evaluated in specified clinical settings, most often including inpatient and outpatient mental health facilities, hospitals, homes, and school environments. Since outcome studies of FBT in adolescent samples have been conducted in outpatient mental health facilities, this is the preferred venue in which to implement FBT with targeted youth and their families. Outcomes resulting from the implementation of FBT have yet to be formally examined within the context of inpatient therapeutic milieus, peer group, multifamily, or exclusive individual applications. We are aware that at least some community-based agencies have been funded to implement FBT in home and inpatient mental health settings, and that their anecdotal findings appear to indicate positive results. However, it is important to emphasize that these programs have reportedly maintained the integrity of FBT implementation while treating families in private rooms as consistent with outpatient implementation. It may be that inpatient settings offer certain advantages over outpatient settings in the treatment of substance abusing youth. For instance, inpatient facilities assure easy access to FBT, prohibit drug use opportunities, and provide opportunities to implement FBT intensively. Nevertheless, in considering FBT for use in inpatient facilities, it is important to ensure that (a) significant others will be able to visit the facility to participate in FBT sessions, (b) patients will have sufficient time in the facility to learn the interventions, (c) treatment providers (TPs) will be able to engage participants in outpatient care subsequent to discharge, and (d) patients will be provided opportunities to practice newly learned skill sets during brief excursions from the facility.

Referrals

The exclusionary criteria in controlled clinical trials involving FBT in youth have been relatively relaxed to permit referrals from a variety of sources, including judges, juvenile justice probation and parole officers, school administrators, and community TPs. Self-referrals are rare, with referrals from family members often occurring in response to pressure from court systems. FBT has demonstrated favorable outcomes with marijuana and hard drug abuse, alcohol abuse and various coexisting problems, such as depression, family dysfunction, stress, incarceration, unemployment, behavior problems, and school attendance. Youth who have been formally diagnosed with mental retardation, severe cognitive impairments, and psychosis have generally been excluded from our controlled trials of FBT. However, when persons with severe cognitive disabilities have been treated with FBT, or other treatments for that matter, the outcomes appear to be relatively poor (see Burgard, Donohue, Azrin, & Teichner, 2000).

General Approach and Structure to Treatment

Outcome Assessment

It is generally recommended that evaluation of FBT include the administration of assessment measures before, during, and after treatment. Sometimes primary measures (e.g., urinalysis) are administered throughout treatment. Assessing treatment outcomes is important because the derived data may be used to guide treatment, assist in determining the adequacy of fit between FBT and the treatment provider, demonstrate program improvements, and justify costs to funding agencies.

In determining which measures to administer, several factors should be considered. First, required consent and assent forms should be obtained consistent with state and federal licensing requirements, and the person administering, interpreting, and recording the respective measures and analyzing this data should be legally and ethically qualified to do so. The measures should be relevant to the presenting concerns.

The gold standard in drug abuse assessment is biological testing. Broadscreen urinalysis testing may be utilized to assess illicit drug use that may have occurred during the past few days, hair follicle tests are ideal to assess illicit drug use that may have occurred during the past several months, and Breathalyzer tests may be used to assess alcohol use that may have occurred within the past day. Our experiences have led us to conclude that biological testing procedures (i.e., urinalysis, Breathalyzer) should occur during treatment when there is reason to suspect drug use, and when contingency management is being implemented (i.e., rewards are provided when youth are drug free as per urinalysis and reports of others). Broad screen or multiple-panel tests (i.e., each panel represents a substance) are recommended instead of select tests of specific substances because youth often experiment with various substances, and their substance use patterns are often irregular. Some TPs do not administer biological testing when youth admit to using substances. However, the administration of broad-screen urinalysis assists in determining if substances that were not reported may have been used. If youth disagree with the results of biological testing, it is important to simply indicate the testing procedures are the best objective estimate of drug use, and subsequently facilitate implementation of consequences that may have been established with the parent through contingency management. Sometimes youth report that biological testing may have come up positive for illicit drugs because something had been "slipped" into a drink at a party or that they were in a room with marijuana smokers and they inhaled the secondhand smoke. In such cases, it is important to initiate any consequences that may have been negotiated during the establishment of contingency contracting, and emphasize that goals should be set to avoid such risky situations in the future. Standardized procedures involving biological testing procedures may be obtained by the companies that sell these products. For instance, Redwood Toxicologies Inc. has a Web-based program relevant to learning to implement biological testing procedures that includes free certification.

Retrospective reports from youth and significant others regarding adolescents' number of days using illicit drugs and alcohol, as well as other problem behaviors (e.g., work and school attendance, days incarcerated), appear to be valid and reliable up to 6 months in retrospect when formal assessment methods are utilized, such as the Timeline Followback method (TLFB) developed by Mark and Linda Sobell. The Sobells maintain a web site at Nova Southeastern University that includes freely accessible information relevant to TLFB implementation.

Satisfaction scales offer utility in achieving goals for treatment. These include the Life Satisfaction (Donohue et al., 2003) and Youth Satisfaction With Parent Scale (DeCato, Donohue, Azrin, & Teichner, 2001) completed by youth and the Parent Satisfaction Scale (Donohue, Decato, Azrin, & Teichner, 2001) completed by parents. Each of these scales may be utilized to determine the respondent's satisfaction in a number of areas that have been validated to be relevant to improvements in substance abuse and conduct disorders (e.g., communication, school, work, chores). Utilizing a 0 to 100% scale, respondents indicate for each of the domains their extent of happiness. Upon scale completion, respondents are queried to indicate how happiness may be improved in specific domains. These scales may be obtained from Dr. Donohue or the immediately aforementioned source articles free of charge.

Depending on various characteristics of the population receiving FBT, other assessment measures may be warranted, particularly measures of psychiatric symptoms and mental health diagnoses, family functioning, satisfaction with treatment, service utilization, and risk of contracting HIV. More information regarding specific assessment procedures used to evaluate the effects of FBT and other EBTs are reviewed in Allen, Donohue, Sutton, Haderlie, and LaPota (2009). In determining assessment procedures to utilize, it is important to ensure that they are standardized; evidence good psychometric properties; and are quick and easy to administer, score, and interpret. Depending on the specific setting in which FBT is implemented, assessment measures vary to accommodate the unique aspects of program referral sources, funding agencies, and state laws.

Orientation Session

Of course, immediately after the initial pretreatment assessment battery is scored and interpreted, an orientation to FBT should be provided to youth and adult significant others that includes opportunities for the youth and family to review the basic treatment structure and approach, review feelings about the referral, receive and provide feedback relevant to the assessment findings, and provide an opportunity to solicit commitments from youth and participating family members to follow established program guidelines (e.g., attend sessions, participate in session exercises and therapy assignments, engage in appropriate communication such as speaking calmly and briefly). To assist in this endeavor, an Orientation Prompting Checklist (Exhibit 1.1) and Communication Guidelines Handout (Exhibit 1.2) are included at the end of this chapter. It is recommended that administrators in community treatment programs review these orientation materials to determine the extent to which their content should be customized to accommodate the unique needs, laws, and culture of the treatment agency. The Orientation session precedes the formal implementation of treatment (see the following Treatment section). As indicated in the previous section, the satisfaction scales that are reviewed in the Orientation session are fully described and freely available in either peer-reviewed journals (DeCato et al., 2001; Donohue et al., 2001, Donohue et al., 2003) or from Dr. Donohue directly.

Treatment

Number of Treatment Sessions   FBT for adolescents usually includes up to 16 treatment sessions, and each session is approximately 60 to 90 minutes in duration. All scheduled sessions are usually implemented within 4 to 6 months, depending on the setting, presenting problems, available funding, and response of youth to treatment. Sessions fade in frequency and duration as therapeutic goals are accomplished.

Persons to Include in Treatment Sessions   The youth referred to the treatment facility for substance abuse is considered to be the identified client in the FBT model. FBT is focused on assisting the youth client in maintaining long-term abstinence from illicit drugs, and accomplishing goals that are consistent with a healthy and prosperous lifestyle. Primary significant others are the legal guardians of the youth client (almost always a parent). At least one primary significant other, and both if available, is expected to attend each session and sign legal consent forms. Secondary significant others include family members and sometimes close friends. Significant others are recruited from the adolescents' social ecology to assist youth in attending their therapy sessions, completing their homework assignments, and providing encouragement and rewards to them when treatment goals are accomplished.

During sessions, significant others can model exemplary skills during role-playing exercises, encourage youth to participate in role-plays or discuss difficult situations, provide insights that are relevant to recovery, and provide youth empathy and support. Adolescent friends and family of youth may be involved in therapy as significant others. However, TPs need to be careful not to involve adolescents in age-inappropriate content, and these young significant others must be committed to facilitating sobriety and other therapeutic goals. Indeed, all significant others should ideally be sober (or evidence a desire to remain sober), have an interest in the youth's well-being, and be relatively well adjusted. Recruiting more than one of these individuals is helpful, although this is often difficult to achieve because youth often have strained relationships with appropriate adults and have established close friendships with other drug users.

Bob Meyers and Jane Ellen Smith detail an evidence-based method of recruiting appropriate significant others of substance abusers into therapy and successfully resolving issues that sometimes come up in this process (see Smith & Meyers, 2004).

Adolescent friends of youth clients who use illicit drugs and alcohol may be valuable to incorporate into treatment, provided they are interested in eliminating their own use of substances. Indeed, the inclusion of these individuals permits TPs to closely monitor their behavior and encourage and assist them in accomplishing a healthy lifestyle that does not include problem behavior. However, these persons must be carefully screened and monitored to ensure that their inclusion in therapy is likely to put youth at relatively less risk of harm than their being excluded from therapy. Of course, recruited significant others must be committed to ameliorate problem behaviors that have the potential to negatively influence youth clients. When significant others are deemed to be appropriate, it is important to tell them that although they may indirectly benefit from FBT, their role in therapy is to aid youth clients in accomplishing treatment goals. Our experiences have generally shown friends of youth clients are especially compliant during treatment sessions so parents feel comfortable permitting their children to spend time with them. Although this compliance may appear disingenuous, such behavior permits practice learning to occur and should be encouraged in therapy.

The role of small children is limited to reviewing the scheduled family activity during the Environmental (Stimulus) Control intervention (see Chapter 10), and providing and receiving positive statements during Reciprocity Awareness and Positive Request interventions (see Chapters 8 and 9, respectively), and the last session (i.e., see Chapter 13).

In each of the remaining chapters, recommendations are provided for TPs to consider in regards to how and when to involve significant others in therapy. Of course, ethical, legal, and programmatic issues will need to be considered in the inclusion of significant others. These issues are customarily reviewed in state and federal laws, and state licensing boards may be queried when relevant laws are unclear. However, legal consultation is highly recommended in the initial development of family-based treatment programming to assist in originating consent procedures and guidelines to review with youth and their participating significant others, such as how various issues that are influenced by relationships will be managed (i.e., establishing firm guidelines in the prevention of "secrets" [e.g., infidelity], reviewing how significant others will be included in record-keeping procedures, consent for treatment, confidentiality).

Content of Therapy Following the aforementioned orientation, there are eight FBT intervention components that are commonly utilized in adolescent-focused FBT. The youth intervention components include:

1. *Consequence Review:* A structured activity in which youth are prompted to extensively review negative consequences of substance use and associated problem behaviors and positive consequences associated with living a drug-free lifestyle. Support and encouragement are provided within the context of motivational techniques.

2. *Level System:* A contingency management program in which primary adult significant others (usually parents) provide contingent rewards for desired behaviors that facilitate youth abstinence from illicit drugs and alcohol and accomplish problem-free behavior.

3. *Treatment Planning:* Involves the youth and the youth's primary adult significant others' choosing the order and extent to which specific FBT intervention components should be prioritized in therapy.

4. *Reciprocity Awareness:* Involves youth and youth's significant others' disclosing things they appreciate about each other, and expressing desired actions.

5. *Positive Request:* Involves the youth and youth's significant others' learning to positively request desired actions from one another.

6. *Environmental (Stimulus) Control:* Involves the youth and youth's significant others' learning to restructure their environment to facilitate interaction with people and activities that are associated with a substance-free lifestyle, while eliminating or managing emotions, people, and activities in the environment that increase risk of drug use and other problem behaviors. Pleasant family activities are also planned and subsequently reviewed.

7. *Self-Control:* Involves teaching the youth and youth's significant others' to identify and manage antecedents (triggers) to substance use and other troublesome behaviors.

8. *Job-Getting Skills Training:* Involves teaching the youth and youth's significant others' how to solicit and do well in job interviews.

Determining the Order and Extent to Which Intervention Components Are Implemented   The order and extent to which the intervention components are implemented in therapy is fully described in Chapter 4 (Establishing Effective Agendas for Treatment Sessions). However, in short, after the Orientation session is conducted, the Consequence Review (see Chapter 5) and Level System (see Chapter 6) are sequentially implemented to assist in gaining motivation for treatment. Treatment Planning is implemented next. The order in which the remaining intervention components are implemented for the first time is mutually determined by the youth and parents during Treatment Planning (see Chapter 7). The extent to which treatments are subsequently implemented, with the exception of Treatment Planning because it is implemented only once, will depend on their effectiveness as determined mutually among the youth, the youth's parents, and the TP. Treatments that appear to be effective are implemented more often than ineffective interventions.

Method of Transitioning Between Treatment Sessions   An agenda is provided by the TP at the start of each session (see Chapter 4). In doing so, TPs initiate agendas by pointing out positive efforts that may have occurred during the most recent session, and briefly mentioning interventions that are intended for review in the current session (including estimated times to complete each intervention). Youth and family members are invited by TPs to modify agendas based on unanticipated circumstances that may have arisen since the last treatment session (e.g., severe arguments, youth wanting to withdraw from school).

Structure of Intervention Chapters   Details regarding how to implement each of the primary interventions are described in Chapters 5 through 12. Each of these chapters include (a) an overview of the intervention approach; (b) goals for the intervention; (c) materials needed to implement the intervention; (d) the specific treatment procedures, including implementation dialogues among youth, TP, and family members; (e) initial and future prompting checklists to guide TPs during treatment implementation; and (f) worksheets and handouts to assist in treatment delivery.

Prompting Checklists Guide Treatment Providers in Sessions The Consequence Review and Treatment Planning interventions each include a single prompting checklist, while each of the remaining interventions include two prompting checklists (initial, future sessions). The initial checklist is specific to the first session the respective intervention component is implemented (e.g., Initial Session Prompting Checklist for Self-Control, Initial Session Prompting Checklist for Environmental Control). The other prompting checklist is used when the respective intervention is implemented in subsequent treatment sessions (e.g., Future Session Prompting Checklist for Self Control). Prompting checklists are included at the end of each of the chapters. Prompting checklists are basically summaries of the specific procedures or steps required to implement the treatments. Because prompting checklists are designed to be used by TPs during sessions, each checklist item is a succinct instructional prompt written in shorthand so TPs can quickly glance at the instruction during treatment and consequently implement what is being prompted. The instructions are listed in the order in which TPs should implement them. During implementation, TPs put the respective checklist on their lap or nearby desk. They briefly glance at the checklist, look up, and proceed to implement what is being prompted with the family. Treatment providers then respond to youth and their significant others as they feel appropriate, implement the next instruction, and so on until all intervention steps in the prompting checklist are complete. Of course, comfort, confidence, and skill in utilizing the prompting checklists is enhanced with continued practice and preparation. Most TPs experience some anxiety in utilizing the checklists initially. However, these anxieties will eventually be overshadowed with successful implementation. Each of these checklists have undergone hundreds of revisions based on the input of TPs in community-based treatment centers and scientists in controlled trials to encourage therapeutic freedom in responding to the concerns of clients. Using these prompting checklists is the best way to ensure that TPs implement all critical components of each intervention and, in this way, assist in ensuring treatment integrity. Until TPs are familiar with the implementation of FBT, they should utilize the prompting checklists faithfully.

The general content or "meat" of each *initial* intervention session prompting checklist pertains to: (a) providing family members a rationale for the treatment (i.e., problem behavior that is expected to be addressed, brief description of intervention, why intervention is likely to work); (b) developing the skill set through participation in simulated role-play scenarios and structured exercises; and (c) assigning homework to practice the learned skill set.

The general format of each *future* intervention session includes: (a) discussing homework assigned during the last therapy session, (b) practicing or behaviorally enacting skill sets that were assigned during the last therapy session, and (c) assigning homework to continue practicing the skill set (if necessary). The number of future sessions implemented for each intervention component is determined mutually between the youth, participating significant others, and TP. Use of these prompting checklists assists in maintaining the integrity of the intervention so that all needed components are implemented, thereby increasing the effectiveness in treatment. For these reasons, TPs are encouraged to closely follow the protocols, but in doing so are also encouraged to use nonprescribed procedures whenever indicated between the prescribed steps.

It is important to emphasize that treatment sessions may include the implementation of several interventions, and that intervention components may be temporarily suspended or abandoned to permit timely implementation of other intervention components. For instance, if the Environmental (Stimulus) Control intervention were being implemented during a treatment session, and a client spontaneously indicated that she wanted to learn to be assertive when talking with her father, the TP could put down her prompting checklist for Environmental (Stimulus) Control, and take out a prompting checklist for the Positive Request procedure (as well as other requisite handouts) to teach her to be assertive. After the Positive Request procedure was implemented, the TP could return to the Environmental (Stimulus) Control intervention if time permitted, end the session, or proceed to another intervention component. This approach to treatment encourages treatment integrity while being flexible to address contemporaneous concerns. In the latter example, the TP's integrity for Environmental (Stimulus) Control would be based on the steps she did or did not complete up to the point at which she stopped administering the respective treatment components (see Treatment Integrity section below).

Treatment Integrity   Although there are a number of ways to define *treatment integrity* or *protocol adherence,* these terms generally concern the extent to which TPs implement a given intervention in a manner that is consistent with the way it was determined to be efficacious. Importantly, programs that utilize standardized manuals and evaluate treatment integrity are consistently rated better than those programs that do not (Moyer, Finney, & Swearingen, 2002). As emphasized by Power et al. (2005), it is imperative that treatment programs conduct comprehensive assessment of intervention integrity or protocol adherence. The methods of measuring treatment integrity vary, although there is some evidence to suggest that examining audiotapes or videotapes of therapy sessions appears to be the most accurate way to assess TPs' adherence to therapeutic protocols (Del Boca & Darkes, 2007).

Therapists utilize two approaches to ensure treatment integrity, with the first focusing on overall adherence in completing the steps necessary to implement the intervention, and the second addressing skill of the TP. Research demonstrates that these methods of assessing protocol adherence in FBT are both valid and reliable in TPs participating in controlled treatment outcome studies (e.g., Azrin et al., 2001) and in community-based TPs (Sheidow et al., 2008). Family Behavior Therapy is especially amenable to the assessment of treatment integrity because all FBT intervention components are specified in the initial and future session therapist prompting checklists. These steps are unambiguous, easy-to-understand instructions that are listed sequentially, permitting TPs to use them as prompts during treatment implementation, and permitting trainers to easily and objectively monitor them during their audio or video reviews of sessions. The prompting checklist method of treatment administration also has practical utility. That is, it encourages TPs to achieve a high degree of treatment integrity (implementation of one step prompts the next step, and so on), while permitting them to compute their own assessment of protocol adherence (their own completed checklist may be used to estimate adherence).

The Treatment Integrity Review Form (Exhibit 1.3) is used to record the results of protocol adherence assessments. In assessing protocol adherence for FBT, TPs examine their completed prompting checklist after the therapy session and divide the number of steps completed by the number of steps that were possible in the sections that were said to be implemented. They then multiply the resulting dividend by 100. The resulting score represents the percentage of steps completed for the respective intervention. Scores above 80% are generally considered to indicate good treatment adherence, while scores between 70% and 79% are considered adequate. Trainers (or other persons or raters examining treatment adherence, such as supervisors) independently complete their own prompting checklists while listening to the session audiotapes, and compute their assessment of protocol adherence in the same way as the TP. Thus, protocol adherence scores may be derived for both the TP and trainer (or other persons or raters examining treatment adherence).

Reliability is determined by dividing the number of agreements between the TP and trainer (number of items or steps both the TP and trainer agreed were either completed or not completed) by the number of disagreements between the TP and trainer (number of items or steps the TP and trainer disagreed were either completed or not completed) *and* agreements between them. The resulting number is multiplied by 100 to yield the percentage agreement score. Eighty percent or higher means reliability between the TP and trainer in assessing treatment integrity is good, while 70% to 79% is adequate.

For example, in the Self-Control Intervention Prompting Checklist for Future Sessions, there are 24 items or steps. If the TP indicated that 24 items were completed, the TP's estimate of treatment integrity would be 100%. If the trainer indicated that 22 of the 24 steps were completed, the trainer's estimate of treatment integrity would be 92%. In computing their reliability, if the TP and trainer agreed that the first 21 items and the last item were performed, there would be 22 agreements. If the trainer stated that the 22nd and 23rd items were not performed, and the TP stated that the 22nd and 23rd items were performed, they would have two disagreements. Thus, reliability would be computed as agreements (22) divided by agreements (22) + disagreements (2) multiplied by 100, or in this case, $22/24 \times 100 = 91.7\%$. Thus, the percentage agreement score would be 91.7 percent, indicating excellent reliability.

In both community and research settings, it is recommended that all therapy session audiotapes be submitted to an appropriate administrator, and that only approximately 10% of these session audiotapes be randomly selected for review by the trainer (or other rater) to enhance feasibility. To assist in the provision of feedback from the trainer to the TP, and enhance treatment integrity, the Treatment Integrity Review Form includes a section where the TP's overall "skill level" can be recorded by the trainer (or rater) utilizing a 1 to 7 Likert-scale: 7 = extremely skilled, 6 = very skilled, 5 = somewhat skilled, 4 = neutral, 3 = somewhat unskilled, 2 = very unskilled, 1 = extremely unskilled. The top of each prompting checklist includes a spot where the name of the trainer may be recorded, as well as the date of the review. Finally, there is a spot at the bottom of each prompting checklist to write notes about the intervention to facilitate qualitative comments about the delivery of therapy.

This highly reliable and valid method of measuring treatment integrity has a number of unique advantages. Indeed, it is psychometrically reliable and valid, administratively feasible, and facilitates learning as TPs use the checklists both as instructional prompts during therapy and to score their own adherence to therapy.

Consumer Satisfaction and Compliance Ratings

After each intervention component is implemented, the youth client is asked to rate the extent to which the intervention was perceived to be helpful (on a 7-point scale), and the TP rates the extent to which the client was compliant (on a 7-point scale; see Table 1.1). These ratings are recorded at the end of each of the prompting checklists, thus permitting an examination of consumer satisfaction (i.e., youth helpfulness) and TP assessed compliance with the family each time a treatment component is implemented. As exemplified below, TPs are prompted to assess these ratings, and to facilitate discussion about how these ratings were derived, and how the intervention component can be improved in the future for the family.

Consumer satisfaction ratings are important to obtain because high scores are indicative of future interest in the respective therapy, whereas low scores may demonstrate a lack of confidence and enthusiasm in the intervention. Of course, assessing consumer satisfaction is also likely to show youth that

Table 1.1. Method of Assessing Consumer Satisfaction and Compliance of Family in Treatment.

Helpfulness Ratings

___a. Solicit youth's rating of helpfulness for the respective treatment component on the following 7-point scale after stating the youth should not feel obligated to provide high scores because an honest assessment helps the treatment provider better address youth needs.

(**7** = extremely helpful, **6** = very helpful, **5** = somewhat helpful, **4** = not sure, **3** = somewhat unhelpful, **2** = very unhelpful, **1** = extremely unhelpful). Youth's Rating: _____.

___b. Solicit how rating was derived & methods of improving the intervention component in the future.

Compliance Ratings

___a. Disclose therapist's rating of the youth and family's compliance on the following 7-point scale (**7** = extremely compliant, **6** = very compliant, **5** = somewhat compliant, **4** = neutral, **3** = somewhat noncompliant, **2** = very noncompliant, **1** = extremely noncompliant). Therapist's Rating: ____

Factors that contribute to compliance ratings are:

    Attendance

    Participation & conduct in session

    Homework completion

___b. Explain how the rating was derived and methods of improving performance in future.

---

the TPs are interested in the youths' opinions about their treatment plan, and this procedure provides opportunities to modify treatment planning to be commensurate with youths' interests. Indeed, low scores may suggest that a treatment is not working or that a treatment is not desired in its current method of implementation and may need to be adjusted. The compliance ratings include three process measures that have consistently been predictive of treatment outcome (i.e., attendance, participation, and homework completion). TPs are also encouraged to consider significant others when compliance ratings are assessed. Providing youth positive feedback lets them know these things are valued. Indeed, with permission from youth, the compliance ratings are provided to referral agents (see Monthly Progress Reports in the appendix of this chapter), thus enhancing the meaningfulness of these ratings and potentially motivating youth to do well.

Concluding Remarks

This chapter provided a general background of FBT, including its historical, theoretical, and empirical underpinnings in youth who have been afflicted with substance abuse and dependence; outcome support to assist in determining appropriate referrals; and strategies to maintain and assess treatment integrity. As indicated, FBT is clearly a robust, empirically supported intervention capable of managing a wide range of problem behaviors. In addition to being relatively easy to learn and monitor, it is exciting to implement. Whereas most of this chapter was focused on the general structure of FBT, the remaining chapters will focus on therapeutic strategies and specific content involved in the effective implementation of this approach.

Supporting Materials for Chapter 1: Introduction to Family Behavior Therapy

Exhibit 1.1. Orientation Prompting Checklist.

ORIENTATION PROMPTING CHECKLIST

Youth ID#: _____   Treatment Provider: _____

Session #: _____   Date of Session: _____

Reviewer (if person completing checklist is different from treatment provider):

_____

Materials Required:

- Summaries of the assessments that were administered pretreatment.
- Completed Satisfaction Scales (e.g., Parent Satisfaction With Youth, Youth Satisfaction With Parent, Youth Life Satisfaction Scale).
- Communication Guidelines Handout.

Begin Time: _____

Program Policies

Review of General Issues Relevant to FBT Context (Youth and Appropriate Significant Others):

____a. Sessions may be audio-recorded so supervisors can monitor therapy for treatment integrity.
- Sessions usually:
  __ 1. Last 60 to 90 min.
  __ 2. Occur once per week.
  __ 3. Last 4 to 6 months.

____b. Explain how prompting checklists will be used during sessions to assure optimum care.
- Show copy of a protocol checklist.

____c. No smoking, alcohol use, or intoxication is permitted during sessions.

____d. Phone calls should be avoided during sessions unless emergency or special circumstance.
- Check-up calls may occur each week between sessions so treatment provider may:
  ___ 1. Ensure youth's needs are met.
  ___ 2. Answer questions.
  ___ 3. Assist in obtaining referrals for additional support.
  ___ 4. Assist w/ implementation of interventions.
  ___ 5. Assist w/ practice assignments.
  ___ 6. Develop plans in working w/ court or other professionals.
- Review the following program policy issues relevant to missing sessions:

___ 1. With consent, others may be notified of missed/late sessions.

___ 2. Treatment provider should be contacted 24 hrs. in advance to reschedule.

___ 3. Provide appointment card w/ scheduled day and times of future sessions (tell to put in conspicuous place).

___e. Assure telephone or other methods of contacting therapist are available.

___f. Assure all persons understand relevant State and federal laws, including confidentiality, and its limits.

Case Review

Review of Youth Experiences and Feelings About Referral (Youth and Appropriate Significant Others)

___a. Review reasons for referral.
  • Empathize w/expressed concerns.
  • Generate solutions to expressed concerns.

___b. Solicit problems experienced, or expected to occur w/ person/agency making referral.

___c. Solicit things that can be done to support family w/person/agency responsible for referral.

___d. Solicit general goals for therapy.
  • Provide support/empathy, and clarify inaccuracies.

Review of Pretreatment Assessment (Usually Youth and Appropriate Significant Others)

___a. Solicit potential concerns w/ pretreatment assessment.
  • Empathize and/or generate solutions to manage expressed concerns.
  • For each target drug that was assessed to occur, do the following (**may need to review w/ youth only**).

  ___ 1. Solicit age and circumstances associated with first use.

  ___ 2. Solicit current circumstances that appear to be associated with higher rates of substance use.

  ___ 3. Solicit current circumstances that appear to be associated with lower rates of substance use.

  ___ 4. Solicit positive and negative consequences of use.

___b. Attempt to obtain commitment from youth to eliminate drug and alcohol use and other identified problem behaviors.
  • If abstinence from substances is refused, attempt to obtain commitment from youth to reduce use.

___c. Show youth completed Life Sat. Scale and Youth Sat. w/Parent Scale (**may need to review w/ youth only**)

  ___ 1. Query why areas that are rated relatively high are rated so.

  ___ 2. Query why areas that are rated relatively low are rated so.

  ___ 3. Query what would need to happen to bring about 100% satisfaction in low areas.

___d. Show parent completed Parent Satisfaction with Youth Scale (**may need to review with appropriate significant others only**).

  ___ 1. Query why areas that are rated relatively high are rated so.

  ___ 2. Query why areas that are rated relatively low are rated so.

  ___ 3. Query what would need to happen to bring about 100% satisfaction in low areas.

___e. Attempt to obtain commitment from significant others to help youth reduce drug use or maintain abstinence.

____f. Provide results for other assessment measures & solicit/answer questions.
  • If disagreements occur, query reasons for disagreement, empathize, and mention other areas will be emphasized in treatment.
____g. Query how youth can be supported in life.
  ___ 1. Show how treatment provider will attempt to provide assistance in these areas.
    • State other youths have indicated therapists have supported in the following ways:
  ___ a. Supportive letters to person or agency responsible for referral, if relevant.
    ___i. Explain youth performance ratings will occur after each treatment is implemented and summarized in letters of support.
    ___ii. Explain ratings based on performance of caregivers and youth.
    ___iii. Explain letters will emphasize youth's progress in accomplishing treatment goals.
    ___iv. State effort will be made to show youth letters before they're sent.
      ___ a. Solicit how supportive letters will be helpful.
        • If a referral agent is not involved, explain information about the youth's participation in treatment may help if future problems occur.
  ___ b. Assistance in maintaining family unity (i.e., keep family together, calm home environment).
    ___ i. Solicit how this would be helpful.
  ___ c. Assistance gaining better jobs w/ greater income.
    ___ i. Solicit how this would be helpful.
  ___ d. Assistance maintaining or "getting out" of trouble (e.g., court, school suspensions) by promoting efforts of youth.
    ___ i. Solicit how this would be helpful.
____h. Solicit greatest motive for being involved in treatment.
____i. Solicit how youth and significant others will be able to motivate themselves to accomplish goals.
____j. Explain success of FBT.
____k. Explain how FBT is expected to be particularly beneficial to youth and significant others.

Communication Policy

Rationale for Communication Policy (Youth and Significant Others)

  • Explain the following:
____a. Lots of material to cover in upcoming sessions.
____b. Important to review guidelines to maintain good communication and get through session material quickly.
____c. Guidelines apply to all family members.
____d. If a guideline is broken, person will be instructed to correct guideline.
____e. Other families have found these guidelines to be effective
____f. Solicit questions.

Review Communication Policy (Youth and Significant Others)

____a. Give participants a copy of Communication Guidelines Handout
  • State the following guidelines and obtain commitments from each family member to comply w/ each one:

___ 1. <u>Avoid interruptions</u>; instead, wait for person to pause or ask if it is O.K. to speak
___ 2. <u>Avoid talking for more than a minute.</u>
___ 3. <u>Avoid saying "no"</u> when someone asks for something, instead say the part you can do.
___ 4. <u>Avoid rolling eyes back</u> or using other <u>negative facial</u> expressions.
___ 5. <u>Avoid swearing, shouting, use of sarcasm, spite, or statements that are hurtful.</u>
___ 6. <u>Avoid talking about</u> <u>past problems</u> or <u>weaknesses;</u> instead, suggest solutions and build on strengths.
___ 7. <u>Stay focused</u> on <u>specific desired actions</u>, not overall criticisms of what negative attitudes are disliked.
___ 8. Speak in a <u>soft</u> and conversational <u>tone of voice.</u>

Helpfulness Ratings

____a. Solicit youth's rating of helpfulness for the respective treatment component on the following 7-point scale after stating the youth should not feel obligated to provide high scores because an honest assessment helps the treatment provider better address youth needs.
(**7** = extremely helpful, **6** = very helpful, **5** = somewhat helpful, **4** = not sure, **3** = somewhat unhelpful, **2** = very unhelpful, **1** = extremely unhelpful). Youth's Rating: _____.
____b. Solicit how rating was derived and methods of improving the intervention component in the future.

Compliance Ratings

____a. Disclose therapist's rating of the youth and family's compliance on the following 7-point scale (**7** = extremely compliant, **6** = very compliant, **5** = somewhat compliant, **4** = neutral, **3** = somewhat noncompliant, **2** = very noncompliant, **1** = extremely noncompliant). Therapist's Rating: ____
   • Factors that contribute to compliance ratings are:
   1. Attendance
   2. Participation and conduct in session
   3. Homework completion
____b. Explain how the rating was derived and methods of improving performance in future.

End Time: _____ Reviewer notes:

Exhibit 1.2. Communication Guidelines Handout.

COMMUNICATION GUIDELINES HANDOUT

1. **Avoid interruptions**. Instead, wait for the person to pause, or ask if it is O.K. to speak.

2. **Avoid talking for more than a minute.**

3. **Avoid saying "no" when someone asks for something**. Instead, tell the person what you can do.

4. **Avoid rolling eyes or using negative facial expressions.**

5. **Avoid swearing, shouting, sarcasm, or statements that are hurtful.**

6. **Avoid talking about past problems or weaknesses**. Instead, suggest solutions and talk about strengths.

7. **Talk about things you want, do not give criticisms about the negative attitudes you dislike.**

8. **Speak in a soft and conversational tone of voice.**

Exhibit 1.3. Treatment Integrity Review Form.

TREATMENT INTEGRITY REVIEW FORM

Name of Trainer (or Rater):_____   Name of Therapist(s) Reviewed:_____
Date of Session Reviewed:_____   Intervention Reviewed:_____

Therapist Protocol Adherence

Adherence according to therapist: % of steps completed according to therapist =_____.

Adherence according to trainer (or rater): % of steps completed according to rater =_____.

Reliability: # of steps agreed upon by therapist and trainer ÷ (# steps agreed upon by therapist and trainer + # of steps disagreed upon by therapist and trainer) × 100 =_____.

Therapist Skill Rating

Trainer: Indicate the extent of therapist skill demonstrated using 7-point scale:

> **7** = extremely skilled, **6** = very skilled, **5** = somewhat skilled, **4** = neutral,
> **3** = somewhat unskilled, **2** = very unskilled, **1** = extremely unskilled

Record Trainer Rating of Therapist Skill Here:_____

Notes (optional):

_____

_____

_____

_____

_____

_____

_____

_____

Exhibit 1.4. Method of Assessing Consumer Satisfaction and Compliance of Family in Treatment.

ASSESSING CONSUMER SATISFACTION AND COMPLIANCE OF FAMILY IN TREATMENT

Helpfulness Ratings

____a. Solicit youth's rating of helpfulness for the respective treatment component on the following 7-point scale after stating the youth should not feel obligated to provide high scores because an honest assessment helps the treatment provider better address youth needs.
(**7** = extremely helpful, **6** = very helpful, **5** = somewhat helpful, **4** = not sure, **3** = somewhat unhelpful, **2** = very unhelpful, **1** = extremely unhelpful). Youth's Rating: _____.

____b. Solicit how rating was derived and methods of improving the intervention component in the future.

Compliance Ratings

____a. Disclose therapist's rating of the youth and family's compliance on the following 7-point scale (**7** = extremely compliant, **6** = very compliant, **5** = somewhat compliant, **4** = neutral, **3** = somewhat noncompliant, **2** = very noncompliant, **1** = extremely noncompliant). Therapist's Rating: ____
   • Factors that contribute to compliance ratings are:
      1. Attendance
      2 Participation and conduct in session
      3 Homework completion

____b. Explain how the rating was derived and methods of improving performance in future.

2

Infrastructure

Overview

This chapter reviews clinic infrastructure and quality assurance procedures for use in Family Behavior Therapy (FBT) training and record keeping. The review underscores standardized forms that were developed to assist in the implementation and management of FBT in community agencies, and are provided as Exhibits 2.1 through 2.10 at the end of the chapter. The forms are also included in the enclosed CD to permit them to be modified to accommodate cultural, legal, and reporting requirements that may differ across treatment agencies. Updated materials may be available through correspondence with Brad Donohue.

Infrastructure and Quality Assurance

There are a number of infrastructural concerns that must be considered when implementing evidence-based treatments (EBTs), such as FBT. First, treatment providers (TPs) need to be qualified to administer FBT, and agency administrators need to be sufficiently prepared to support FBT training and sustainability. This section, therefore, identifies methods of determining, securing, and sustaining appropriate resources, training, and quality assurance programming.

Treatment Providers and Supervisors

One TP is required to implement FBT when adolescents are considered the identified client. Treatment providers should be state-licensed and legally qualified to provide therapeutic and/or substance abuse services, or practice under the supervision of a state-licensed mental health or substance abuse service provider with such qualifications. TPs should ideally be counselors, therapists, psychologists, or substance abuse treatment providers who have experience serving the population that is being targeted in treatment, and must have an interest in conducting FBT. Supervisors should ideally have experience in conducting EBTs, particularly cognitive–behavioral therapies, and must have professional therapeutic experience serving the population that is being treated.

Assuring a Sufficient Number of Clients

It is possible to secure resources to learn and implement FBT, and subsequently, to evidence difficulties soliciting a sufficient number of client referrals. This is usually not a fatal blow since it is probably important for TPs to assume small caseloads when first learning to implement EBTs. However, within 6 months of initiating training in FBT, it is important that TPs maintain full caseloads to assure program sustainability. Along these lines, a number of strategies may be helpful in soliciting referrals. First, administrators of potential referral agencies may be approached to determine their needs and assess the extent of their interest in FBT. Some of these agencies include juvenile justice programs, family and juvenile court, juvenile group homes, juvenile prisons and correctional institutions, family service agencies, large corporations that are responsible for the mental health care of their employees, and private practitioners. In doing so, it is important to query which specific juvenile populations or problem behaviors the funding or referral agency is most interested in treating, and determine if plans can be made to accommodate these needs with the implementation of FBT.

After potential referral agents (agencies) are identified and their program needs are initially assessed, it is important to conduct succinct professional presentations at their facilities aimed at showing them how FBT can be administered to satisfy their referral needs. To assist in this endeavor, the FBT Presentation to Assist in Obtaining Referrals checklist is included at the end of this chapter as Exhibit 2.1. This checklist includes sequential instructions that may be utilized to prompt correct responding in the preparation and implementation of formal meetings to solicit referrals. This form may need to be customized to accommodate the unique needs of each referral agency. In the first section of this form (i.e., "Preparation for Presentation"), prompts are provided to determine if the agency representative would be interested in having a 30- to 45-minute presentation that is designed to enhance cohesion, communication, and positive relationships within the referral agency itself. These meetings are designed to be fun and foster an experiential appreciation of FBT. For instance, "Reciprocity Awareness for Coworkers" might be developed from the "Reciprocity Awareness" intervention (see Chapter 8). In the latter example, coworkers would be substituted for family members, and the referral agency staff would be prompted to exchange things they loved, admired, or respected about each other in small groups. For the "Positive Request" intervention component (see Chapter 9), the TP could model how this communication technique may be used to ask for a raise, or ask a coworker to substitute a shift. The larger group could then be split into pairs to practice while the TP provides feedback. Finally, for the Self-Control component (see Chapter 11), the TP could model the management of someone taking a pencil off her desk without permission. The group could then be split into pairs to practice the Self-Control procedure while the TP walks around providing feedback. Of course, these presentations permit the referral agency staff to experience the relative strengths of FBT firsthand while enabling the treatment provider to establish rapport with the referral agents. Similar activities can be performed to solicit referrals from school administrators (i.e., "I've Got a Great Classroom" instead of Reciprocity Awareness—teacher and students are the participants).

Other preparatory instructions (prompts) are included in the FBT Presentation to Assist in Obtaining Referrals checklist. For instance, there are prompts to obtain basic contact information from the referral agent, as well as to gather important materials from your program to distribute to the referral agency (i.e., forms for the referral agent to complete when making referrals, brochures that describe your program, business cards, sign-up sheets to solicit future contact information with members of the agency). Also relevant to preparation, there are prompts to gather treats that may be distributed to participants during the recruitment presentations (e.g., donuts, coffee).

The Presentation to Assist in Obtaining Referral checklist also includes specific instructions to perform when conducting the client recruitment presentation itself. The presentation is initiated with a 15-minute description FBT, including introductions, solicitation of contact information, description of FBT and its benefits, and steps involved in making referrals. To assist in this endeavor, a sample template of a recruitment brochure is included as Exhibit 2.2. As can be seen, the template includes written prompts in all capital letters where idiosyncratic information about your agency may be recorded, such as your contact information, directions to your treatment facility, and criteria necessary for youth to be included in your program. Of course, this form should be distributed to the referral agents to assist them in making referrals.

The presentation ends with the experiential exercise that was mentioned earlier in this section. Participants are usually encouraged to democratically choose the exercise they are interested in reviewing among Reciprocity Awareness, Positive Request, or Self-Control. However, the exercise may be determined by the referral agency's administrator a priori. The purpose of these exercises is twofold: (a) establish rapport and have fun, and (b) demonstrate the power of positive reinforcement offered within the FBT model. The TP should provide clear and succinct instructions.

Methods of Learning FBT

There are a number of training options available in learning FBT. The most inexpensive method of training involves studying this book. Someone who is familiar with the treatment of substance abuse and EBT implementation, particularly behavior therapies, may find this method sufficient. Along these lines, cost-free films will soon be available from Dr. Donohue that depict appropriate implementation of FBT utilizing actors, and continuing education units are available after this book is read and a brief quiz is passed (see back of this book). When more intensive training is desired or needed, interactive continuing education opportunities are also available through independent TPs who have received extensive training in FBT and have expressed an interest in the provision of on-site training. A list of these providers may be obtained from Dr. Donohue. There are no standard fees, as training fees are negotiated between the treatment agency wishing to implement FBT and the trainer. Alternatively, Dr. Donohue currently teaches a course in FBT, and maintains a web site that includes information about FBT, at the University of Nevada, Las Vegas. FBT trainers generally utilize the following consultative approach, although instruction may vary.

Consultative Approach to Learning FBT   Of course, clinical expertise and adherence to evidence-based protocols like FBT are enhanced by interactive ongoing training (Bartholomew, Joe, Rowan-Szal, & Simpson, 2007). Intensive training in FBT initially involves a series of conference calls from a reputable trainer and the administration of structured questionnaires to participating TPs and their administrators to assist in customizing the FBT training experience to fit the agency's culture. There are currently three training packages available that are thematically organized as follows:

1. *Drug- and Other Problem Behavior–Specific Training Module:* Includes Level System (Chapter 6), Environmental (Stimulus) Control (Chapter 10), and Self-Control (Chapter 11).

2. *Family Relationship and Job Getting Training Module:* Includes Reciprocity Awareness (Chapter 8), Positive Request (Chapter 9), and Job-Getting Skills Training (Chapter 12).

3. *Comprehensive FBT Training Module:* Includes all FBT interventions listed above.

   Note: Program Orientation (Chapter 1), Agendas (Chapter 4), Treatment Planning (Chapter 7), and Consequence Review (Chapter 5) are included within each training package.

The drug- and other problem behavior–specific module typically requires a 2.5-day initial workshop, the family relationship and job-getting training module requires a 2-day initial workshop, and the comprehensive FBT module requires a 3.5-day initial workshop. All workshops are followed by ongoing teleconference training calls that usually last about an hour. These teleconference calls initially occur once per week and fade in frequency over the course of 3 months to a year. TPs who receive the comprehensive training package are encouraged to additionally participate in a 2-day booster workshop that is usually scheduled to occur 6 months after the initial workshop. Of course, the comprehensive FBT training module is recommended but requires greater time and resources. Most treatment agencies fund their training experience through federal and state grants and private foundations.

Initial Workshop   During the initial workshops, FBT interventions are usually taught in a conceptually driven sequence. For instance, in the comprehensive training package, the Session Agenda is taught first, then Consequence Review, Level System, Treatment Planning, and finally the remaining skill-based interventions in no particular order. After introductions, trainers usually present a slide show demonstrating the theory and empirical background supporting FBT, as well as a general overview of its treatment components and agenda for the workshop. Each intervention component is first modeled by the trainer utilizing the initial session prompting checklist while participating TPs sequentially take turns portraying the role of a client, each for about 5 minutes. Rather than asking questions during these role-plays, TPs are instructed to "act out" problems during the role-plays, which helps maintain flow and contextual appreciation of issues that are relevant to clinical management (Rowan-Szal, Greener, Joe, & Simpson, 2007). For instance, if a TP were curious to learn what the trainer would do if an adolescent client said he didn't want to do a therapy assignment, the TP would tell the trainer he didn't want to do the assignment when asked to do so by the trainer in the role-play. The roles are then reversed, with the trainer portraying the role of a relatively compliant client and the trainees assuming the role of a TP, each for about 5 minutes. TPs are instructed to "work out" their mistakes as if they are in a real session. Positive feedback is offered by the trainer and other TPs after each role-play has finished. The trainer points out clinical skills that were effectively demonstrated, and suggests ways to improve them further, whenever necessary. After initial session protocols are modeled, the trainer and TPs role-play future sessions in a similar manner. Trainees are also sometimes encouraged to "break out" into pairs to role-play the interventions while the trainer walks about the room providing encouragement, guidance and instruction throughout.

Ongoing Training and Case Monitoring   After the initial training workshop is conducted, the TPs and their supervisor participate in weekly 1- to 2-hour teleconference meetings with the FBT trainer. Of course, if an outside trainer was not involved in training, these meetings would include only program staff, with the supervisor taking on the additional role of the trainer. The meetings usually occur once per week for about 60 to 90 minutes initially and fade in occurrence as TPs master FBT. These ongoing training sessions are feasible because supervisors usually manage their legal and ethical responsibilities during these sessions. That is, supervisory tasks and training tasks are reviewed conjointly. Audiotape recordings of intervention sessions and case records of each of the clients are brought to these meetings. The supervisor is taught to utilize a standardized form to monitor cases (Exhibit 2.3, Record of Ongoing FBT Training Form), and a prompting checklist to guide the administration of activities during these meetings (Exhibit 2.4, Case Review for Ongoing FBT Training Form). To assist in maintaining confidentiality of clients, it is recommended that trainers are "not" provided names or other information that would identify clients, and that appropriate information releases are obtained from clients to permit agency staff to share confidential information about them with the trainer. As noted from Exhibit 2.3, the Record of Ongoing FBT Training form includes basic descriptive information about each client, as well as important details relevant to legal and ethical issues that may need to be reviewed during the ongoing training meeting, such as incidents or emergencies, court-related activities, outstanding notes, and recommendations. There are also prompts to record information that is relevant to treatment integrity, such as whether treatment integrity feedback was provided to TPs from persons who listened to randomly selected session audiotapes (usually the trainer but also from co-TPs or supervisors), or if session audiotapes were reviewed during the ongoing meeting. Thus, for each client, the supervisor has an ongoing record of the TPs' efforts in providing FBT.

The Case Review for Ongoing FBT Training Form (Exhibit 2.4) focuses on improving implementation of the FBT interventions, including discussion of therapist style, role-playing to teach therapeutic skills, and descriptive feedback on adherence rating forms, and provides positive feedback for successful efforts to implement treatment. Monitoring adherence to treatment protocols is essential when trainees are first learning to implement EBTs (Madson, Campbell, Barrett, Brondino, & Melchert, 2005) but is also important for more seasoned TPs, as there is always the potential for drifting from standardized procedures over time. Therefore, all TPs receive feedback regarding the quality and extent to which they provided therapy with integrity, with more frequent feedback for those with less experience. As can be seen in Exhibit 2.4, the Case Review for Ongoing Training Form, each therapist reviews the number of cases seen during the past week, and TPs are encouraged to use structured problem-solving exercises to assist them in generating solutions when clients are not attending therapy sessions as prescribed. The supervisor decides the order of case review with input from TPs. Priority is typically given to inexperienced TPs (Morgan & Sprenkle, 2007) or to complicated cases, particularly those where there is a threat of self-harm or harm to others. Treatment providers report case feedback using the Case Review for Ongoing Training form. For cases that are reviewed for the first time, TPs disclose basic identifying information, including the client's demographic information; reason for referral; family constellation, including the number of children who may be living in the home and their ages; diagnostic information; drug use history; personal strengths and areas of growth; a brief conceptualization of how presenting problems developed and are maintained; and a tentative treatment plan. These case presentations last less than 10 to 15 minutes. Random sections of session audiotapes or areas warranting particular attention are then reviewed for about 5 minutes. The supervisor may permit TPs to present particular sections of tapes. However, it is important to appreciate that TPs sometimes may be less inclined to volunteer sections where they experienced greatest relative difficulty.

For cases previously presented, only brief descriptive information is provided by the TP to identify the case to the supervisor. TPs then present the reason for referral, current session number, estimate of the percentage of scheduled sessions attended, any family members present during the session, the treatment module(s) completed, and plans for the next session. When necessary, the TPs, supervisor, and trainer, if available, also discuss methods of incorporating other family members into future sessions, and solutions to help resolve problems that occurred during the session. The supervisor initiates a case review that lasts approximately 10 minutes and includes a random review of the session tape, and sometimes a review of clinical records for quality assurance.

In cases where youth clients were not seen, the supervisor and TP may discuss family support systems that may be recruited, problems that possibly influenced session nonattendance, and strategies to increase attendance at subsequent sessions. This case review supervision format encourages TPs to be independent and improves their skills in retaining clients in therapy, while allowing for appropriate oversight of cases.

At the end of the ongoing training/supervision session, supervisors place session audiotapes in a locked filing cabinet for evaluation of protocol adherence. At least one session audiotape (or about 10% if possible) of the pool of tapes available is randomly selected for review by the trainer to assist in the assessment of protocol adherence (see Chapter 1). However, when TPs are inexperienced or evidence difficulties or low attendance in their treatment sessions, they are also encouraged to review session audiotapes for treatment integrity utilizing the respective prompting checklists. Of course, conducting treatment integrity checks enhances clinical skill sets by familiarizing TPs with the intervention protocols.

Booster Workshop   The booster workshop that is performed in the comprehensive training module is similar to the initial workshop, with the exception that the trainer does not model each FBT intervention. Rather, FBT TPs take turns modeling/practicing in the therapist's role (5-minute blocks), with the trainer serving as the client. The trainer increases the difficulty level of the role-play commensurate with TP experience level. The trainer provides feedback between each role-play. In this way, inexperienced TPs are able to view senior TPs implementing the interventions in difficult scenarios, while still practicing FBT at an appropriate level of difficulty. Furthermore, experienced TPs have opportunities to sharpen their skills at an advanced level.

Record Keeping

It is important to ensure that clinic operations and other contextual factors are managed effectively when implementing FBT. Of course, quality assurance is greatly enhanced when treatment is administered with integrity, and some of the methods that were reviewed earlier in this chapter assist in this process. However, case management procedures such as record keeping are also extremely important in assuring quality care in clients. Several forms are included in this chapter to assist in efficient record keeping that is relevant to FBT. These forms are standardized and have undergone several years of revision based on the feedback of TPs and administrators in both community and clinical research settings. Some agencies and practitioners may prefer to modify these forms or be comfortable with their own record-keeping system. Indeed, some treatment providers may be obligated to use electronic record-keeping systems. Nevertheless, utilization of standardized record-keeping forms may decrease errors and enhance consistency between the persons who complete them. Of course, these forms are legal documents; thus, it is strongly recommended that appropriate program representatives and legal counsel examine each of these forms to ensure that they are legally and ethically appropriate and consistent with state laws and relevant licensing boards.

Client records are organized in a folder that includes a Table of Contents for Client Record form (Exhibit 2.5) that may be used to guide agency staff through the record. The forms may be incorporated easily into electronic filing systems, and particular forms may be modified or omitted when redundancy occurs within existing systems. The table of contents lists the following documents (of course, other documents may be necessary, and these documents may require revision or exclusion based on state laws and agency culture):

1. *Termination Report*: There is no standardized treatment termination report, but treatment agencies usually complete their own treatment termination reports immediately after the client is severed from the treatment program. The content of these documents varies due to extenuating circumstances, but generally include demographic information about the client, reason for referral, type of treatment provided, response to treatment, reasons for program termination, status at the time of termination/discharge, and discharge plans. Although the duration of FBT usually occurs up to 4 to 6 months, treatment agency staff must determine when appropriate termination is warranted.

2. *Table of Contents for Client Record* (Exhibit 2.5): Shows how the client record is organized. Forms on the left side of the chart record are listed in numerical order (top to bottom) in the left column, and forms on the right side of the chart are listed in numerical order in the right side.

3. *Log of Contacts Form* (Exhibit 2.6): Summarizes all legal communication with the client or appropriate others that is in the record, and includes the date, duration of contact, person making the contact, and type of contact.

4. *Monthly Progress Report to Referral Agency Form* (Exhibit 2.7): Sent to referral agents (if appropriate) once per month upon consent of clients to show how clients are progressing in therapy. These reports may assist in motivating clients to do well in accomplishing their treatment goals through the establishment of accountability. These standardized reports reveal common information typically required by most referral agents, such as the number of sessions attended during the past month and up to that time, promptness to sessions, nonattendance rates, treatments addressed, and compliance/effort of clients during the past month. However, there is also space available in the form to record outstanding notes that are relevant to the case, such as therapeutic progress in therapy.

5. *Outside Correspondence*: As determined by the treatment agency, this section includes all written outside correspondence provided to others and received by others, such as emails, court reports, and letters.

6. *Treatment Plan* (see Chapter 7, Intervention Priority Worksheet, Exhibit 7.3): Shows which FBT treatments were preferred by clients and how treatments will be implemented. Treatment agency staff are especially likely to have their own treatment plan forms to either complement or replace the Intervention Priority Worksheet.

7. *Demographic Form*: Shows relevant demographic and contact information. The content of these forms is idiosyncratically determined by appropriate treatment agency staff.

8. *Informed Consent and Releases to Provide/Receive Information*: The content of all consent forms is determined consistent with state and federal laws, and these forms are required for the protection of clients. The treatment agency fully determines the content of these forms.

9. *Standard Treatment Session Progress Notes* (Exhibit 2.8): A record of content reviewed during each FBT session. The form was designed to be quick and easy to complete, while including relevant information specific to the implementation of FBT. Treatment providers are prompted to indicate the date and time of the session, who was present, and the session number. To assist in appropriate supervision and safety of clients, TPs are prompted to record if any "adverse events" (e.g., issues that threaten the safety of the individual) occurred during the session, and if the supervisor was notified within 24 hours. All FBT interventions are listed, permitting them to be circled if they were implemented. Relevant information about each intervention may be recorded quickly in response to standard fill-in-the-blank prompts, such as duration of implementation (which is derived from the start and finish times of each prompting checklist), the protocol adherence or treatment integrity score (percentage of steps completed as derived from the prompting checklist), helpfulness and compliance ratings (derived from the Ratings section at the bottom of each prompting checklist), and if homework was complete or incomplete, and assigned. Of course, the latter information assists TPs in maintaining protocol adherence. There is also space to record information that is not specific to effort demonstrated during the implementation of intervention components, such as therapeutic progress in therapy, and experienced life stressors.

10. *Extra–Treatment Session Progress Notes* (Exhibit 2.9): Consists of clinical information that is not typically recorded in the Standardized Treatment

Session Progress Notes, including telephone contacts, court appearances, emails, content in letters, and so on.

11. *Treatment Session Worksheets:* Include all worksheets that are completed by clients.

12. *Testing Results:* Include all testing results and measures completed by clients.

Method of Checking Quality Assurance of Client Records

To assist in maintaining appropriate records, we have developed a monitoring system to accompany the aforementioned forms (see Exhibit 2.10, Monitoring Form to Assist in Appropriate Record Keeping.). This form is completed by a staff member who is familiar with client record-keeping procedures, such as a TP or ideally an administrator of the agency. In addition to printing the name of the reviewer and TP responsible for the chart, the reviewer lists the date of review as well as the date that the necessary revisions to the record are due if errors are determined when reviewing the record. Briefly, the reviewer examines each form (listed in the left-most column) to determine if the following errors are present: (a) form is missing, (b) form is sloppy, (c) a required date is not recorded, (d) a time or duration is not recorded, (e) supervisor signature is missing, (f) client signature is missing, (g) there is relevant information missing, and (h) the identification number (or name) of the client is missing. If an error is detected in the record, the reviewer indicates the error with a check mark in the appropriate column and row corresponding to the form and error type. If an "NA" is indicated in the column representing the type of error and row representing the form, the respective error for that form is not applicable.

Several potential errors are not specific to particular forms. Rather, these errors are systemic and include (a) the order of forms is incorrect, (b) the Log of Contacts and Standard Treatment Progress Notes or (c) Log of Contacts and Extra–Treatment Session Progress Notes do not match, and (d) the Monthly Progress Reports do not include a cover sheet and fax confirmation. These errors are indicated with a "yes" or "no" response.

This overall method of monitoring client records is relatively easy to teach and highly effective in reducing errors that are common to record keeping. However, it is important that TPs are encouraged to show reviewers how they have corrected errors during the presence of their supervisors or that their supervisors actively support the chart record reviewers to assist in account-ability. The time required to monitor client records in this manner will vary depending on a number of issues, such as the extent of treatment received, experience and conscientiousness of the TP responsible for the record, and involvement of legal entities. However, most records may be completed in about 10 minutes the first time the monitoring system is implemented, and about 5 minutes thereafter. Most records should be monitored on a monthly or every other month basis to assist in maintaining quality assurance while balancing parsimony when resources are limited.

Concluding Remarks

Recognizing inherent difficulties involved in the adoption of evidence-supported interventions within community settings, FBT was developed to be relatively easy to learn and implement, flexible to concurrently address multiple problem areas, and include interventions that are fun to implement and consumer driven. A relative strength of FBT, as noted in the National Registry of Evidence-Based Programs and Practices (2008), is its inclusion of the many standardized forms reviewed in this chapter. However, it should be emphasized that some of these forms may be inappropriate in their current form and thus require adjustments to fit the agency's culture. Electronic forms are listed in the CD-ROM attached to the backside cover. The forms are set up to make it easy to make changes. Of course, because reporting requirements may vary across state and local governments, treatment agency representatives should consider qualified legal representation in the adoption and revision of these forms, including standardized procedures underlying their use.

Supporting Materials for Chapter 2: Infrastructure

Exhibit 2.1. Prompting Checklist for Recruitment Presentation.

FBT PRESENTATION TO ASSIST IN OBTAINING REFERRALS

PRESENTER PROMPTING CHECKLIST

Preparation for Presentation

☐ Review presentation options w/referral agent.
- Indicate FBT-related activities can be performed pro bono w/the agency to enhance cohesion, communication, and positive relationships among the agency staff members (about 30 to 45 min.)
  - Use Reciprocity Awareness in small groups w/coworkers instead of family.
  - Use abbreviated Positive Request w/coworkers instead of family.
  - Use Self Control w/c-workers instead of family.
- Indicate the presentation describing FBT can be conducted in about 10 to 15 min. (and includes donuts and coffee if funding permits).

☐ Establish what presentation will include w/referral agent and for how long.

☐ Obtain address and contact information for presentation.
- Street address (Map Quest if necessary)
- Phone number
- Contact person (typically a supervisor)

☐ Obtain FBT program forms:
- Forms necessary for agencies to make referrals (approx. 5 for each agent).
- Program brochures describing your program for agency attendees.
- Sign-up sheet for individuals who attend meeting (record names, emails, phone #s).
- Personal business cards.
- Protocol checklists for interventions to be implemented w/agency staff (if relevant).
  Note: Paper clip business cards to program brochures.

☐ Purchase small token gifts to distribute to attendees for answering questions about presentation.
- Candy, gum, snacks, coffee/drinks, and/or costume jewelry for attendees to give to their clients.

☐ Purchase drinks, donuts, snacks, token gifts, etc. for meeting, if funding permits.

Day of Presentation

☐ Add 15 min. to estimated drive time to avoid tardiness.

Presentation Introduction

☐ Introduce self and affiliation (include position held).

☐ State gratitude for permitting presentation.

☐ Distribute sign-in sheet for attendees.

☐ Provide the following to all presentation attendees:

- Forms necessary for agencies to make referrals (approx. 5 for each agent).
- Program brochure describing program for agency attendees.
- Sign-up sheet for people who attend meeting (record names, emails, and phone #s).
- Personal business cards.

☐ State who program targets (e.g., adolescents w/ drug abuse and their families).

☐ Provide the following list of benefits:

☐ Relatively low program costs for participation.

☐ Clients and family members choose from list of evidence-based and skills-building interventions.

☐ Indicate the typical anticipated # of sessions (i.e., about 16 sessions within 4 to 6 months).

☐ Mention client's significant others are involved, as appropriate.

☐ Open communication w/ referral agent is desired.

- Monthly progress notes may be sent to referral agent if desired, and w/ release from youth and youth's parents (regarding therapy attendance, compliance, effort, progress).
- Monthly calls made to referral agent (re. therapy attendance, compliance, effort) w/ releases.
- Referral agent notified of missed sessions w/in 24 hrs. if release obtained.

☐ Advocacy for clients in scheduled court hearings (if relevant).

Treatment Review

☐ Highlight FBT Tx. modules (time is limited so curtail extensive description):

1. **Consequence Review:** Determining and facilitating motivation from youth about illicit behavior, particularly substance use.

2. **Level System:** Establishing and implementing rewards from the youth's social ecology for staying clean and out of trouble.

3. **Treatment Planning:** Mutually determining which treatments are most relevant to accomplishing the youth's goals while balancing needs of family.

4. **Environmental (Stimulus) Control:** Arranging environment to spend more time w/ people, places, and situations that do not involve drugs and trouble, and less time w/ people, places, and situations that do involve drugs, including management of these situations.

5. **Reciprocity Awareness:** Family exchanges things they love, admire, and respect about each other to enhance overall tone in the relationship.

6. **Positive Request:** Skills in requesting things and compromising.

7. **Self-Control:** Recognizing and managing negative emotions and troublesome behavior, including substance use, through thought stopping, reviewing negative consequences, problem solving, and positive imagery for having done desired actions.

8. **Job-Getting Skills Training:** Skills relevant to soliciting job interviews, preparing for job interviews, and doing well in job interviews.

Referral Form Review (refer to the form necessary to make a referral):

☐ State criteria necessary to make a referral.

☐ Show how to complete the referral form.

☐ Tell agents to call the clinic after referral is faxed to assure its receipt.

Referral Process Review

☐ Let agency know what to expect once a referral is received at FBT clinic.

☐ Solicit questions.

☐ Solicit referrals and completed sign-up sheet.

FBT Experiential Exercise

☐ Solicit if group wants to do Reciprocity Awareness, Positive Request, or Self-Control for Coworkers.

☐ Engage the group in the respective exercise, if desired.

    - It will be necessary to make adjustments to the prompting checklist for the exercise to be implemented (e.g., Reciprocity Awareness Therapist Prompting Checklist).

☐ Solicit what was liked about exercise and disclose that similar exercises occur in FBT w/ families.

After Presentation

☐ Send thank you letter w/ referral forms to contact person (typically supervisor).

Example Letter:

On behalf of the staff at (AGENCY NAME), we would like to thank you for your support of our treatment program and look forward to working with you in the future. We have enclosed some additional referral forms for your staff. We can be reached at (AGENCY PHONE NUMBER) if you have any questions or need anything.

Sincerely,

TEAM MEMBER'S NAME AND TITLE

☐ Send thank you email w/ an electronic version of the referral form to all attendees of presentation

Example Email:

Thank you for your support of our program. We have attached an electronic version of our referral form so you can conveniently print when you need to fax a referral to our office at AGENCY FAX NUMBER. We can be reached at (AGENCY PHONE NUMBER) if you have any questions or need anything.

We look forward to working with you,

Sincerely,

TEAM MEMBER'S NAME AND TITLE

Exhibit 2.2. Recruitment Brochure.

Contact Information:

****INSERT CONTACT
PERSON'S NAME AND
TITLE HERE****

****INSERT CONTACT
PERSON'S NAME AND
CONTACT INFO. HERE****

****AGENCY NAME AND
ADDRESS HERE****

Directions:

****PUT DIRECTIONS FROM A
FEW MAJOR STREETS OR
LOCATIONS HERE****

****COMPANY LOGO
HERE****

Please enjoy learning about our program,
which includes Family Behavior Therapy,
an evidence-based program listed in
SAMHSA's National Registry of
Evidenced-Based Programs and Practices
and other national clearinghouses.

The development and dissemination of
Family Behavior Therapy was funded by
grant awards from the National Institutes of
Health and the Substance Abuse and Mental
Health Services Administration.

45

Who Is Eligible?

Any adolescent who meets the following criteria can be referred for an evaluation to determine program eligibility:

- Adolescents who have recently been identified to use illicit drugs,

- Adolescents who have someone who is willing to participate in the client's treatment.

ADD OTHER CRITERIA HERE

What are the costs? **PUT COSTS HERE** OR OMIT SECTION**

How do I make a referral?

INSERT TELEPHONE AND FAX NUMBER HERE

Services Include:

- ****LIST # AND MONTHS OF TREATMENT HERE, IF RELEVANT****

- Involvement of family members.

- Evidence-supported Family Behavior Therapy targets:
  - Alcohol & drug abuse
  - Behavior problems
  - Mood disorders
- Family dysfunction
- Under/unemployment.
- Poor communication skills
- Anger management
- Poor school performance

ADD MORE INFORMATION HERE THAT IS SPECIFIC TO YOUR PROGRAM

PUT AGENCY LOGO HERE

Exhibit 2.3. Record of Ongoing FBT Training Form.

RECORD OF ONGOING FBT TRAINING FORM

Identification number of youth:_____

Relationship(s) of adult and child significant others:_____

Age(s) of children living in the home:_____

Unique or Important Characteristics about case (to jar memory)_____

Primary treatment targets (including specific illicit drugs):_____

Reason for referral:_____

Date & Week					
Incidents addressed	Yes, No	Yes, No	Yes, No	Yes, No	Yes, No
Court activities addressed	Yes, No	Yes, No	Yes, No	Yes, No	Yes, No
Feedback provided about protocol adherence from someone who listened to an audiotape of session	Yes, No	Yes, No	Yes, No	Yes, No	Yes, No
Session audiotape reviewed during ongoing session	Yes, No	Yes, No	Yes, No	Yes, No	Yes, No
Outstanding recommendations made					
Outstanding notes					

Exhibit 2.4. Case Review for Ongoing FBT Training Form.

CASE REVIEW FOR ONGOING FBT TRAINING FORM

Preparation for Case Review Meetings

a.   Include up to 6 treatment providers and 1 supervisor (possible trainer).
b.   Meetings usually last about 1 hr. (up to 4 providers) to 90 min. (4 to 6 providers).
c.   Require 1 audiotape recorder for audiotape review.
d.   Require providers to bring audiotapes for each therapy session during week.
e.   May require providers to bring treatment records for each active client (or have quick access).
f.   Require providers to bring copies of this form to guide case review.

Protocol for Case Review

a.   Supervisor or lead provider distributes new referrals to providers.
b.   Providers summarize phone calls made to enlist and retain clients.
  1.   Report client ID# numbers contacted.
  2.   Report outstanding issues, if any, for each client/family member contacted.
c.   FBT trainer (if present) or supervisor gives feedback relevant to protocol adherence for a session audiotape that was scored for adherence since last ongoing training.
  1.   Provide strengths in style and methods used by provider to accomplish adherence.
  2.   Provide strengths in style and methods of accomplishing adherence.
  3.   Provide things to enhance protocol adherence.
  4.   Provide things to enhance protocol adherence, if possible.
d.   Each provider reports:
  1.   Caseload (i.e., how many clients each provider is assigned to treat each week).
  2.   # clients seen since last case review.
  3.   Any incidents (emergencies) that need to be addressed immediately.
e.   Cases presented by providers using "CASE REVIEW" format (see below).
  1.   Supervisor or lead provider prioritizes which cases to review and for how long:
    a.   Cases that are difficult/evidencing incidents or potential problems have top priority.
    b.   Cases that have received relatively less attention in recent past are prioritized.
  2.   Supervisor /lead provider completes "Record of FBT Cases" form for each assigned case.
f.   Randomly assign 1 session audiotape for adherence review by trainer (if present) and 1 session audiotape for a provider, prioritizing which provider conducts the review based on:
  1.   Providers attempting to learn intervention.
  2.   Providers experiencing difficulties w/ protocol adherence.
  3.   Providers who didn't maintain active caseload during previous week.
h.   Supervisor completes protocol adherence form (kept, e.g., in supervision binder).

Note: Monthly Progress Notes should probably be reviewed the last week of every month.

SEE THE FOLLOWING CONTENT ITEMS FOR HOW CASES ARE TO BE REVIEWED (CASE REVIEW FORMAT)

Content for Presenting a Case for the First Time by a Provider (About 5 to 10 Min.)

a. Useful info about client (i.e., approx. age, # of previous tx. programs attended).
b. Reason for referral.
c. #, and ages, of children in home.
d. Drug of choice and brief summary of assessment tools/measures administered.
e. Synopsis of strengths obtained from pretreatment assessment.
f. Synopsis of areas warranting greatest improvement from pretreatment assessment.
g. Conceptualization of case (i.e., how did probs. develop, how are they maintained).
h. Treatment plan (or tentative treatment plan).
i. Plans for next session.
j. Random review of session tape (optional).
    1. Supervisor determines what sections are reviewed and for how long.

Content for Presenting a Case That Has Been Presented Previously (About 5 to 10 Min.)

a. Client # and idiosyncratic info about client to jar memory.
b. Reason for referral.
c. Approximate percentage of scheduled sessions attended.
d. Family members present in last session and methods of including more family in future.
e. FBT treatment components completed thus far.
f. Notable problems that occurred during the session.
g. General comments on how client is doing and overall improvement.
h. Plans for next session.
i. Random review of session tape (optional).
    1. Supervisor/lead provider determines what sections reviewed and for how long.

Content for Presenting a Case That Has Been Presented Previously, but Did Not Attend Scheduled Session During Past Week (About 5 Min.)

a. Client # and idiosyncratic info about client to refresh memory.
b. Reason for referral.
c. Approximate percentage of scheduled sessions attended.
d. Family support available to attempt to bring about session attendance.
e. Notable problems that may have influenced nonattendance.
f. Plans to increase future attendance.

Exhibit 2.5. Table of Contents for Client Record.

TABLE OF CONTENTS FOR CLIENT RECORD

TREATMENT FILE

Client Name:_____

Primary Clinician Name and Credentials:_____

Date of Intake/Admission:_____

Left Side of Chart Record (listed from top to bottom)	Right Side of Chart Record (listed from top to bottom)
1. **Termination Report** (added to chart by treatment provider <u>once client is terminated</u>)	9. *Standard Treatment Session Progress Notes*
2. **Table of Contents**	10. **Extra-Treatment Progress Notes**
3. **Log of Contacts**	11. **Completed Treatment Session Worksheets**
	12. **Testing Results**
4. **Monthly Progress Reports** (added by treatment provider each month)	
5. **Outside Correspondence** (i.e., emails, court reports, letters to and from client, etc.)	
6. **Treatment Plan** (added by treatment provider once treatment plan is developed)	
7. **Demographics Form**	
8. **Consent/Releases to/for Information**	

Exhibit 2.6. Log of Contacts Form.

LOG OF CONTACTS

Date of Contact (mm/dd/yy)	Duration of Contact (e.g., 12:00 PM– 11:00 PM)	Outside Person Involved in Contact/Attempted Contact (e.g., client, case worker, probation officer)	Type of Contact	Staff Involved in Contact

Key for type of contacts:

TC = telephone contact   **M** = meeting   **CH** = court hearing

E = email   **F** = fax   **Text** = text message

LM = left message   **TA/NA** = telephone attempt, no answer

Exhibit 2.7. Monthly Progress Report to Referral Agency Form.

MONTHLY PROGRESS REPORT	Client ID:_____ Referral Agent's Name:_____ Client Name:_____

DATES OF PROGRESS: _____ TO _____

Date treatment began: _____

# of Sessions Attended During Month	# of Session Late During Month (15 min. or more)	# of Session Cancelled or No-Showed During Month	# of Sessions Rescheduled During Month	Total Number of Sessions Attended to Date

Treatments performed during month:	Treatment Addressed During the Month (Check = Yes)	Avg. Provider Rating for Client's Compliance (1 = Needs Improvement 2 = Adequate 3 = Very Good)
Program Orientation (review of program policies and communication guidelines).		
Consequence Review (instilling motivation in youth client through review of negative consequences)		
Level Sytem (teaches youth client to develop and manage goals that are consistent with treatment plan, and establishes rewards for goal accomplishment).		
Treatment Planning (youth client, parent, and provider determine relevant treatment interventions).		
Environmental (Stimulus) Control (assist youth client in recognizing triggers to substance use and other problem behaviors, and reviewing methods of escaping and/or avoiding such triggers—teaches how to structure environment to be healthy.		

Reciprocity Awareness (improves positive exchanges among family members and overall tone in the relationship).		
Positive Request (teaches family how to make requests of others that increase likelihood of getting needs met, and also resolving conflicts effectively).		
Self Control (assists youth client in terminating thoughts that lead to drug use and other problem behaviors, learning relaxation strategies to reduce stress, learning to brainstorm and perform alternative actions, positive imagery for desired behaviors).		
Job-Getting Skills Training (assists family in gaining satisfactory employment)		
Last Session Review (review all implemented treatments with family and discuss how family can plan to use developed skills to keep youth client)		

Outstanding Notes:_____

_____

_____

_____

_____

Name of Provider(s): _____

Provider Signature/Title: _____

Supervisor Signature/Title: _____

Exhibit 2.8. Standard Treatment Session Progress Notes.

STANDARD TREATMENT SESSION PROGRESS NOTES

Client ID: _____ Date: ___/___/___ Time: from ___:___ AM / PM to ___:___ AM / PM Session Number: _____

Persons Present in Session: _____

Did any adverse incidents (threats to safety) occur during the session? Yes/No
If yes, was supervisor informed within 24 hrs.? Yes/No

Print First and Last Name of All Staff Present: _____
Treatments Implemented

Modules	Duration in Minutes	Percentage of Protocol Steps Completed (e.g., 9 steps completed from a prompting checklist that includes 10 steps = 90%)	Client's Rating of Intervention Helpfulness (1 = extremely unhelpful 7 = extremely helpful)	Provider Rating of Client Compliance (1 = extremely noncompliant 7 = extremely compliant)	Homework Due* I = incomplete C = complete	Homework Assigned (indicate with a check)
Session Agenda						
Program Orientation						
Consequence Review						
Level System						
Treatment Planning						
Reciprocity Awareness						
Positive Request						
Environmental (Stimulus) Control Self Control						

Self-Control						
Job-Getting Skills Training						
Last Session Review						
Specify if Other:						

* If no homework due, leave blank.

Strengths Noted During the Session:

_____

_____

_____

_____

_____

_____

_____

_____

Important Notes Outside of Protocol (if relevant):

_____

_____

_____

_____

_____

_____

_____

Date of Next Session : ____/____/____ **Time of Next Session: from** ____:____ AM / PM
to ____:____ AM / PM

Name of Treatment Provider Completing Session Progress Note (including degree & title):

_____

Signature of Treatment Provider (including degree & title): _____

Exhibit 2.9. Extra–Treatment Session Progress Notes.

Client ID: _____

EXTRA-TREATMENT SESSION PROGRESS NOTES

Excluding treatment sessions, this is a summary of all contacts with
youth client, <u>including emails, telephone contacts, court contacts, etc.</u>
Each note should include date/duration of contact, and type of contact made (if any).
End all notes by printing name (first/last), title, degree, and signature of writer.

Date, Time (from–to)	Notes

Exhibit 2.10. Monitoring Form to Assist in Appropriate Record Keeping.

Monitoring Form to Assist in Appropriate Record Keeping

Reviewed By: _____   Client ID #: _____

Review Date: _____   Due Date to fix errors: _____

	Form Is Missing	Writing Is Sloppy	Date Not Recorded	Time Not Recorded	Supervisor Signature Missing	Clinician Signature Missing	Client Signature Missing	All Relevant Information Not Completed	Client ID missing
Table of Contents		NA	NA	NA	NA	NA	NA	NA	
Log of Contacts					NA		NA		
Informed Consent		NA		NA	NA				
Demographics Form			NA	NA	NA	NA	NA		
Authorization to Release				NA					
Authorization for Release				NA					
Treatment Plan				NA	NA	NA	NA		
Standard Tx Session Progress Notes					NA		NA		
Extra-Treatment Progress Notes					NA		NA		
Monthly Progress Report									
Termination Report*				NA			NA		

NA = not applicable to form listed at left of column

1. Are all the forms in the correct order?   Yes_____   No_____

2. Do the log of contacts and standard tx. session progress notes match?   Yes_____   No_____

3. Do the log of contacts and Extra-Treatment Progress notes match?   Yes_____   No_____

4. Does the Monthly Client Progress Report include a cover sheet and fax confirmation sheet?   Yes_____   No_____

Signature of Therapist: _____   Date: _____

CHAPTER 3

Therapeutic Style, Techniques, and Implementation Strategies

Overview

As will be demonstrated in the subsequent chapters, the content of FBT is well organized, conceptually grounded, and empirically justified, reflecting more than two decades of refinement in clinical research and community settings. However, the successful implementation of FBT is, of course, dependent on the therapeutic approach and conduct of the treatment providers (TPs). Therefore, this chapter underscores the general disposition and style of TPs, provides the context underlying its content, and reports important guidelines that may be utilized to assist in preparing FBT sessions. The last section highlights several methods of organizing and implementing treatment materials, such as treatment prompting checklists, worksheets, and handouts that may be used to guide TPs during treatment sessions.

Chapter at a Glance

> Therapeutic style and approach

> Organization of treatment materials

Therapeutic Style and Approach

Emphasis on Positive Feedback and Encouragement

Positive Introductions   Treatment providers introduce themselves by their first and last names and professional title. Business cards are distributed upon first contact if available, and adults are addressed formally (e.g., Ms., Mrs.) unless explicitly told otherwise. During introductions, TPs are trained to immediately compliment family members (e.g., "I love how you blended those colors into your outfit. You've got a real sense of style."). Sincere compliments assist in quickly gaining rapport and have long-lasting effects in therapy. TPs should be pleasant, humorous, entertaining, praiseworthy, and supportive, smiling and letting youth and their families know their coming to therapy is appreciated. Indeed, many youth may indicate they are not motivated for therapy, either explicitly in words or through their body language (e.g., looking down or away). Therefore, one of the primary initial goals for TPs is to make therapy fun and engage youth and their families with token gifts, soda, coffee, candy bars, and other snacks. By creating a positive environment upon first interaction, youth are less inclined to get upset and noncompliant to therapeutic procedures. Indeed, positive statements are capable of removing tension and motivating youth and their families to accomplish goals.

Positively Focused Agendas   Clients are often unfamiliar with the directive therapeutic process underlying FBT. Indeed, FBT is unique to many of the traditional approaches to treatment that may permit client discontents to determine the direction of therapy. For instance, TPs avoid asking the family how they're doing or how their week was at the start of therapy sessions because such queries sometimes invite winded derogatory tangents that are inconsistent with goal-oriented treatment planning. Instead, TPs are taught to bias their initial session queries to solicit positive responses that are focused on goal attainment (e.g., "How were you able to make an effort to have a good time with your dad at the ballgame last week?"). As will be extensively reviewed in Chapter 4, formal agendas are implemented at the start of each therapy session to make it easy to focus on treatments that are strategically conceptualized to address primary underlying issues. Each agenda includes a summary of the youth's (and significant others') achievements that occurred during the past session and mutual determination of therapy session content by the youth, parent, and TP.

Differential Reinforcement   Treatment protocols rely heavily on TPs' utilizing differential reinforcement when teaching youth and their families. True differential reinforcement involves descriptively praising *observed* behaviors that are desired and functional, while ignoring concurrently *observed* behaviors that are undesired or dysfunctional. However, in therapy sessions it is often not possible to differentially reinforce *observed* behaviors, unless they are relevant to communication (e.g., smiling, giving a compliment, stating interest in accomplishing a goal). Therefore, during therapy sessions it helps to praise youth when they report or express actions that are *desired*, while ignoring those actions that are *not desired*. For instance, a youth indicated that he reluctantly smoked marijuana on his 17th birthday, but initially attempted to tell the person who offered the marijuana that he did not smoke anymore. The TP quickly praised this youth for attempting to avoid marijuana use and subsequently prompted the youth to attempt to generate several methods of refusing drug offers in case this experience was to happen again. In this example, alcohol use is completely ignored while the attempt to refuse alcohol is praised. Such responses decrease the likelihood of arguments and defensive reactions from clients, while priming them to be more accepting of goal directed suggestions that are consistent with treatment planning.

It is also important to descriptively praise pleasant feelings and functional thoughts, as well as behaviors that increase their occurrence. For instance, the solicitation of positive feelings may permit opportunities to *descriptively* praise desired behaviors and thoughts while ignoring undesired ones. The following dialogue between a TP and her adolescent client exemplifies this point:

Diane: I actually had a good time at the party, and I didn't use!

TP: That's wonderful. Tell me what you enjoyed most about the party?

Diane: Well, one of my friends, Tara, was in a big fight with her father. I took her aside and we talked it out. When she smiled it made me feel happy to know she had someone like me willing to listen. We spent the rest of the time talking about boys, and places we'd like to visit after high school. Wish my mom was able to listen to me.

TP: I'm glad you spent time helping Tara get through a tough situation. That says a lot about your character. It also shows me the party itself was not the reason for your enjoyment, but rather the interaction you had with your friend.

Diane: Yeah. I can enjoy myself with her anywhere. We're really close now.

TP: I'm glad to hear you're thinking about graduating high school.

Diane: Figure I might as well give it a shot. Otherwise I'll end up in a crummy job and won't be able to go very far in my travels, right?

TP: Somehow I think you'd make it work even without a job, but it sure makes it easier to get where you want to go when you have a formal education. I think it's very mature of you to consider these factors. Earlier you told me you wished things were going better in your classes. Tell me a few things you can do to get things back in your control.

In the latter example, the TP solicited something Diane enjoyed about the party to associate good feelings with abstinence, and to descriptively praise drug-incompatible behaviors and thoughts that influenced positive feelings to occur. Praise also facilitated an easy transition into goal setting. On the other hand, the TP was able to completely ignore Diane's negative comment about her mother since this comment was not functional. Indeed, the TP may address communication skills with Diane and her mother later in therapy.

Descriptive Praise   It is important to practice descriptive praise so it can be quickly and spontaneously utilized throughout therapy. Along these lines, a culture of positive feedback must be created within the treatment agency. Fortunately, practice exercises are fun and may be performed easily during existing daily activities. One exercise ("catching my coworkers being good") is implemented within regularly scheduled program meetings. A list is passed out requesting all attendees to record something they love, admire, or respect about coworkers. At the end of the meeting, a designated member of the team reads the statements to the group, and discussion of the recorded events naturally occurs. TPs also practice "catching others being good" throughout the day in spontaneous situations (buying tickets from a teller for a sporting event). In this exercise, TPs record praiseworthy statements that are provided throughout the day, and subsequently review them with their supervisor once a week.

A related exercise involves having TPs think of hypothetical situations in which they descriptively reinforce clients with various adjectives, particularly ones that are seldom used by others in daily conversations (e.g., stupendous) so praise doesn't get stale. It is helpful to make these imagined scenarios difficult, such as how to descriptively reinforce an adolescent who swears at his mother, but did not do so until his mother yelled at him:

I'm glad to hear you avoided swearing at your mother at first. I'm proud of you for wanting to have restraint and recognizing that swearing was not the way to go. Next time you get angry at your mother for yelling at you, what could you do?

In this example, the TP descriptively praises the youth's intentions to avoid confrontation while ignoring behaviors, thoughts and feelings that are associated with swearing. Thus, shaping the youth into realizing his initial thoughts to avoid yelling are indeed his true intentions. This positive context is also likely to increase the youth's receptivity to brainstorming alternatives to undesired behavior. Drawing attention to the undesired behavior, swearing, may bring about defensiveness from the youth that is not conducive to positive behavioral change.

Eliminate Blame and Facilitate Communication Although individuals learn poorly, and often become defensive, when their flaws are pointed out, substance-abusing youth and their parents have a tendency to place blame on others when undesired behavior occurs. Of course, casting blame leads to arguments, upset, and stress, and ultimately interferes with the prevention of future undesired behavior. Therefore, when clients err, TPs are trained to excuse their problem behaviors as having occurred due to situational circumstances that were to some extent out of their control. This approach is consistent with *positive practice.* Positive practice includes two steps and is a relatively benign way of disciplining youth for undesired behaviors. The first step is to teach parents to blame the situation or environment when their youth engage in undesired behaviors. For example, a parent may indicate that her teenager didn't complete a homework assignment because the youth must have thought the assignment was not due for another week, or that the lawn was not mowed because it hadn't rained and the grass probably didn't look as tall as usual. It is important to let parents know that it is important to be sincere when they blame undesired behaviors on situational contexts so their kids truly believe they are not the kind of people who perform such behaviors (i.e., "This is very unusual for me" rather than "Maybe I am a kleptomaniac."). After undesired behaviors are excused, TPs teach parents to determine with their children what could have been done to prevent the respective undesired behaviors from happening, and subsequently assist the parents in telling their children to practice the generated solutions. If ideas are wanting, TPs may provide solutions or ideally instruct parents to use the Self-Control procedure to generate solutions (see Chapter 11). Using the Self-Control intervention teaches several skill sets, including anger management, problem solving, and positive imagery.

It is sometimes helpful to empathize with family members when derogatory comments are stated, and subsequently instruct the involved parties to make *positive requests*. Importantly, empathizing only with the person stating the derogatory comment or only the person receiving the derogatory comment may lead to inequity in the immediate interaction, potentially resulting in an argument. For example, if a youth was hurt because he believed his father did not stick up for him when he was criticized by his teacher, the TP could lead the youth into a Positive Request after the provision of empathy to both the father and son.

Evan: You didn't say anything. You just stood there, Dad!

TP: You sound very hurt, Evan, and bring up an important issue worthy of resolution. Dad, I can see you're saddened for your son. Evan, please give your father a chance to respond by making a Positive Request. You can use this Positive Request Handout.

Evan: What could I possibly ask him for? It's already done.

TP: Well, you could either ask for an explanation to understand what happened, or you can ask him to react in another way next time. You've made positive requests a few times before, so go to the first step in the handout and make your request.

Evan: It hurt me that you didn't do anything, so just please tell the teacher that you want to hear what I have to say next time.

Father: I was going to . . .

TP: Dad, I appreciate you wanting to let him know what happened, but let's try to let him finish his request. This way you both are more likely to understand where the other is coming from more accurately. After his request, you'll be able to fully respond. Do the next step, Evan.

In the aforementioned example, the youth is more likely to express feelings in a positive way, and eventually engage the father in compromise. Indeed, upset and derogatory statements often lead to defensiveness, which in turn decreases effective resolution.

Another useful strategy in the management of derogatory comments is to terminate them quickly, and immediately instruct the perpetrator of the comment to alternatively make a positive request. The following dialogue demonstrates an adolescent being disallowed by the TP to tell her father that she doesn't like how he monitors her when she's away from home.

Chelsey: Dad, I don't like how you always . . .

TP: Oh, I forgot something (raises hands behind head and smiles)! I forgot to emphasize that I'd like you both to indicate what you want to have happen. Here is a copy of the Positive Request Handout. Chelsey, look at the handout and tell your dad something you want him to do.

Chelsey: He doesn't listen.

TP: Dad, you do your best to listen to what Chelsey has to say. Chelsey, go ahead and make your request starting with *please*, being specific about what you want, and telling him when you'd like it done. That's what it says in your handout for step number one, right?

Chelsey: Yeah. Dad I want you to . . .

TP: Way to be positive. Practice by saying *please*.

Chelsey: Dad, please let me stay out later on Saturdays.

TP: Nice letting him know what day you were hoping to stay out later. Now, give him a time to work with?

Chelsey: Until 3:00 a.m. would be great.

Dad: There's no . . .

TP: Dad, remember you'll have a chance to make a counter-request or offer. Let's let Chelsey finish so she can practice. What's the second step, Chelsey?

In the preceding example, the TP does a nice job terminating the sentence as soon as it was clear that Chelsey was going to focus on what was not liked about the father. Rather than permitting them to engage in another argument, the TP recognized poor communication early and terminated it early. Raising the hands assists in distracting the dyad, doing so behind the back and with a smile is not associated with anger and aggression, and specific brief instructions to practice a positive request one step at a time is likely to scaffold the youth into a positive outcome. Indeed, if the youth and parent are able to come to an effective compromise, they are positively reinforcing themselves to resolve their differences in an appropriate manner.

Learn by Doing

Role-Play as an Assessment Tool   Role-playing is an excellent method of assessing social skills. Briefly, the TP describes a hypothetical scenario that warrants the respective skill set. For instance, "Show me what you'd do if Gord offered you a line of cocaine at that party. I'll be him." An initial prompt is subsequently provided by the TP, who pretends to be in character (i.e., "Go ahead, this is good stuff"). The TP can provide additional prompts, if necessary (i.e., "Don't be a scared"). Scenarios can be altered to include obstacles or important details; for example, "Now, I want to see how you manage a similar drug offer where Gord is upset because you don't want to skip a class with him to use under the bleachers. Show me what you could do in this situation. (*Pause*) I can't believe you're not going to bail out of school with me. We can come back before English and you won't even miss your test. Come on."

Instructing significant others to engage in the role-plays as participants usually helps with generalization, as friends are often familiar with various difficulties that youth clients experience at home. Instructing peer significant others to comment on the performance of youth during role-play assessments is also a useful strategy. For instance, in the earlier stages of therapy, a peer might respond with the following statement before a role-play, "I think Valerie wouldn't be able to confront him." TPs need to be sensitive to problems that may occur due to role-playing in front of others, such as anxiety and poor response to criticism. In general, significant others may be included in role-plays as clients gain confidence and skill in their performance.

TPs make spontaneous adjustments during role-plays so that particular reactions of clients can be observed. For example, a TP might increase emotional upset in a role-play if a client was able to effectively settle an argument, or decrease emotional upset if a client appeared to be intimidated.

It is important to ask youth who they would like to involve in role-plays prior to conducting them. For instance, it is generally not a good idea to involve parents in role-plays with youth when the skills to be assessed involve illicit or intimate behaviors, such as requesting the use of condoms or prematurely asking to be paid more money to complete a chore.

Role-Play as an Intervention Tool Most of the FBT intervention components utilize role-playing to teach behavioral skills. Scenarios generally involve negative assertion in avoiding punishment (e.g., responding to upset or criticism in others), positive assertion in soliciting reinforcement (e.g., asking a peer for a date or a parent to use the car), and refusing offers to use illicit drugs or alcohol. Skills can be verbal (e.g., tone of voice, conversational content), physical (e.g., eye contact, facial expression), cognitive (e.g., generation of ideas, thought content), and affective (i.e., upset, happy, excited). Affective skills can often be observed behaviorally through voice inflections, facial expressions, physiological symptoms (e.g., perspiration), conversational content, and so on, whereas cognitive skills must be interpreted through the reports of clients. Thus, cognitive skills are in some ways more difficult to teach. It is usually best for TPs to conduct role-plays with only one person and gradually involve others as skills improve.

TPs first model the respective skills and encourage, prompt, and assist youth and their significant others in rehearsing them in simulated hypothetical scenarios (e.g., being offered to smoke marijuana). The intensity and difficulty of problem scenarios increase as youth and their significant others improve their confidence and skill. Indeed, role-playing provides an opportunity to increase self-efficacy (due largely to knowledge of improved skills and TP praise), and increases the likelihood that participants will attempt the modeled behaviors outside therapy. Role-playing is more likely to be successful when the following steps are consecutively employed by TPs:

1. Choose a problem scenario that is relevant (generated by client).

2. Brainstorm skills that may be used to manage the problem scenario.

3. Model skills w/ client pretending to be antagonist in role-play.

4. Solicit what client liked about modeled performance.

5. Solicit what client would do to enhance modeled behavior.

6. Instruct client to model skill w/TP as relatively compliant antagonist.

7. Solicit what client liked about personal performance.

8. Solicit what client could do to enhance performance.

9. Perform additional role-plays w/client modeling skills in progressively more difficult scenarios until skill level is overlearned.

Generating problem scenarios that are relevant to youth is likely to increase clients' interest. Motivation to conduct role-plays is also enhanced when clients participate in the generation of skills that may be used to assist in solving social problem scenarios, and skills are relevant to their *real-life* situations. Clients should then be encouraged to generate skills while TPs assist in improving the quality of their responses. Of course, once appropriate skills are brainstormed, it is extremely important that TPs model skills prior to instructing clients to do so. Indeed, skipping this step is very likely to lead to awkward circumstances. For instance, seeing TPs model skill sets demonstrates what is expected, which lowers anxiety and ultimately permits clients to perform better during role-plays.

Asking critical significant others to express what they liked about role-play performance safeguards against potential disclosure of limitations and demonstrated weaknesses that often occur. Along these lines, it may be necessary for TPs to redirect clients and their significant others to focus on demonstrated strengths while ignoring weaknesses or skill deficits. Instructing significant others to provide positive feedback followed by methods of enhancing skills shows how role-playing can be fun, nonthreatening, and constructive. It also shows clients that the role-plays will emphasize positive behaviors.

The TP should instruct clients to do role-plays rather than ask them to do so. For example, the TP might say, "I'll be your mom. Ask if you can stay out later Friday night. Hi, Jennifer, what did you want to talk about?" In the preceding example, the TP's prompt does not give the client a chance to get anxious.

Of course, the TP responds to the client's first attempt with descriptive praise, but does not solicit or provide constructive feedback. In fact, when clients critique their own performances, TPs usually dismiss these critiques initially (e.g., "If you were nervous, I sure didn't notice."). In the latter example, the client gains very little if the undesired behavior is verified, while the potential gains in disagreeing with the criticism are substantial. In later role-plays, when youth demonstrate confidence in their performance, TPs may increase difficulty in role-play scenarios, provide instructions to enhance role-play performance, and solicit constructive feedback from the client and others.

Therapy Assignments

Most of the FBT intervention components require youth and their significant others to practice, at home, the skills they have reviewed during therapy sessions. Such practice is extremely important, as it facilitates opportunities for youth to consequently obtain descriptive praise, encouragement, and corrective feedback from TPs in subsequent treatment sessions. Home practice assignments also provide opportunities for clients and TPs to identify issues that make it difficult to execute newly acquired skill sets in *real-world* settings so solutions to these issues can be reviewed during treatment sessions. There are several strategies TPs may use to increase the likelihood their clients will complete therapy assignments on time.

First, TPs should model successful implementation of the respective skills and ensure that clients effectively demonstrate these skills in simulated scenarios prior to implementing them at home. These in-session role-plays should address obstacles that are likely to be encountered when the target behaviors are performed at home. Providing clients and their significant others with descriptive praise in the role-playing process enhances their confidence and interest in performing the skills at home. These reviews involve youth providing their parents with the completed recording forms and parents praising youth for actions that are consistent with therapy assignment completion (e.g., effort completing target behaviors, completion of the recording form) and encouraging youth to complete target behaviors in the future. For instance, in portraying a father reviewing his son's performance of a Positive Request homework assignment, the father might say, "I love how you made a positive request with your sister earlier today, and I'm proud you recorded each of the steps of this request in this form. Keep up the great work." Modeling the recording process (i.e., reviewing homework completion) permits clients to prepare for problems that may subsequently occur in the home, such as noncompliance, being too critical, and recording errors.

TPs should role-play hypothetical scenarios in which youth fail to complete therapy assignments. In this regard, TPs explain that the missed therapy assignments must have occurred due to very good reasons that were uncontrollable (e.g., more chores or school work than usual), and that youth need to complete the recording process in retrospect. Another strategy in managing failed homework completion is to instruct parents to tell youth to complete the recording forms *as if* they had completed the target behaviors. That is, they report what they would have liked to have done if they were able to implement the assigned skills. This permits youth to think about the application of skills and provides parents with opportunities to descriptively praise and encourage their youth for desired actions. Retrospective completion of an incomplete therapy assignment also shows that the assignment is important and must be complete prior to moving forward in the therapy session.

It is important to query family members to indicate where they will keep the forms that will be used to record their completion of therapy assignments, and ideally suggest a private location that will be visited on a daily basis, such as a bathroom or bedroom mirror. Other methods of increasing the likelihood of therapy assignment completion include calling family members a couple of days after the assignment is prescribed and descriptively praising efforts to complete the assignment, as well as determining solutions to problems that may have interfered with therapy completion. Other strategies include *instructing* clients to provide their completed therapy assignment forms rather than *asking* if they've completed the assignment during reviews of homework assignments that occur during treatment sessions. Instructions establish the expectation that assignments have been performed, whereas queries suggest that these assignments are optional and thus may not have been completed.

Management of Significant Others

How Can I Involve Significant Others in Therapy?   Parents sometimes request youth clients to be seen individually in therapy. When this occurs, they should be informed that their participation is imperative. Indeed, they can be told that their actions may or may not have contributed to the youth's problem behaviors. However, their participation is absolutely part of the solution. Indeed, at least one legal guardian is expected to attend all therapy sessions.

Other significant others are also encouraged to participate in therapy to some extent, such as older siblings and other family members and friends who are interested in helping youth clients accomplish their treatment plan. Of course, in doing so, it is important that their behavior must be found to support youth clients, and it is necessary to obtain appropriate consent to involve significant others in therapy. Indeed, a visiting grandparent, uncle, or friend at school should always be welcome to participate in treatment, however spontaneously. These persons are important because they assist in drawing a connection between therapy and the home environment and act as therapeutic change agents. To assist in managing confidentiality while permitting intimate issues in therapy to be addressed with attending significant others, both youth clients and legal guardian(s) assist in determining session agendas, and TPs do not introduce sensitive background information. Rather, clients dictate the extent to which their personal information is disclosed, and TPs may temporarily excuse significant others from sessions whenever appropriate. Children rarely attend sessions because the content of most treatment components is not appropriate for their age group. However, they are extensively involved in Reciprocity Awareness and parts of other treatments (i.e., reviewing the scheduled family activity during Environmental Control).

Responsibilities of significant others may include:

1. *Motivating and assisting youth clients in therapy session participation and completion of therapy assignments.* Parents are usually responsible for transporting youth to therapy sessions, and they can be encouraged to consequence therapy attendance and compliance with contingent rewards. At the very least, significant others can be contacted after appropriate consent forms are completed to find and subsequently encourage youth clients to attend scheduled therapy sessions when they are "missing" at home. Parents may utilize the therapists' ratings of youth compliance (see Chapter 1) during each treatment component to assist in determining the extent of reinforcement provided to youth. The provision of rewards can be formalized through the Level System (see Chapter 6), and friends of youth clients can be invited to therapy sessions to bring about a pleasant and rewarding learning environment.

2. *Modeling and providing encouragement for behaviors that are associated with a healthy, non-drug-associated lifestyle.* Youth peers are especially valuable along these lines, as they are often motivated to try hard during treatment sessions to impress parents in thinking they are good influences. From their perspective, such behavior is likely to lead parents to permit their children to spend more time with them. Peers also relate well with youth clients, and thus may be utilized to interpret difficult-to-understand material that is reviewed during treatment sessions. Instructing parents to model skill sets

during treatment sessions demonstrates for youth clients that their parents accept responsibility for amelioration of youth problems and are willing to improve their own skill sets in doing so.

How Can TPs Implement Sessions When Significant Others Are Unavailable? Youth are very unlikely to attend particular therapy sessions without their parents. However, when they do, it is usually later in treatment, after rapport has been established. In these cases, TPs will need to decide, even with parental consent, if it is appropriate to conduct the therapy session without the legal guardians. When therapy is decided to be appropriate without significant others, agendas will need to be determined between TPs and youth clients, and sessions will need to emphasize interventions that do not require the participation of significant others, such as the Consequence Review, Self-Control, Positive Request, and Job-Getting Skills Training. For other treatments (i.e., Environmental Control), TPs will need to indicate *not applicable* (NA) for each of the prescribed therapeutic steps listed in the respective protocol that warrant the participation of significant others. For instance, if a TP were implementing Environmental Control, "NA" would be marked next to each therapeutic step in the prompting checklist that was relevant to gathering information from significant others. These instructional steps would not be considered when computing treatment integrity (see Treatment Integrity section in Chapter 1). Some interventions can be modified when significant others are not present. For instance, when implementing the Reciprocity Awareness intervention, the TP could instruct the client to imagine a significant other is sitting in one of the empty chairs and pretend to state something that is loved, admired, or respected about this person. This provides youth opportunities to practice statements of appreciation in preparation for *in vivo* situations.

How Can TPs Manage Significant Others When They Become Upset During Treatment Sessions? Significant others of youth clients often lack skills that are relevant to problem solving, anger management, and effective communication. Therefore, they are likely to evidence problem behaviors (e.g., upset, swearing) during treatment sessions. Whenever appropriate, an attempt should be made to explicitly address these issues in therapy to assist in preventing these problem behaviors from negatively affecting youth clients. For instance, if significant others become agitated, TPs can initiate

HEARD (Hear, Empathize, Alternatives, Review, Decide). Basically, the TP instructs the upset individual to summarize the problem in a sentence or two, empathizes with the individual's concern, assists the individual in generating alternatives to the problem, assists the individual in reviewing the pros and cons of each generated solution, and prompts the individual to decide which options to implement. The acronym includes the evidence-supported problem-solving steps initially developed by D'Zurilla and Goldfried (1971).

Other strategies to managing upset include instructing significant others (or clients) to explain how they may have to some extent contributed to the problem that is causing them upset, and/or blame the problem behavior on some aspect in the environment. For instance, if a mother was upset that her child came home late, she could indicate that her child may have had a difficult time convincing her friends to take her home on time, or that she didn't tell the child to be home at a specific time. The family should be told that it is not important whether the potential explanations are accurate, but rather that they provide opportunities to engage in communication while reducing perceptions of blame. This strategy does not impede the implementation of consequences for undesired behaviors, if appropriate. Rather, it facilitates appropriate discipline to occur with relatively less upset and better communication.

Assist Significant Others in Staying Focused on Youth   Of course, significant others may be encouraged to learn skills while assisting clients in FBT, such as learning to perform Self-Control, Positive Request, and Job-Getting Skills. Indeed, this provides them opportunities to be intimately familiar with the treatment of youth clients, permits them to model skills, and usually enhances family relationships. However, sometimes significant others become so excited with therapy that they may attempt to shift therapy focus to their own issues, rather than the client's. This problem is usually avoided when TPs follow FBT protocols with integrity. That is, all steps involved in all TP prompting checklists are focused on clients. Therefore, if adherence is good, significant others will not have opportunities to dominate intervention sessions.

Establish Effective Methods of Communication   Arguments may be prevented by establishing communication guidelines early in therapy and utilizing prompts to engage in communication skills training exercises when triggers for arguments occur (e.g., anger). Communication Guidelines were first mentioned in Chapter 1 in the description of the Orientation Session. Specifically, a list of basic communication guidelines is provided to clients (see Communication Guidelines Handout in Chapter 1). Other guidelines may be added, although the ones that are listed are usually sufficient. TPs distribute copies of the guidelines and attempt to get commitments from each of the participating family members that they will attempt to comply with each of the guidelines. TPs then obtain permission from family members to redirect them to correct guidelines when they are broken, and potentially engage them in performing Positive Requests (see Chapter 9) to resolve these potential conflicts. The latter strategy makes it much easier to quickly terminate dysfunctional communication.

Enhance Compliance in Therapy

Review Compliance After Each Treatment Is Implemented As initially described in Chapter 1, TPs review the compliance of youth clients after each therapy component is reviewed during each therapy session. The response scale (7 = extremely compliant, 6 = very compliant, 5 = somewhat compliant, 4 = neutral, 3 = somewhat noncompliant, 2 = very noncompliant, 1 = extremely noncompliant) is based on attendance to the treatment session, participation in the respective intervention, and completion of the therapy assignment. The resulting score is recorded in the session progress note, and the referral agent is provided a summary of these scores in a monthly progress note upon permission from clients. There is also a standardized prompt for TPs to tell clients how they can enhance compliance in the future. These ratings are an effective prescriptive approach to assist in motivating clients and their family members to do well in therapy when youth are mandated for treatment by court or school and the ratings are shared with these parties (upon appropriate consent).

Call Youth Clients and Their Parents Between Therapy Sessions to Encourage Attendance and Participation Telephone calls are routinely utilized to enhance therapy attendance and, as mentioned earlier, assist in the completion of therapy assignments. Telephone calls should occur 2 or 3 days prior to the scheduled session. The initial orientation telephone call is made prior to admittance or enrollment in the program. The content of this call focuses on briefly describing FBT, discussing how significant others may be involved, generating solutions to obstacles that might interfere with session attendance, having parents indicate directions to the clinic to ensure that they know how to get to there and what time the session will happen, soliciting positive features associated with their expectations of FBT, and providing empathy for expressed concerns that are relevant to presenting problems. Subsequent calls are usually conducted a couple of days prior to therapy sessions and involve positive discussions about the client's progress in therapy, reviewing therapy assignments, and encouraging future session attendance. TPs sometimes call clients immediately after sessions to review things that were performed admirably in sessions and provide encouragement. Our previous studies indicated that it was important to contact either the youth only or both the youth and parent, but not the parent only. We have found initial session attendance is improved by 29% using teletherapy (see Donohue et al., 1998).

Use HEARD to Manage Therapeutic Noncompliance   Instances of therapeutic noncompliance (e.g., refusing to perform intervention techniques, refusing to come to treatment) are often unpredictable, and may be treated with the HEARD intervention (hear, empathize, alternative, review, decide) that was reviewed earlier in this chapter. For instance, if a youth was uninterested in conducting a Self-Control trial, he could be instructed to indicate why he is uninterested in performing the trial at the current time. After listening and empathizing with generated concerns, the TP could facilitate a review of various alternatives that assist in maintaining abstinence from drugs or other relevant problem behaviors (e.g., doing the trial later, emphasizing another intervention).

Organization of Treatment Materials

To assist in preparing for FBT sessions, TPs can create a three-ring binder that includes TP prompting checklists, handouts, and worksheets for each of the FBT intervention components. The workbook permits TPs to quickly access requisite forms during treatment sessions. The best order in which to list the interventions in this binder is consistent with the order in which these interventions are reviewed in this book. Each intervention might represent a section in the binder. Each section or intervention would first include several initial prompting checklists, followed by several future session prompting checklists (if future sessions are possible), followed by worksheets and hand-outs for the respective intervention (if relevant). For example, the first section of the binder would be for the agenda. This intervention has only one prompting checklist, and there are no forms for this intervention, so there would be no worksheets or handouts listed in this section. The next section would be the Level System. This section includes both initial and future session prompting checklists, and worksheets. Therefore, Initial and Future Session Level System prompting checklists would be followed by the worksheets in this section of the binder. This manner of presentation would continue until Concluding Treatment and Planning for Success (see Chapter 7).

Once organized, TPs maintain multiple copies of each of the forms in the binder. The number of copies will depend on the number of sessions performed each week, although most TPs prefer to have approximately 5 to 10 copies of each form in their binders. The binders permit TPs to rapidly obtain materials they need during treatment sessions, and are essential when therapies are implemented in the homes of clients or other off-clinic locations. An alternative strategy to using binders is to create a similar system in a filing cabinet, which may be easier to maintain in a clinic or hospital setting.

Concluding Remarks

It becomes clear in this chapter that the style of FBT is uniquely positive, making it particularly refreshing for clients who have experienced aversive backgrounds and trauma. Although insufficient by itself, descriptive praise and other therapeutic strategies reviewed in this chapter complement the effective delivery of FBT content. Therefore, the style of FBT is superimposed onto its content, which is extensively reviewed in each of the remaining chapters.

4

Establishing Effective Agendas for Treatment Sessions

Overview

A structured agenda is developed between the treatment provider (TP) and participating family members at the start of each treatment session. Agendas are initially drafted by the TP prior to the treatment session. In doing so, the TP initiates the session by stating a few positive comments about the family's performance that occurred during the previous session, and subsequently reports interventions that may be considered during the current session. To assist in time management, the TP provides an estimate of how much time it might take to implement each intervention that is provided for consideration. Family members are encouraged to suggest potential modifications to the agenda, including the order in which therapies are implemented as well as the omission or addition of therapies. This prescriptive approach helps to reduce spontaneous, and often tangential, dialogue that may be irrelevant and poorly integrated into treatment planning. Indeed, this strength-based approach helps family members to stay focused on processes that are likely to facilitate goal accomplishment. Although session agendas usually require 5 or 10 minutes to implement, their absence may result in a relative lack of flow and general inefficiency during the session.

Goals for Intervention

➤ Review positive efforts that occurred during the preceding session.

➤ Determine interventions to implement during the current session.

Materials Needed

> Session Agenda Therapist Prompting Checklist (Exhibit 4.1)

Procedural Steps for Implementation

Preparing Initial Drafts for Session Agendas

Immediately prior to each treatment session, TPs review their progress notes to assist in remembering interventions that were implemented during the previous session, as well as the family's response to these treatments. Of course, this review aids TPs in brainstorming interventions that should be considered during the next treatment session. In doing so, TPs consider the treatment plan (see Chapter 7) and the family's response to implemented treatments (as per assessment measures, reports from youth, youth's family, and professionals, and behavioral observation). Other considerations in determining which interventions to present to the family for consideration include TP implementation factors, such as comfort and skill in delivering the particular treatments. TPs should suggest, whenever consistent with treatment planning, therapies they are capable of implementing with precision and certainty.

To assist in determining which interventions to implement, TPs utilize the general guidelines that are specified in Table 4.1. As the table indicates, an agenda is always implemented at the beginning of each session. An Orientation is provided during the first session, and the Consequence Review and Level System treatments are implemented during the next two sessions to assist in motivating youth to achieve treatment goals. The Level System is implemented during most of the remaining sessions to some extent because the established contingencies need to be monitored on an ongoing basis. Once motivational interventions are established, youth and parents construct the Treatment Plan. Of course, the Treatment Plan assists family members in understanding the remaining therapies that are available and permits them to determine which treatments will be implemented during future sessions (with the exception of the Level System since this treatment will occur during most of the remaining sessions). Because Treatment Planning is succinct, there is usually time for Reciprocity Awareness at the end of the fourth session, and occasionally thereafter based on the treatment plan. This intervention is fun, and often results in tears of happiness, thus acting to positively demonstrate need for the forthcoming skill-based treatments (i.e., Self-Control,

Table 4.1. Usual Order of Interventions and Estimated Times for Implementation

Intervention	When Implemented	Approximate Duration (All treatment sessions are scheduled between 60 and 90 mins.)
Agenda (Chapter 4)	First session, and every session thereafter	<5 mins.
Orientation Session (Chapter 1)	First session only	55 mins.
Consequence Review (Chapter 5)	Second session only	45–55 mins.
Level System (Chapter 6)	Third session and every session thereafter	First (initial) LS session (constructing levels) = 55–85 mins. All remaining (future) sessions (reviewing contract) = 15–30 mins.
Treatment Plan (Chapter 7)	Fourth session only	25 mins.
Reciprocity Awareness (Chapter 8)	End of fourth session and occasionally thereafter	Initial RA session = 30 mins. Future RA sessions = 20–40 mins.
Positive Request (Chapter 9)	Based on Treatment Plan or spontaneously to prevent arguments	First (initial) PR session (including rationale and teaching how to do PR) = 30–40 mins. Remaining (future) PR sessions (reviewing PR or making requests during session) = 20–40 mins.
Environmental (Stimulus) Control (Chapter 10)	Based on Treatment Plan	First (initial) EC session (setting up the lists) = 55–70 mins. Remaining (future) EC sessions (reviewing lists) = 20–40 mins.
Self-Control (Chapter 11)	Based on Treatment Plan or when drug use or significant problem behavior is indicated	First (initial) SC session (teaching how to do SC) = 55–70 mins. Remaining (future) sessions (reviewing SC) = 20–40 mins.
Job-Getting Skills Training (Chapter 12)	Based on Treatment Plan or when job is needed	First (initial) JG session = 40–55 mins. Remaining (future) PR sessions = 15–40 mins.
Last Session (Chapter 13)	Last session only	About 40–55 mins.

Environmental Control, Positive Request). These treatments, as well as the Level System, are referred to as *core* therapies because they target the elimination of illicit substance use and other target behaviors. Throughout therapy, these interventions will be revisited based on need, as the skills that are targeted in these interventions are not typically mastered during the course of one session. Of course, the last session reviews treatment gains and assists in generalization of therapeutic gains. Thus, TPs are guided by the aforementioned guidelines, but are free to make adjustments on a session-by-session basis during the agendas.

TPs are encouraged to record scheduled interventions, as well as their anticipated time to implement, in the Session Agenda TP Prompting Checklist prior to each session. Also in preparation for each treatment session, TPs record outstanding accomplishments that occurred during the past session in the Session Agenda Prompting Checklist (Exhibit 4.1) so these positive points are available for review at the start of the next session. Outstanding accomplishments often include extreme effort during one of the therapies, accomplishing a difficult goal, family members exchanging meaningful positive comments, honesty in reporting substance use, and desire to learn new methods of relapse prevention.

Developing Session Agendas With Family Members

At the start of each therapy session, the TP reports a few outstanding accomplishments that occurred during the past session in the progress notes. The intent of this latter step is to immediately get the family focused on their positive aspects. This approach is often novel to disgruntled family members who may wish to express their discontents with other family members as treatment sessions are initiated. However, TPs must not relinquish ground in defending their positive perspective. To assist family members in being constructive it may be necessary to implement communication guidelines (see Chapter 1) and assure upset family members that the issues will be prioritized in the therapy session during the review of prescribed treatments that have been shown to be effective in families that have experienced similar problems.

TPs initiate each agenda by reporting and soliciting outstanding efforts and accomplishments that may have occurred since their last session. The family is always recruited to participate in the provision of affirmative comments. It is within the TPs' discretion to determine how long the positive reviews occur, although they are usually limited to a few minutes.

TPs then report the interventions that have been planned for the session, including a brief explanation of why the interventions were selected, and an estimate of how much time it will take to implement each therapy. Potential modifications to the agenda are solicited, although family members usually agree with the prescribed agendas. When youth disagree with their parents about the session agenda, TPs are advised to listen to expressed concerns and provide empathy. Most intervention components are capable of assisting in the management of spontaneously reported problems. Therefore, TPs should attempt to clarify how the planned therapies might be adjusted to accommodate expressed concerns prior to changing prescribed agendas.

The example dialogue that follows presents a typical exchange among TPs, clients, and significant others in completing the session agenda.

TP: Amazing session last week. I'm particularly proud of Paul due to his efforts in accomplishing all of his goals. I really enjoyed watching you learn Self-Control. I also appreciate you, Mom, for having the patience to listen to his trial and later praise his effort in doing this technique. You really seemed to love his success.

Paul: I was surprised she didn't give me the third degree.

TP: So what did you enjoy, specifically?

Paul: She was just cool. She just trusted me to do my thing.

TP: Great, tell her that. I'd like to observe her reaction.

Paul: I liked how you were on my side and didn't feel an urge to interrupt.

Mom: I was proud of you, and I'm particularly proud of your being here today.

TP: I thought we could go over the Level System for about 20 minutes today, and finish up with the Self-Control to take advantage of Paul's great work last time. We could do Self-Control trials until the rest of the session to have him really prepared, Mom.

Mom: Sounds good to me.

Paul: Yeah, let's just do it. Mom promised she'd take me to Tina's after the session.

Concluding Remarks

The agenda assists in establishing a positive, focused tone for each treatment session, and is necessary for several reasons. First, positive statements at the start of each session assist in putting treatment progress into proper perspective, and often aid in the prevention of negative tangents that proliferate in unstructured therapies. In our interviews with youth and their families we have been told the invitation to change agendas is very much appreciated, particularly by adolescents because they are not provided such opportunities. This latter point reflects consumer-driven therapy, as TPs and their clients share in the determination of FBT implementation. It is important that TPs move through the agendas swiftly and be prepared to manage tangents and "war" stories about undesired behaviors that may have occurred since the family's last treatment session. Finally, it is important that the agendas are reviewed quickly to permit greater time for the TP to initiate treatments.

Supporting Materials for Chapter 4: Establishing Effective Agendas for Treatment Sessions

Exhibit 4.1. Session Agenda Therapist Prompting Checklist.

SESSION AGENDA
THERAPIST PROMPTING CHECKLIST

Client ID:_____ Clinician:_____ Session #:_____ Session Date:_____

Begin Time:_____

Establishing the Session Agenda (Usually the Youth and Adult Significant Others)

___ 1. State/solicit outstanding efforts and/or accomplishments occurring during last session.
___ 2. State planned interventions to be implemented in session & how long each will take.

Scheduled Interventions	Estimated Time
1. _____	_____
2. _____	_____
3. _____	_____
4. _____	_____
5. _____	_____
6. _____	_____

Note: Complete aforementioned table prior to session.

___ 3. Provide opportunity for youth/significant others to modify proposed agenda.

End Time: _____   **Notes: _____**

_____

_____

_____

5

Probing Negative and Positive Consequences to Determine Core Motivation

Youth who have been referred for substance abuse are notoriously unmotivated to participate in psychotherapy. Therefore, Family Behavior Therapy (FBT) includes motivational enhancement procedures throughout the content of its interventions. However, the primary method utilized to instill motivation for treatment is the Consequence Review. This intervention is based on the assumption that youth are more likely to discontinue substance use and other problem behaviors when the aversive consequences of these behaviors are perceived to be greater than their reinforcing aspects. To assist in accomplishing this initiative, youth are seen individually for about an hour prior to initiating treatment. In a facilitative, nonconfrontational manner, treatment providers (TPs) solicit from youth how, exactly, consequences of substance use and other problematic behaviors negatively affect them. TPs actively listen to youth responses without judgment, requesting youth to elaborate on their circumstances and reflecting their appreciation for youth concerns. Later, TPs assist youth in drawing connections between their negative consequences and the negative consequences that have been reported by other youth. This strategy assists TPs in prompting additional negative consequences, while providing a therapeutic context that is relatively free of aspersions and negative bias. After TPs listen to youth concerns, they provide empathy and facilitate discussion of positive alternative behaviors that can be targeted in treatment. During subsequent therapy, when motivation is relatively low, TPs may point out these negative consequences and quickly focus on alternative goal-directed behavior.

Goals for Intervention

> Increase the youth's motivation to abstain from illicit drugs and alcohol and associated problem behaviors.

Materials Needed

> Consequence Review Therapist Prompting Checklist (Exhibit 5.1)

> Consequence Review Worksheet (CRW, Exhibit 5.2)

> Consequence Review List of Annoyances Worksheet (LAW, Exhibit 5.3)

Procedural Steps for Implementation

Rationale (Youth Client)

As indicated in the Consequence Review Therapist Prompting Checklist (Exhibit 5.1), the Consequence Review is initiated with the TP providing a brief rationale for this intervention in an individual session with the youth. The TP first specifies illicit substances that the youth has been identified to use that have been identified to be problematic by adults or the youth him- or herself. If coexisting problems have been identified, the TP also reports these behaviors. To enhance the youth's receptivity to this intervention, the TP tells the youth that these behaviors will be difficult to eliminate because they have most likely been associated with powerful positive consequences. It is explained that the strength of positive consequences for the listed behaviors are enhanced because negative consequences are often delayed, and people tend to avoid thinking about them. Therefore, the Consequence Review intervention is aimed at assisting the youth in gaining intimate awareness of these negative consequences, including those that may occur in the distant future, and those that are due to the reaction of others. Of course, it is also important to indicate why the youth is especially likely to do well with this intervention and validate that the youth is interested in trying it out.

The following dialogue exemplifies an effective implementation of the Consequence Review rationale.

TP: From the questionnaires and interviews we did last week, I learned that you and your mother reported that you are using pot and cocaine and missing classes at school. I believe these things will be difficult for you to eliminate because there are very strong positive consequences that are presently outweighing the negative ones. Some of the negative consequences will not occur until much later in your life, and if you're like me, you probably try to avoid thinking about them. Today, I'd like to get a better understanding of the negative consequences you've experienced from using pot, cocaine, and missing school. We'll also review consequences you feel may occur in the future and those that are due to the reactions of others. You'll notice I'm not going to judge you. I will simply ask for your perspective. I think this will be a great exercise because you're very bright and have good insight. How do you think this might help you?

Youth: I'm not sure. It will probably be good to talk about school, but I'm not going to use drugs anymore. So I don't think we need to do it for that.

TP: I understand. I'd like to hear your perspectives on missing school. I know you're motivated to want to get clean from drugs, but I think it will help me to understand what's motivating you to stay clean. This will help me to know what to say if your motivation goes down due to extenuating circumstances beyond your control.

Youth: OK.

TP: Let's get started. You've got a great maturity about you.

Reviewing Negative Consequences (Youth Client)

Based on prior assessments, the TP determines which substances the youth has been identified to abuse, and records these substances in the first column of Consequence Review Worksheet (CRW, Exhibit 5.2). Substances other than marijuana and alcohol may be summarized as "hard drugs." It is also helpful to list primary problem behaviors in this first column (e.g., vandalizing a house, arguing with parents, missing school). Indicating specific behavioral experiences (e.g., throwing rocks at a bus, swearing at a sister) rather than vague behavioral categories (e.g., vandalism, arguments) usually makes it easier for youth to draw connections between their behavior and the consequences of these behaviors, particularly when they are expected to be defensive in providing negative consequences associated with their problem behaviors. On the other hand, behavioral categories may lead to a greater range of consequences and richer discussions when youth are relatively insightful and cognitively bright. The specific behaviors, or behavioral categories, that are listed should also be those that are most relatively problematic. The number of problem behaviors selected for review will be determined based on several factors, including the extent to which the youth is motivated to participate and time availability. However, selecting two to four behaviors is usually sufficient.

The TP shows this list to the youth and indicates how the behaviors were derived (e.g., urinanalysis, report from parent), and obtains the youth's initial rating of unpleasantness for each of the listed behaviors using a scale from 0 (not at all unpleasant) to 100 (couldn't get any more unpleasant). These ratings are recorded in the second column of the CRW next to their respective problem behavior. The initial ratings are important because they assist in determining the extent to which youth are motivated to make efforts to eliminate problem behaviors. A low rating (e.g., 40 or below) is indicative of someone who is probably not likely to make great efforts to terminate problem behavior. When youth report that a behavior is not at all unpleasant (i.e., 0), the TP may skip the review of consequences for this behavior, as the youth is probably not ready to consider unpleasant consequences for this behavior. Instead, when this happens, the youth's motivation to terminate the behavior will be treated later using other FBT interventions that incorporate extrinsic rewards (i.e., Level System). It is also possible to challenge youth when ratings are 0. For instance, youth can be reminded that negative consequences include the reaction of others to the respective behaviors, or point out negative consequences that were reported by them earlier. In any event, youth almost always report at least some degree of unpleasantness with each of the listed behaviors. The following dialogue exemplifies a TP attempting to solicit a youth's initial rating for marijuana use when the youth indicates the rating is 0.

TP: OK, let's get started. On a scale of 0 to 100, tell me how unpleasant your marijuana use is for you at the present time. A 0 equals not at all unpleasant, and a 100 means it couldn't get any more unpleasant.

Robby: I guess a 0.

TP: You seem hesitant.

Robby: I would say it is 0, but I don't think that's what you want me to say.

TP: I want you to indicate what you really feel. I'm not sure if you know, however, that many youth base their ratings on how other people react to their drug use, as well as other factors. For instance, you said your mom nags you when you're high from pot. Is this something that should be considered in your rating?

Robby: Well, it would be a 10 if you put it that way. My mom's always giving me a hard time.

The TP asks the youth to report what is unpleasant about each of the behaviors that were rated above 0 in unpleasantness. Most youth rate drugs or other undesired behaviors more than 0. For each behavior, the TP records the information that is provided in the Initial Unpleasant Consequences column of the CRW next to its respective rating. It is extremely important that the TP responds to the youth in a nonjudgmental manner, with emotionless affect and neutral acknowledgment of the information (e.g., "Got it," "I understand"). The information is recorded verbatim to prevent subsequent misunderstandings when discussion ensues. It is appropriate to ask youth to clarify ambiguous responses and query for additional negative consequences (e.g., "If I got you right, you said your pot use was bad for your lungs; are there any other negative consequences?"). Youth should not be asked to provide greater details at this time in the intervention, however. The following dialogue exemplifies a TP's attempting to solicit initial negative consequences about a youth's marijuana use when the youth initially indicates there is nothing wrong with marijuana. In this example, notice how the TP always prompts: "Anything else?"

TP: What is unpleasant about marijuana use for you?

Robby: Nothing, really.

TP: You rated it a 10 earlier, which would imply you thought something was unpleasant. Is that right?

Robby: My mom's constantly bitching at me for it.

TP: I'll put that down. Anything else?

Robby: No.

After the initial consequences are generated for each behavior, the TP may examine the response quality of negative consequences for each problem behavior. Obviously, substantively aversive responses that are described in great detail suggest the youth has thought a lot about the problem behaviors and is perhaps experiencing distress and readiness to attempt treatment goals. However, having only a few responses that are perhaps nonsubstantive and relatively benign may indicate the youth is probably unmotivated to attempt treatment goals. For instance, if a youth initially indicates cocaine is "bad for your lungs," and upon being queried if there is anything else, responds, "not really," this youth has probably not thought much about the negative consequences of terminating cocaine use. This relative lack of insight also suggests the youth is primed to do well in this intervention.

Regardless of the extent of motivation evidenced from the solicitation of initial negative consequences, the next step is to solicit details for the negative consequences that were generated initially, and to prompt additional ones. For each consequence that is listed in the Initial Consequences column of the CRW, the TP prompts the youth to describe why, specifically, the consequence is negative. The TP should respond to youth responses with neutral affect and statements that are relevant to appreciating the youth's concerns without bias. For instance, the youth might be asked to explain why poor health is unpleasant or why it is aversive to argue with parents. When done right, the solicitation of negative consequences resembles a conversation, with one consequence leading to discussion of other similar consequences. For instance, if a youth thought being grounded at home was aversive because it kept him away from his friends, he could be asked to explain what he was missing, and how that affected his friendships. These consequences are recorded in the Prompted Consequences column of the CRW. The following dialogue exemplifies a TP's attempting to prompt additional negative consequences about a youth's marijuana use. Notice how the TP uses exact terminology expressed by the youth.

TP: You indicated that you thought your mom's bitching at you is unpleasant to you. What is unpleasant about this for you exactly?

Robby: I don't know. She's just annoying to me.

TP: Anything else?

Robby: She usually tries to do everything she can to keep me at home, but she usually forgets and I go out anyway.

TP: You said usually. Does this mean sometimes you do get stuck at home?

Robby: Yep.

TP: If that's unpleasant for you, should I write that down?

Robby: Sure.

TP: What's so bad about being restricted from going out? That is, what are you missing?

Robby: Everything. My friends, my girlfriend, going out and having a good time.

TP: What do you like to do that you're not able to do?

Robby: We hang out and play cards. Sometimes we just watch TV, or play pool. Sometimes I like to go over to my girlfriend's and we go to her room. Just us, you know what I mean?

TP: I think I have enough to write down. Thanks for sharing that with me. Anything else?

After prompts are performed for all consequences, youth are asked to complete the Consequence Review List of Annoyances Worksheet (LAW, Exhibit 5.3). It is explained that the first column includes a list of negative consequences that youth have considered aversive or at least annoying. The youth is instructed to rate each of the listed annoyances on the aforementioned scale from 0 to 100 (0 = not at all unpleasant, 100 = couldn't get any more unpleasant). The youth is also instructed to rate each annoyance on a scale from 0 to 100 regarding its likelihood of occurrence in the future (0 = completely unlikely, 100 = will happen). All annoyances that are rated relatively high in both unpleasantness and likelihood (both ratings usually > 70) should be inserted into the Prompted Consequences column of the CRW next to the behavior problem for which it is most relevant. Along these lines, youth should be queried to assist in determining which problem behaviors are most influenced by the annoyances. For instance, if a youth indicated that jail or detention center would be most likely to occur due to being caught using cocaine, "jail or detention center" would be recorded to the right of the Initial Consequences for "cocaine." In determining which annoyances to include, it is generally appropriate to include annoyances that are rated greater than

70 in unpleasantness and likelihood. However, the TP has discretion in determining which annoyances are selected. Thus, if none of the annoyances are rated with 70 or greater, the TP may decide to include an annoyance that is rated 50 in both unpleasantness and likelihood. Similarly, the TP may decide to exclude annoyances that are rated greater than 70 in both likelihood and unpleasantness because the youth had previously generated a sufficient number of negative consequences or because all but one of the annoyances were rated 100. The TP should also not list annoyances when the youth indicates the annoyance will not result from any of the listed problem behaviors. The following dialogue exemplifies a TP's attempting to utilize the LAW to prompt additional negative consequences.

TP: Looking at your ratings, you have a lot of things that are rated as unpleasant, but only a couple that are also rated as being relatively likely to occur. For instance, you indicated that suspensions at school and getting in trouble at home were rated a 70 for unpleasantness and likelihood.

Robby: That's right, none of those other things are going to happen to me if I'm careful.

TP: If you look at this paper for a moment (showing CRW), you can see I've listed several behaviors in the first column. Of these, which do you think is most likely to lead to suspensions from school?

Robby: Getting caught at school smoking is the only thing they can get me for, and that would mean I'd get punished at home.

TP: O.K., I'll put these things in the row that corresponds to marijuana use.

After all annoyances are appropriately listed in the Prompted Consequences column, the TP attempts to solicit details about each of the annoyances within the context of the respective problem behavior. For instance, the TP might query a youth to indicate how, specifically, jail or detention center might occur due to cocaine use. The TP might also query additional negative consequences and prompt youth for greater elaboration and response clarity. In reviewing negative consequences associated with the recently added annoyances, the TP may also think of new prompts that are relevant to gathering additional information about the initial negative consequences. For example: "If I understand correctly, continued cocaine use might lead to jail, and that would be aversive to you because you would lose your freedom to do what you want, you'd not be able to visit your friends or girlfriend, and it would give you a record so you'd have a hard time getting a satisfying job later. Earlier, you said your teacher doesn't respect you, and that bothers you because she doesn't know you well enough to jump to that conclusion. Do you think others might be more likely to judge you prematurely if they knew you went to jail, and would that be aversive to you if that happened?" The following dialogue exemplifies a TP attempting to solicit unpleasant details about a couple of annoyances in the Prompted Consequences column of the CRW.

TP: Help me to understand how getting suspended at school and getting in trouble at home for smoking pot would be unpleasant for you.

Robby: As soon as my mom hears anything from my science teacher, she automatically assumes I'm wrong and starts to think how she can punish me in a bad way. My science teacher also seems to get some kind of pleasure out of that. I don't want to sound like a nerd or anything, but I also end up falling farther back in my classes and I'm starting to worry that I won't graduate with my friends.

TP: That's a lot of information. Let me make sure I have it correct. Your teacher would give you a suspension if he caught you, and that would result in punishment from your mom at home, and you also might not graduate on time. I normally don't do much interpretation when I'm getting the information down, but it also seems to me like you don't like giving your science teacher the satisfaction of your getting in trouble.

Robby: It really pisses me off.

TP: What kind of trouble at home is unpleasant for you?

After the prompted consequences are recorded in the Prompted Consequences column, the TP should read aloud the consequences that are listed in the Initial and Prompted Consequences columns for each of the respective behaviors, and assure these consequences are accurately recorded. After each series of consequences for each problem behavior is objectively reported to the youth, the TP should provide empathy. The following dialogue exemplifies the TP reading the negative consequences that are listed in the Initial and Prompted Consequences columns of the CRW, and subsequently providing empathy.

TP: I appreciate the information you were willing to share about the negative consequences of your marijuana use. Let me read some of these things back to you, and make sure I have it correct. First, you don't like your mom's bitching about your use, as well as her sometimes keeping you separated from your friends when they're doing fun things like hanging out. When she does this you also don't get a chance to spend private time with your girlfriend. There are also other things that are unpleasant to you about marijuana use, such as potentially getting suspended at school. This would be bad because you don't want your science teacher to get any satisfaction from this, which you feel he does. Suspensions from school also get you in trouble from your mom, like you indicated to me earlier, but also being restricted from using your car. Suspensions also get you further behind so you might not be able to graduate with your friends. Did I get that right?

Robby: You missed me not being able to play pool, but that's not that big of a deal.

TP: I appreciate that, thanks. For you to mention that it must be important. I'll put that down. I wanted to let you know I think it's terrible that you have to be concerned about getting suspended and not being able to graduate from school on time. I remember graduating high school with my friends and it was a great thing that I'll never forget. You deserve to graduate with your friends and girlfriend. I also think that at 17, it is important for you to spend time away from home with your friends. I was particularly disappointed to hear you don't get along with your mom when you get caught. The relationship between a mom and her firstborn son is sacred, and to have it go sour when you're in your last year at home is not good.

The TP concludes the review of negative consequences by reading the initial and prompted consequences for each problem behavior, and subsequently obtaining a final rating using the aforementioned scale of unpleasantness (0 = not at all unpleasant, 100 = couldn't get any more unpleasant). Youth responses should be recorded in the Final Ratings column of the CRW in the row corresponding to its respective problem behavior. For most problem behaviors the final rating will be higher than the initial rating. When these changes occur, the youth should be asked to explain why the ratings went up. Of course, most youth indicate the changes were due to reviewing the negative consequences in detail while the TP listened to relevant concerns without judgment. Such responses are usually good prognostic indicators of success, demonstrating the youth's appreciation for the TP and willingness to attempt sobriety and good conduct.

In rare cases, however, final ratings may be lower than the initial ratings. When this occurs, TPs can either not bring these changes up in discussion, or query youth to explain why the initial ratings decreased. Decreases are usually reported by youth to be due to realizing the negative consequences "weren't really that bad." In hearing this information, the TP should simply thank the youth for their candid assessment while being emotionless. Indeed, youth who report responses such as the one represented in the latter example often do so to assess the TP's reaction, figuring the TP was expecting the ratings to go up (i.e., get the TP aroused, see what the TP will do). Ratings that are relatively low for problem behaviors (i.e., usually final ratings < 50), or those that are at least 20 units lower than initial ratings, are indicative of the need to emphasize interventions that stress external rewards (i.e., Level System). Indeed, such youth are usually not receptive to psycho-education-based approaches.

The example dialogue that follows shows a TP comparing the initial and final ratings that were provided by a youth for marijuana use.

TP: I see here that your initial rating for marijuana use was 20 and now you rated it a 60. What led you to decide to change this rating?

Robby: I never really thought about how it is affecting my relationship with my mother. You're right. This is my last year at home and if I leave with our relationship like this I'm not sure we'll ever have an opportunity to get that back.

TP: That's a great point. She loves you, but I don't see her ever compromising what she feels is in your best interest. She loves you very much, that's for sure. Are there any other things that led you to change your score?

Reviewing Positive Consequences (Youth Client)

The final step of this intervention involves a discussion with the youth about how the youth's behavioral patterns can be changed to turn the negative consequences into positive consequences. The TP may ask the youth to provide a plan for each behavior that is listed in the CRW ("What can you do to stop your use of cocaine?"), or can present this query in an open-ended format ("What can you do to change some of these negative consequences into positive ones?"). Of course, throughout the ensuing discussion, the TP should provide encouragement and support and make suggestions to assist the youth in accomplishing alternative behaviors. The example dialogue that follows shows an TP formulating a plan with the youth to increase positive consequences for marijuana use by maintaining abstinence and other prosocial behaviors.

TP: Well, we've reviewed a lot of negative consequences that are occurring for marijuana use. I'd like you to tell me what you can do to bring about more positive consequences for staying clean. Like a better relationship with your mom, and showing your teachers what you are capable of achieving at school.

Robby: You said it. I just need to stay away from pot.

TP: That's a good point. Staying away from situations in which it is present will be a big first step. How will you be able to make that happen?

Robby: I could cut out parties and hanging out in a few places where I know people are going to smoke.

TP: Outstanding. How will you motivate yourself to get to school?

Robby: Think about how I'd be showing a few of the teachers that I'm not a loser like they think I am.

TP: I understand how you would think that, and it may be true to some extent. However, it's hard to get motivated in the long run thinking how you're proving you're not a loser. A lot of people who show their anger, like maybe your science teacher, do so because at some level they're disappointed because they think they're losing control of someone who has a lot of potential and they can't really do anything about it.

Robby: That makes sense. I used to have a good relationship with Mr. Johnson before my grades started getting worse.

TP: Beautiful, see that shows the kind of character you have in yourself. Maybe you could think about your past successes when you're down, and motivate yourself by thinking of getting those experiences back. Anything else you can do to make it easier to bring about more positive experiences while staying clean?

Concluding Remarks

The Consequence Review provides a structured opportunity for TPs to constructively listen to the youth about the things that are troubling them about their various behavior problems without judgment and redirection. Although the friends of substance-abusing youth are often good listeners, they are rarely experienced enough to motivate them to consistently desire abstinence, and usually don't have the repertoires to assist them in achieving their goals. Thus, the Consequence Rehearsal is guided by the art of listening and positive redirection. As a 16-year-old once stated to the lead author, "I think you're the first adult other than my dead grandfather who listened to what I had to say without judging me."

Supporting Materials for Chapter 5: Probing Negative and Positive Consequences to Determine Core Motivation

Exhibit 5.1.   Consequence Review Therapist Prompting Checklist.

CONSEQUENCE REVIEW
THERAPIST PROMPTING LIST

Client ID#: _____ Clinician: _____ Session #: _____ Date of Session: _____

Materials Required:

- Consequence Review Worksheet (CRW)
- List of Annoyances Worksheet (LAW)

Begin Time: _____

Rationale (Youth Client)

___a.   Report drugs and troublesome behaviors identified to be problematic by youth and/or others.

___b.   State drug use & troublesome behaviors will be difficult to eliminate due to powerful positive consequences.

___c.   State negative consequences are usually delayed, avoided, or suppressed.

___d.   State this intervention aimed at gaining better awareness of neg. consequences of youth behavior.

___e.   Explain why youth is likely to be successful w/this intervention.

___f.   Query how youth expects intervention to be helpful.

Reviewing Negative Consequences (Youth Client)

___a.   Insert at least 1 drug and up to several problem behaviors in 1st column of CRW.

___b.   Obtain & record initial unpleasantness ratings for drugs & prob. behaviors in 2nd column of CRW.

- 0 = not at all unpleasant, 100 = couldn't get any more unpleasant.

___c.   Obtain & record initial consequences for drugs and prob. behaviors from youth in 3rd column of CRW.

___d.   Prompt & record additional neg. consequences & solicit details re. unpleasantness in 4th column of CRW.

___e.   Instruct youth to complete LAW.

___f.   For annoyances in LAW rated relatively high in both unpleasantness & likelihood (both usually > 70) ask youth to indicate the drug or behavior problem listed in CRW that is most likely to lead to the annoyance.

- e.g., "jail" might result from "stealing" behavior listed in CRW.

___g. Record each solicited annoyance in 4th column of CRW in the row representing the respective behavior.
  • If youth indicates an annoyance will not result from listed behaviors, do not include it in CRW.
___h. Obtain & record more details regarding unpleasantness for prompted consequences in 4th column of CRW.
___i. State consequences for each drug and troublesome behavior and after each provide empathy.
___j. State consequences for each drug and troublesome behavior and after each obtain final ratings.
  • 0 = not at all unpleasant, 100 = couldn't get any more unpleasant.
___k. Record each final rating in the 5th column of CRW next to its respective problem behavior.
___l. For each final rating that is rated higher in unpleasantness than its initial rating, query why this is so.

Reviewing Positive Consequences (Youth Client)

___a. Discuss how youth can change behavior to make neg. consequences turn into positive consequences.
  ___1. Provide encouragement and support.
  ___2. Provide suggestions to assist youth in accomplishing alternative behaviors

Conduct Ratings

___a. Disclose therapist's rating of client's compliance on 7-point scale (**7** = extremely compliant, **6** = very compliant, **5** = somewhat compliant, **4** = neutral, **3** = somewhat noncompliant, **2** = very noncompliant, **1** = extremely noncompliant).   Therapist's Rating: ____
  • Factors that contribute to compliance ratings are:
    1. Attendance
    2. Participation & conduct in session
    3. Homework completion
___b. Explain how rating was derived, and methods of improving performance in future.
___c. Solicit client's rating of helpfulness for Consequence Review on 7-point scale after stating client should not feel obligated to provide high scores, as an honest assessment helps therapists better address client needs.
  (**7** = extremely helpful, **6** = very helpful, **5** = somewhat helpful, **4** = not sure, **3** = somewhat unhelpful, **2** = very unhelpful, **1** = extremely unhelpful).   Client's Rating: _____.
___d. Solicit how rating was derived, & methods of improving intervention in future.

End Time: _____   **Note: Reviewer notes can be written below:**

Exhibit 5.2. Consequence Review Worksheet.

TARGET BEHAVIORS	INITIAL RATING	INITIAL UNPLEASANT CONSEQUENCES	PROMPTED CONSEQUENCES	FINAL RATING

Exhibit 5.3. Consequence Review List of Annoyances Worksheet.

CONSEQUENCE REVIEW

LIST OF ANNOYANCES WORKSHEET

ANNOYANCES	RATING OF UNPLEASANTNESS (0–100)	RATING OF LIKELIHOOD (0–100)
1. Jail or detention center (attacked while sleeping, beaten up, raped)		
2. Poor health		
3. Negative relationships with others (screamed at or insulted by adults)		
4. Hurting/upsetting others		
5. Arguments with others		
6. Disrespect from others		
7. Doing bad in school		
8. Getting in fights		
9. Suspensions and detentions		
10. Get in trouble at home		
11. Not being able to get a job (having no money)		

6

Establishing and Rewarding Goal Attainment With Family Support

Overview

Youth who are seen by FBT treatment providers (TPs) are often unmotivated to improve their conduct and maintain abstinence from illicit substances. Therefore, a family-supported Level System (LS) is implemented to reward youth when they achieve therapeutic goals. The intervention is initiated with the provision of a rationale to the family. It is explained that the LS will involve the development of a contract in which the identified youth client will receive desired rewards that have been previously approved by the caregiver(s) when goals are accomplished throughout treatment. The TP subsequently determines rewards that are contemporaneously being provided to the youth, which are often provided noncontingently. For instance, a youth may be receiving an allowance of $5.00 each day while using illicit drugs. Caregivers also sometimes provide rewards inconsistently or ignore desired behaviors while being critical when undesired behavior occurs. To assist in establishing a contingency that is both fair and motivating to the youth, the TP encourages the youth to indicate how existing rewards may be enhanced. Later, caregivers are assisted in creating three reward levels of increased magnitude. For instance, relevant to money, Level 1 rewards are those that are currently provided to the youth (e.g., $3.00 each day); Level 2 rewards are somewhere between what is currently provided to the youth and what is ideally desired by the youth (e.g., $4.00 each day), and Level 3 rewards are those rewards that are ideally desired by the youth (e.g., $5.00 each day). The TP then obtains, from the caregiver, three levels of conduct (behavioral goals) for several target behaviors that are listed in a worksheet. Most Level 1 behavioral goals represent a slight improvement in the youth's conduct (e.g., attending four of six classes), Level 3 goals represent ideal conduct (e.g., attending all classes with satisfactory conduct and achievement according to teacher), and Level 2 goals represent greater improvement in conduct than Level 1, but less behavioral improvement than Level 3. Various worksheets are available to assist in the establishment of target behaviors (goals) and rewards. The TP concludes by integrating the target behaviors and rewards into a contract, and teaching the caregivers to monitor behavioral goals and to contingently provide rewards on a daily basis consistent with the contract. If the youth accomplishes all goals for the day, the youth may receive all rewards the following day. Accomplishing all behavioral goals for 7 consecutive days permits the youth to advance one level, whereas substance use drops youth to level one. Bonus rewards may additionally be earned for consecutive days in which all goals are accomplished. The LS usually requires between 55 and 85 minutes to implement the first time, and about 15 to 30 minutes to implement during subsequent sessions.

Goal for Intervention

➤ Establish an effective contingency management (CM) system in which youth earn rewards from their family members for completion of target behaviors that are incompatible with substance abuse and its associated problem behaviors.

Materials Needed

➤ Level System Therapist Prompting Checklist Initial Session (Exhibit 6.1)

➤ Rewards Worksheet (Exhibit 6.2)

➤ Goals Worksheet (Exhibit 6.3)

➤ Level System Recording Form (Exhibit 6.4)

➤ Record of Chores (Exhibit 6.5)

➤ Daily School Progress Report (Exhibit 6.6)

➤ Level System Therapist Prompting Checklist Future Sessions (Exhibit 6.7)

Procedural Steps for Implementation

Initial Session

Providing Rationale (Youth and Adult Significant Others)   Utilizing the Level System Therapist Prompting Checklist (Exhibit 6.1), the TP initiates the LS by providing the family a rationale for this intervention. The TP explains that the LS is designed to motivate youth to avoid drug use and other behaviors that have been associated with trouble by establishing a contingency system in which caregivers reward youth for staying clean and out of trouble. Although not necessary, if the family is interested it is appropriate to further explain that three levels of increased standards of youth conduct will be established. As the youth accomplishes goals in therapy the youth will advance through these levels, resulting in greater reinforcement from caregivers. The TP reports how the LS is expected to be particularly beneficial for the youth and youth's caregivers, and the family is asked how they expect the LS to be effective. Of course, questions should be solicited and answered as appropriate.

If the youth indicates that this system is unnecessary, it may be that the youth is attempting to avoid commitments that are established with reward contingencies (perhaps due to a relative lack of motivation or guilt about past undesired behaviors). When this occurs the TP should indicate that the youth deserves rewards when earned, and the LS will support the youth when motivation to quit substance use or improve troublesome behavior is low. When caregivers oppose the LS, it is usually because they have a hard time appreciating the importance of extrinsically "rewarding" youth for doing beneficial behaviors they should be intrinsically motivated to desire (i.e., youth should be self-motivated). Such responses are usually squashed by reminding the caregiver that work is probably attended every day at least to some extent due to being paid, that the establishment of work ethic is a gradual process, that it will probably take some time for the youth to appreciate a new set of natural reinforcers, or something along those lines. If this does not work, it is important to temporarily excuse the youth from the session and inform the caregiver that the system can be modified or terminated if it is not working. The following dialogue demonstrates an appropriate implementation of an LS rationale with a mother who believes her daughter should do what she's told without rewards. The daughter also expresses the system is unnecessary.

TP: Today we're going to learn develop a system in which Jasmine will get rewarded for avoiding drugs and alcohol and also behaviors that seem to get her in trouble. She will get more rewards than she is currently receiving, but she will also have to earn these rewards by improving her conduct.

Youth: I don't need any rewards. I need to do this myself. My mom's already been through enough.

TP: I insist. You deserve it, and it will be a great way of earning a little extra money and privileges to take your sister out to dinner or something. At least do it for her, right? When times are tough, and your motivation is low, you could benefit from the extra support this system will establish for you.

Youth: That's fine.

Mom: Wait a second. I actually think she should do this on her own. Why should I have to reward her for doing the right thing? I didn't get any rewards from my parents when I was a kid.

Youth: I don't want anything from you, Mom!

TP: Well, think about what you said for a moment, Mom. Did your caregivers really not give you any rewards for your behavior?

Mom: Well, not for staying clean from drugs.

TP: Rewards have been shown to be effective for lots of things, and your daughter may have experienced circumstances in her environment that make her situation unique from yours.

Mom: You're right. She's been through a lot.

TP: It's my fault for not emphasizing how Jasmine was exposed to an illicit substance at a very early age, and this has made it hard for her to eliminate substance use. We all work best when we are reinforced. Even though we may like our jobs, we probably wouldn't work for free. Jasmine's good conduct and sobriety will be like her full-time job, and I think your rewards will be important to maintaining her enthusiasm.

Mom: That makes sense.

TP: I really think the Level System is going to be great for you both because there is a lot of love in your home that I think will be emphasized when we alter the contingencies of reinforcement a little. Do you have any more questions?

Determining Desired Reinforcers From Youth (Youth Only) The TP excuses all family members with the exception of the youth, then shows the Rewards Worksheet (see Exhibit 6.2) and points out the broad-based daily reward categories that are listed in the far left column (i.e., Potential Daily Rewards). It is explained to the youth that daily rewards are those that have the potential to be provided by the caregiver(s) every day if earned. The youth is first queried to reveal which of the listed Potential Daily Rewards are desired. For each reward that is desired, the youth is queried to explain how the reward is currently provided by the caregivers on a daily basis. Youth responses are recorded in the second column of the Rewards Worksheet (Currently Receiving) next to the respective reward category. There is also a prompt to solicit one or two "other" potential desired daily rewards in the Potential Daily Rewards column. "Other" potential daily rewards are developed in a similar manner as the prerecorded Potential Daily Rewards. Sometimes potential daily rewards that are solicited from youth need to be adjusted so they can be provided on a daily basis. For instance, if a youth indicated that he received an allowance of $10.00 per week, this reinforcer could be converted to approximately $1.50 per day. For each of the desired rewards, the TP attempts to determine how it can be modified to be "ideal." That is, if a youth had a cell phone package that permitted 1 hour of cell phone use per day, an ideal reward for cell phone use might be an unlimited minutes plan. In determining ideal rewards, youth should be encouraged to not consider whether their caregivers can provide these rewards or not. This is important, because caregivers are often very excited to increase the attractiveness of their rewards if desired target behaviors are evidenced in their children, and it is imperative that youth be highly motivated to improve their conduct. Solicited ideal rewards are listed in the third column (Ideally Desired) of the Rewards Worksheet next to the potential reward that is currently provided.

Bonus rewards are provided to youth once in awhile (e.g., a trip to amusement center), usually because these rewards are relatively costly or difficult to provide. Thus, the distribution of bonus rewards in the LS follows a different set of guidelines than daily rewards. Bonus rewards are provided according to the number of consecutive days in which the youth accomplishes all goals that are targeted in the LS (see next section for the method of determining goals). In soliciting bonus rewards, the TP first determines which bonus rewards are desired by the youth, and subsequently solicits how the youth thinks these rewards can be modified to be "ideal." Ideal bonus rewards are recorded in the "Ideal Rewards" column of the Rewards Worksheet where appropriate.

The following dialogue exemplifies successful solicitation of two daily rewards (i.e., "money," "transportation") from an adolescent who is accustomed to getting what she desires from her caregivers without having to do much to earn these rewards.

TP: I'd like you to look at these potential rewards and tell me which ones you would like to receive, or continue to receive.

Kim: I get all of these already.

TP: Fantastic for you. Tell me which ones you'd like to continue to receive. We might modify them to make them even more attractive to you.

Kim: All of them, although I need more money and rides to places.

TP: Great, let's take money first. How much do you currently get?

Kim: As much as I ask for usually.

TP: What's the most you've been given in a typical week, not counting special events.

Kim: About $100.00.

TP: So that would be about $14.00 a day. What do you currently get regarding transporation?

Kim: My mom takes me to my friends' houses whenever I ask, as long as it's before she goes to sleep.

TP: So what's the latest she's given you a ride?

Kim: She's picked me up at 12:00 A.M. before, but she doesn't usually like that.

TP: So it looks like if I put down rides whenever asked before 12:00 A.M. that would be what you are currently receiving.

Kim: Yep.

The TP would continue to determine how the caregiver is perceived to support the youth in providing each of the daily reinforcers that are listed in the Potential Daily Reinforcers column. The TP would then attempt to obtain, for each solicited reinforcer what is ideally desired on a daily basis, as indicated in the following dialogue.

TP: Looking at what we have for money. You are currently receiving up to $14.00 every day on average, at least when times are good. What would make that ideal for you?

Kim: I don't know, 20 bucks. My mom probably couldn't afford that anyways. I'm fine with how it is right now.

TP: I'll put it down for her to consider. Your mom can always change the value if she wants. For transportation you indicated that she could give you a ride pretty much anytime prior to her bedtime, which is usually 12:00 A.M. What would make transportation ideal for you?

Kim: My own car, or to be able to use her car at least.

Determining Goals With Caregiver (Adult Significant Others Only)   After the youth is excused and the caregiver enters the room, the TP shows the Goals Worksheet (see Exhibit 6.3). The caregiver is told that the LS will be used to target the youth's problem behavior in three phases, or levels. The TP refers the caregiver to each of the Behavioral Domains that are listed in the first column of this worksheet and explains that three standards of behavioral conduct will be targeted for each of the listed domains. The first level will reflect a slight improvement over existing conduct, the third level will represent ideally desired conduct, and the second level will represent conduct that is between the first and third level. For each behavioral domain, the TP first solidifies a first-level goal with the caregiver (i.e., slight improvements in target behavior), then the third-level goal (ideal behavior for the respective behavioral domain), and finally the second-level goal. If there is no room to improve a particular behavioral domain, this domain should not be targeted in treatment. For instance, if a youth is going to school every day and earning all A's on his report card, the domain of "school" would be skipped. Each of the solicited goals should ideally be positive, goal-oriented, and objectively measurable on a daily basis. Solicited goals may vary between youth due to a number of factors, including the severity of behavioral disturbance evidenced. The Goals Worksheet includes partial or complete first-, second-, and third-level goals that are prerecorded to assist in rapidly determining relevant targets in the LS. It is important for TPs to stress to caregivers, however, that any prerecorded goals, partial goals, or goal prompts may be modified to accommodate the unique needs and culture of the caregiver's family. For instance, the "work" behavioral domain and its prerecorded goal prompt "___ hours worked/day" may be ignored (crossed out on the form).

In developing goals for the first domain (i.e., illegal/troublesome behavior), all three levels necessitate the absence of misconduct reports, including detentions and suspensions from school and arrests from police. However, other misconduct can be additionally targeted. For instance, if a youth were getting into a fight once every other month, a slight improvement in behavior for this youth might be physically getting along well with others throughout the day, whereas an ideal goal in this domain might additionally be the performance of a desired social skill or prosocial behavior while getting along physically and verbally with others throughout the day. The second-level response might additionally involve getting along with others physically and verbally throughout the day. In this example, each level demonstrates an improvement in conduct. Of course, the number of potential illicit behaviors targeted in this behavioral domain at any level may be overwhelming. Therefore, it is highly recommended to target no more than two or three illicit behaviors at the same time.

The following dialogue demonstrates the establishment of three goal sets for illicit behavior in a mother who has a child who has been arrested several times in the recent past.

TP: If you look at the first behavioral domain, illicit behavior, you can see that all three levels will require your child to evidence no reports for illicit behaviors from adults or authorities. Some caregivers add additional targets that are more specific, particularly during the second and third levels. Would no reports of illicit behavior represent a slight improvement in your son's behavior?

Mother: That would be an understatement.

TP: Let's go to the third level. What would you ideally desire from your son on a daily basis that is relevant to illicit behavior?

Mother: I would like him to make more friends with nice kids who don't use drugs or get into trouble.

TP: I think any caregiver would desire that for her child. What if we required him to get involved in a social activity or club where he would be likely to meet someone with these qualifications?

Mother: How about him being a member of the school baseball team again. He used to love this, and I know his coach would let him back on the team if he got himself together in a good way again.

TP: That's a great idea. We could always modify it a little later in case your son can think of some equally satisfying alternative. What if for Level 2 we required him initiate a conversation about how he is trying to restructure his social network to include clean friends who don't get into trouble. Although he could probably validate the actions he brings up, I think the important part of this would be that he'd be talking with you again about prosocial activities. This would provide you opportunities to praise his efforts, or at least stated efforts. He would have to evidence no reports of misconduct at all levels.

As indicated above, most of the behavioral domains should demonstrate improvements in conduct as levels advance. However, this is not required. For instance, it is also possible to keep the expected standards of behavior the same for two or three levels. For instance, relevant to the second behavioral domain (i.e., substance use), it is clear that abstinence from all illicit substances is the most desired substance use goal, as alcohol and illicit drug use is illegal for adolescents, substance intoxication may weaken motivation and skills that are relevant to resisting other illicit behaviors, and so on. Moreover, many persons are philosophically opposed to rewarding youth for staying clean from one drug (e.g., cocaine) while permitting another drug (e.g., marijuana or alcohol) to occur. Therefore, it is recommended that all illicit substances, including alcohol, are targeted for abstinence at all three levels. It may also be appropriate for other behavioral domains to include the same goals as levels increase. For instance, it may be determined that a youth who has dropped out of school and is working full-time may require 8 hours per day of employment for all three levels.

Curfew. Two curfew times are typically recommended for each level, one for weekends and the other for weekdays. Weekdays usually include Sunday through Thursday because school occurs during the next day and youth need to be well rested to perform well in school. Youth are thus usually permitted to stay out later on Friday and Saturday nights because youth do not have to get up early the next morning to perform well in school. Exceptions to this guideline occur when youth are employed and need to work the next morning. The first, second, and third levels for curfew are partially completed. The TP simply fills in the blanks with the caregiver desired curfew times (e.g., slight improvement for first level = 1:30 A.M. curfew for weekends). As indicated above, it is also possible to keep the second and third levels the same for curfew, have one curfew for all 7 days, or for the parent to temporarily adjust curfew times to be more or less stringent whenever desired due to extenuating circumstances (e.g., summer, holidays). It should be mentioned that this is also true for other goals in the LS, as well.

Reporting whereabouts. Monitoring youth throughout the day and evening has been indicated to prevent delinquent and drug use behavior. Daytime monitoring is typically managed by school administrators or employers. However, with the exception of evening employment, youth are often unmonitored during evenings. In the LS, youth are required to inform their caregivers about their whereabouts throughout the evening, or when they are not in school, work, or involved in adult-monitored activities. Most caregivers find it acceptable for their children to report their whereabouts in a telephone call because they can assess voice tone and speech patterns and background noises that are consistent with intoxication (i.e., text is not advised as an appropriate check). However, some caregivers may require personal contact or some combination of telephone and personal contact (e.g., phone calls every hour, in person contact every 4 hours). There are prompts in the "informing caregivers of whereabouts" row corresponding to the first, second, and third levels where the TP may record the maximum number of minutes that may occur before the youth is required to inform the caregiver of whereabouts. The worksheet also specifies that for each level, youth are required to inform, or get permission from, caregivers when leaving one location and arriving at another.

Communication. When TPs query caregivers to indicate a slight improvement in the communication of their youth, most indicate no swearing, lying, or yelling at them. Along these lines, the standard first-level goal for the behavioral domain "communication" is "talking calmly and truthfully throughout the day," whereas caregivers are encouraged to additionally choose a minimal number of minutes of conversation for second- and third-level goals. Caregivers may also include additional goals, whenever desired. However, we've found these behavioral communication sets are usually sufficient.

Chores. The caregiver is assisted in recording chores in the "Record of Chores" form. As can be seen in Exhibit 6.5, chores may be inserted in the left column of each of the three levels. The TP then solicits what day each of the chores need to be performed, and records an "X" in the appropriate row. The caregiver should be informed that the Record of Chores form will be referenced each night when reviewing the LS to assist in knowing which chores were due for completion.

Work. Employment is strongly encouraged because it is incompatible with substance use and illicit behavior, and it is positively associated with self-esteem, reduced stress and other beneficial psychological factors. If youth are enrolled in school, employment becomes less important, and is sometimes skipped (i.e., not required in the LS). However, whenever possible, employment (or attempts to gain employment) should be encouraged to some extent (i.e., part-time if enrolled in school, full-time if not enrolled in school, making attempts to get a job). There is a prompt for each level in this behavioral domain to record the specific number of hours required for work in the Goals Worksheet. Caregivers should be told efforts to gain employment include making calls to potential employers, completing job applications, buying appropriate clothing for job interviews, attending vocational training, and so on. These efforts can be easily monitored. For instance, youth can be required to show caregivers their completed applications or purchased clothes, make telephone calls in front of caregivers, and have caregivers drive them to potential job interviews. Similarly, attendance at work may be monitored to some extent by calling youth during their work shifts on the company line, talking with their boss, and so on.

School. With very few exceptions, youth should be encouraged to attend traditional high schools or alternative vocational schools. However, when these school formats are refused by youth, home schooling and general education development (GED) classes may be viable options. School performance is targeted as the number of classes attended each day, and the number of these classes that are judged by the parent to require satisfactory conduct and achievement. Class attendance and school conduct and achievement are monitored utilizing the Daily School Progress Report (see Exhibit 6.6). In this form, all enrolled courses are listed in the left column (for GED and home schooling, the youth can substitute total number of hours in class). The youth is instructed to bring this form to each teacher, and teachers are instructed to record whether the youth's conduct and achievement were satisfactory for the day. Caregivers are also encouraged to interact with teachers through written notes that may be recorded at the bottom of this form. When initially establishing the daily school progress report, it is important to contact each teacher to review the system, and encourage participation. We have found most GED classes difficult to monitor. Moreover, when we checked youth attendance in GED classes, we were often informed that youth did not attend these meetings. Many youth appear to evidence difficulties motivating themselves for self-study, or lack assertiveness skills in seeking assistance with GED related problems. Therefore, we generally recommend the GED not be targeted in Levels 2 and 3 unless there are very good reasons to support this choice.

Other. Caregivers have the option of targeting "other" goals in the Behavioral Domain category. Ideally, these targets should contribute to the youth's development and be educationally based. For instance, caregivers may want to target the participation of their youth in a club at school, music lessons, or sport team.

Determining Reinforcers With Caregiver (Adult Significant Others Only)   The caregiver is shown the Rewards Worksheet (Exhibit 6.2) that was completed with the youth. The desired daily rewards that were said to be currently provided by the caregiver are pointed out, as well as the rewards that were ideally desired by the youth on a daily basis. For each of these rewards, the TP queries the caregiver to suggest rewards that may be provided on a daily basis if all third-level goals are performed. Caregivers are often upset with their youth, making it difficult for them to think of their youth as deserving such rewards. Therefore, it is sometimes helpful to suggest caregivers imagine that their child is behaving "perfectly." These rewards are recorded as "Caregiver Third-Level Rewards" in the Rewards Worksheet. The TP then solicits rewards that are a slight improvement over currently administered daily rewards that may be provided to the youth on a daily basis if the youth performs all first-level goals. These rewards are recorded as "Caregiver First-Level Rewards." Finally, the TP solicits moderate rewards that may be provided by the caregiver on a daily basis if all second-level goals are performed. The solicited first-level rewards are transferred to the First-Level System Recording form in the Daily Rewards section. The TP may later transfer second- and third-level rewards to the Second- and Third-Level System Recording Form, respectively (usually performed in the office after the session).

In a similar manner, the TP discloses all bonus rewards that were desired by the youth in the Rewards Worksheet (listed as ideal rewards in bonus section of the Rewards Worksheet), and explains that these rewards are usually provided less frequently than the daily rewards. It is important to determine if the caregiver is capable of providing these ideal rewards (or if they need to be modified somewhat) so youth may be reinforced for engaging in consecutive days in which all goals are accomplished for an extended time. Endorsed bonus rewards are recorded in the left column of the "Bonus Rewards Section" of Level System Recording Form for Level 1. These same bonus rewards can be inserted into the Second- and Third-Level System Recording Forms immediately after the session. For each of the bonus rewards, the caregiver is asked to estimate the number of consecutive days the youth will need to perform all goals in order to earn each bonus reward. The number of consecutive days needed to earn each bonus reward is recorded in the Level System Recording Form for Level 1 in the Bonus Reward section, and these numbers are later transferred to the Bonus Reward sections of the Second- and Third-Level System Recording Forms after the session.

It is also helpful to briefly show the caregiver that the "Goals" section of the LS Recording Form includes brief summaries of all First-Level Goals that are more specifically defined in the Goals Worksheet. It should also be shown how "chores" in the LS Recording Form is more specifically defined in the Record of Chores Worksheet, and this worksheet should be referenced when reviewing the level system with the youth at the end of each night. Similarly, the first-level daily reward "good at school" in the LS Recording Form is more specifically defined in the Goals Worksheet, although the Daily School Progress Report needs to be reviewed each night to determine if classes were attended with sufficient conduct and achievement. There is no sense reviewing Second- and Third-Level System Recording Forms since these levels are similarly reviewed later, when the youth's conduct improves.

Reviewing the Level System Daily Review (Youth and Adult Significant Others)   After the youth is invited back into the office, it is explained that at the end of each day the caregiver will review the youth's completion of goals, and based on the youth's performance let the youth know which rewards were earned. The youth and caregiver are briefly shown all Level 1, 2, and 3 goals listed in the Goals Worksheet and all Level 1, 2, and 3 daily rewards listed in the Rewards Worksheet. The Daily School Progress Report and Record of Chores Worksheet are reviewed. For youth who attend school, or will attend school, it is emphasized that the LS Recording Form includes a brief reference to "good at school" in the goals section, but that this goal is fully defined in the Goals Worksheet. The youth and caregiver are shown how to complete the Daily School Progress Report for all courses. It is explained that courses are recorded in the far left column, that each teacher records if conduct and achievement were satisfactory or not, and that each teacher signs the form after completing it. Prior to leaving the session, the youth should be provided five copies of the School Progress Report form for teachers to complete (one report per day). Goals and rewards that are listed in the LS Recording Form should be compared with those in the Goals and Rewards Worksheets because the LS Recording Form is a summary of these contingencies, and thus the goals and rewards look a little different. It is important to explain that all goals will need to be performed by the youth for the reviewed day in order for the youth to receive any respective rewards during the next day. It is further explained that the caregiver must prevent the youth from experiencing any of the respective level rewards if all goals for the respective level were not performed by the youth during previous day.

The additional benefits of accomplishing all goals for extended periods of time should be emphasized. That is, the youth will advance one level each week all goals are accomplished, and additional bonus rewards may be earned as indicated. Prior to reviewing bonus rewards, it should be explained that evidence of substance use or reports of illicit behavior, such as detentions and suspensions at school, and police reports, will result in the youth going back (or remaining in) Level 1. Caregiver approved bonus rewards that are listed in the Rewards Worksheet and summarized in the first LS Recording Form should be shown. During this time, the youth learns the number of consecutive days in which all goals will need to be accomplished in order to receive each of these bonus rewards.

It is explained that the caregiver has discretion to determine if the youth can be permitted to rectify (i.e., "make up") goals that were not performed during the day. Make-up behaviors need to be slightly more difficult to achieve than the goals that were not accomplished, and make-up behaviors need to be performed prior to receiving rewards the following day. From the youth's perspective, make-ups are important because they provide opportunities to gain lost reinforcement during the following day, and because they permit consecutive "perfect" days (i.e., a day in which all goals are accomplished) to continue. Consecutive days lead to greater bonus rewards and advancement in levels. Make-up opportunities are important because the youth is assisted in gaining motivation to naturally correct their behavior. For instance, if a youth did unsatisfactory class work in math but accomplished all other goals, he would not be able to obtain any of the daily rewards the next day. In this situation, the caregiver might consider permitting the youth to make up for this is oversight by doing the class work at home in addition to extra math problems. The caregiver simply marks an "M" to indicate "make-up" in the LS Recording Form for the day and goal instead of indicating completion of the goal with a check, as usually recorded when goals are accomplished in a timely manner. Make-ups are not possible for substance use and illicit behavior.

After the general guidelines are sufficiently reviewed, the TP models how to review the LS Recording Form with the youth while pretending to be the caregiver. The TP informs the family that a hypothetical day will be modeled. Along these lines, it is important for the TP to pretend as if the youth completed most behaviors but missed a couple of behaviors that could be made up by the youth if desired. The TP descriptively praises the youth for hypothetically performed goals, and provides encouragement for a couple of goals that were not accomplished. The TP also queries if the youth would like to make up goals that were not accomplished. Along these lines, the TP should firmly, but supportively, indicate how the youth may make up the goals that were not accomplished.

Prior to soliciting positive feedback from the family about the modeled performance, it is imperative that the TP let the family know make-ups are often not permitted. The TP shows the completed LS Recorded form, and points out how checks and the letter "M" were used to indicate goal performance for the respective day. After soliciting and answering questions, the TP instructs the caregiver to conduct the LS daily review for the present day.

The TP prompts correct responding and answers questions throughout the interaction. Of course, the caregiver is praised for accurate responding after the review, and the youth is descriptively reinforced for compliance and other desired behaviors that may have occurred during the interaction.

The TP instructs the caregiver and youth to sign the contract, and provides them with copies of the completed LS Recording form, Chores Recording form, Daily School Progress Report, and the reviewed worksheets (i.e., Rewards, Goals). A time to review the LS is established, and the youth is informed that if the LS is not brought to the caregiver by the scheduled meeting time rewards will not occur during the next day.

Future Sessions (Youth and Adult Significant Others)   All future LS sessions correspond with the Level System Therapist Prompting Checklist Future Sessions (Exhibit 6.7), and are initiated with the TP instructing the family to show the completed LS Recording form. The TP descriptively praises the youth for completing outstanding goals, and descriptively praises the caregiver for monitoring the completion of goals. This is often a serious problem, as some caregivers erroneously assume youth are telling them the truth. Therefore, caregivers are assisted in learning to monitor the conduct of their children utilizing problem-solving strategies when monitoring skills are poorly demonstrated. Of course, relevant to monitoring, youth sometimes indicate their displeasure of not being trusted when their caregivers "check up" on them. In responding to such comments, it is important to immediately empathize with youth after they make these statements and suggest check-ups will reduce in frequency as goals continue to be accomplished and trust is reestablished.

It is important to assure caregivers are providing earned reinforcers as negotiated. When earned rewards are not provided by caregivers it is important to indicate the importance of doing so, and encourage caregivers to retrospectively make up for these losses. If youth engage in undesired behaviors that are not listed in the LS, caregivers should be encouraged to consequence such behaviors using disciplinary strategies outside the LS, and later consider the integration of these behaviors into the LS as target goals.

Caregivers sometimes permit youth to access reinforcers that are not earned. Such violations threaten the integrity of the LS and must be immediately addressed by asking caregivers to report how they think this problem may exacerbate the LS. This strategy is useful in determining the extent to which caregivers may need to be educated about the basic tenets of CM. More often youth "sneak" reinforcers without caregivers' knowledge. In such cases, it is usually helpful to determine how youth were able to access unearned rewards and initiate methods of preventing such behavior in the future. Level system reviews are always concluded with the TP asking the family if the LS needs to be modified, and negotiating such changes between youth and caregivers.

Concluding Remarks

The benefits of CM programs in treating children and adolescents are generally quite positive across a wide array of conduct problems. CM approaches in adolescent substance abuse have usually involved powerful rewards that are practitioner assisted (i.e., earning vouchers for abstinence as verified by negative urinalysis testing). The reviewed LS is therefore unique in its emphasis on family generated and maintained contingencies. When our research team initiated the development of this CM, there appeared to be a clear lack of reinforcement available in the families we were treating. For instance, families were often from impoverished neighborhoods and/or evidenced long-standing histories of contingency *mismanagement*. Some caregivers lacked basic contingency management skills, and parental attention was usually inconsequential due to years of strained relationships with their children. We quickly noticed it was common for youth to obtain their reinforcement elsewhere. Some of the youth evidenced a greater income than their parents selling drugs, and when parents implemented aversive punishments, their youth sometimes left the family to live with substance-abusing peers. Educational deficits made it difficult for caregivers to understand our initial contingency management systems (i.e., point systems). These anecdotal discoveries led us to encourage the development of simple reinforcement menus and monitoring forms. Through trial and error, we determined the behavioral goals (i.e., target behaviors) that seemed to be most associated with improved treatment outcomes. We also discovered that even when youth initially did not appear to be motivated to change their behavior because the rewards appeared to lack power, these youth ultimately responded well, perhaps due to the system's emphasis on objectivity and fairness. Indeed, they seemed to be reinforced by TPs "going to bat" for them during LS reviews. Finally, although the implementation of urinalysis once or twice a week is ideal to assist in the detection of substance use, when funding does not permit such testing, rewards may be made contingent on other signs of substance use (i.e., not coming home on time for curfew, smell of marijuana on jacket, unsteady gait, alcohol on breath). Reviewing signs of substance use assists parents in learning to monitor and react to substance use, thus reducing upset and arguments that often contribute to future substance use. Therefore, we believe the overall benefits of this LS extend far beyond the simple provision of contingent rewards for desired behaviors.

Supporting Materials for Chapter 6: Establishing and Rewarding Goal Attainment With Family Support

Exhibit 6.1. Level System Therapist Prompting Checklist Initial Session.

LEVEL SYSTEM
THERAPIST PROMPTING CHECKLIST
INITIAL SESSION

Client ID#: _____ Clinician: _____ Session #: _____ Date of Session: _____

Begin Time:

Providing Rationale (Both Youth and Adult Significant Others):

___ a. Level System (LS) is designed to motivate youth to avoid drug use and trouble.
___ b. LS involves giving youth rewards for staying clean and out of trouble.
___ c. Explain how youth is expected to benefit from LS.
___ d. Query how LS can benefit youth.
___ e. Solicit questions and provide answers.

Determining Desired Reinforcers from Youth (Youth Only):

___ 1. For each desired Potential Daily Reward in Rewards Worksheet assess what is currently provided by caregiver.
   • Record in "currently receiving" column of Rewards Worksheet.
___ 2. Solicit "Other Potential Daily Rewards" in Potential Daily Rewards section of Rewards Worksheet.
   • Record in "Currently Receiving" column of Rewards Worksheet.
___ 3. For each desired Potential Daily Reward in Rewards Worksheet assess what is ideally desired.
   • Record in "ideally desired" column of Rewards Worksheet.
___ 4. For each desired Potential Bonus Reward in Rewards Worksheet assess what is ideally desired from caregiver.
   • Record in "Ideally Desired" column of Rewards Worksheet.

Determining Goals w/Caregiver (Adult Significant Others Only)

___ 1. Assist caregiver in determining a 1st Level Goal (i.e., slight improvements in youth's behavior) for each "Behavioral Domain" in Goals Worksheet.
   • Record goals as "1st-Level Goals" in Goals Worksheet.
   • Record all Level 1 chores in Record of Chores Worksheet (insert "X" for days chores are to be completed).
   • Record all courses in "Daily School Progress Report."

___ 2. Assist in determining a 3rd-Level Goal (i.e., ideal behavior for youth) for each "Behavioral Domain" in Goals Worksheet.
   • Record these goals as "Third-Level Goals" in Goals Worksheet.
   • Record all Level 3 chores in Record of Chores Worksheet (insert "X" for days chores are to be completed).
   • Record all courses in "Daily School Progress Report."

___ 3. Assist in determining a 2nd-Level Goal (i.e., behavior somewhere between slight improvement and ideal behavior) for each "Behavioral Domain" in the Goals Worksheet.
   • Record these goals as "2nd-Level Goals" in Goals Worksheet.
   • Record all Level 2 chores in Record of Chores Worksheet (insert "X" for days chores are to be completed).
   • Record all courses in "Daily School Progress Report."

___ 4. Disclose how all 1st-Level Goal summaries listed in 1st-level Goals section of Level System Recording form correspond w/those in Goals Worksheet.
   • Each 1st-Level Goal is defined in the Goals Worksheet.
   Note: "Chores" in the LS Recording form are defined in the Record of Chores Worksheet.
   Note: "Good at school" in LS Recording form specifically defined in Goals Worksheet and dependent on Daily School Progress Report.
   • 2nd- and 3rd-Level Goals may be listed/reviewed in Goals section of 2nd- & 3rd-Level System Recording forms later.

Determining Reinforcers With Caregiver (Adult Significant Others Only)

   • Show copy of Rewards Worksheet.

___ 1. Indicate youth-desired daily rewards the youth reports earning currently.
___ 2. Indicate youth desired daily rewards the youth would ideally like to receive.
___ 3. Solicit ideal daily rewards to be earned by youth for doing all Level 3 goals.
   • Record as "Caregiver 3rd-Level Rewards" in Rewards Worksheet.
___ 4. Solicit daily rewards that are a slight improvement over rewards currently offered (1st level).
   • Record as "Caregiver 1st-Level Rewards" in Rewards Worksheet.
___ 5. Determine daily rewards that are moderate compared w/1st-and 3rd-level rewards (somewhere in the middle).
   • Record as "Caregiver 2nd-Level Rewards" in Rewards Worksheet.
___ 6. Transfer all Caregiver 1st-level rewards in Rewards Worksheet to 1st-Level System Recording form.
   Note: 2nd- and 3rd-Level Rewards can be transferred to 2nd- and 3rd-LS Recording forms later.
___ 7. Disclose potential bonus rewards youth ideally desires, & for each determine bonus reward acceptable to caregiver.
   • Record as bonus rewards in "Bonus Rewards" section of Level System Recording form for Level 1.
   Note: Bonus rewards can be inserted into the 2nd- and 3rd-LS Recording forms later.

___ 8. Determine number of consecutive days youth will need to perform all goals to earn each bonus reward.
   • Record # of consecutive days needed to earn each bonus reward in Level System Recording form for Level 1.
   Note: # of consecutive days needed for each bonus reward can be inserted into 2nd- & 3rd-Level System Recording forms later.

Reviewing the Level System Daily Review (Youth and Adult Significant Others)

___ 1. <u>Explain</u> all daily goals for a given level must be performed by youth to obtain daily rewards for same level the next day.
___ 2. Review the daily rewards that are listed for each of the 3 levels in Rewards Worksheet.
___ 3. Review goals for each of the 3 levels in Goals Worksheet.
   ___ a. Explain how to utilize Daily School Progress Report.
   ___ b. Explain how to determine "chores" in Record of Chores Worksheet.
___ 4. Explain caregiver must restrict all daily rewards if all goals for respective level were not performed during previous day.
___ 5. Show bonus rewards in LS Recording form and # of consecutive days in which all goals need to be accomplished to earn them.
___ 6. Explain youth will advance 1 level for each week in which all goals are accomplished.
___ 7. Explain youth will drop 1 level for each week substance use or a report of misconduct is evidenced.
___ 8. Explain it is caregiver's discretion to determine if youth can "make up" goals that weren't performed.
   • Make-ups need to be more difficult to achieve than original goals.
   • Make-ups should be performed prior to providing rewards during the following day.
   • Make-ups are not permitted for drug use or illicit behavior.
___ 9. Model how to review LS Recording form in role of caregiver w/youth for hypothetical day, including:
   ___ a. Praising performance of target behaviors.
   ___ b. Making arrangements to provide rewards during next day.
   ___ c. Providing next day encouragement for goals that were not accomplished.
___10. Instruct caregiver to review LS Recording form w/youth for current day.
   ___ a. Praise/prompt caregiver for performance of target behaviors.
   ___ b. Praise/prompt caregiver for making arrangements to provide rewards next day.
   ___ c. Praise/prompt caregiver for providing encouragement for goals that were not accomplished.
___11. Schedule a time for youth and caregiver to review level system at home each night.
___12. Instruct youth and caregiver to sign contract.

Conducting Ratings

___ a. Disclose therapist's rating of client's compliance on 7-point scale (**7** = extremely compliant, **6** = very compliant, **5** = somewhat compliant, **4** = neutral, **3** = somewhat noncompliant, **2** = very noncompliant, **1** = extremely noncompliant).   Therapist's Rating: ____

- Factors that contribute to compliance ratings are:
  1. Attendance
  2. Participation & conduct in session
  3. Homework completion

___ b. Explain how rating was derived, and methods of improving performance in future.

___ c. Solicit client's rating of helpfulness for Level System on 7-point scale after stating client should not feel obligated to provide high scores, as an honest assessment helps therapists better address client needs.

(**7** = extremely helpful, **6** = very helpful, **5** = somewhat helpful, **4** = not sure, **3** = somewhat unhelpful, **2** = very unhelpful, **1** = extremely unhelpful).   Client's Rating: _____.

___ d. Solicit how rating was derived and methods of improving intervention in future.

End Time: _____   **Reviewer notes:**

Exhibit 6.2. Rewards Worksheet.

REWARDS WORKSHEET

Type of Reward	Currently Receiving	Ideally Desired	Caregiver 1st-Level Reward	Caregiver 2nd-Level Reward	Caregiver 3rd-Level Reward
Potential Daily Rewards					
Money					
Transportation					
Type of meal/dessert					
Cell phone use					
TV/video/games/Wii					
Time w/friends and activities					
Privacy time					
Other Potential Daily Reward:					
Potential Bonus Rewards	NA	NA	NA	NA	NA
Clothing	NA		NA	NA	NA
Magazine subscription	NA		NA	NA	NA
Bike/motorcycle/scooter/car	NA		NA	NA	NA
Letter to probation officer or others	NA		NA	NA	NA
Pet/fish	NA		NA	NA	NA
Trips w/family/friends	NA		NA	NA	NA
Own car	NA		NA	NA	NA
Phone	NA		NA	NA	NA
Gifts (computer, weights, stereo, CD player)	NA		NA	NA	NA
Own room	NA		NA	NA	NA
Sport/fitness/club membership/lessons (horseback riding, scuba, guitar)	NA		NA	NA	NA
Pet/pet supplies	NA		NA	NA	NA
Laundry	NA		NA	NA	NA
Non-drug/alc. party/get-together/barbecue	NA		NA	NA	NA
Overnight sleepover	NA		NA	NA	NA
Concerts	NA		NA	NA	NA
Other Bonus Rewards:	NA		NA	NA	NA

Exhibit 6.3. Goals Worksheet.

GOALS WORKSHEET

Behavioral Domain	1st-Level Goals	2nd-Level Goals	3rd-Level Goals
Illegal or troublesome behavior—good conduct	Absence of misconduct reports	Absence of misconduct reports, and _____ _____.	Absence of misconduct reports, and _____ _____.
Substance use—substance free	Abstinence from illicit drugs and alcohol	Abstinence from illicit drugs and alcohol	Abstinence from illicit drugs and alcohol
Curfew	Weekdays: Weeknights:	Weekdays: Weeknights:	Weekdays: Weeknights:
Caregiver informed of whereabouts	Every _____ mins. When changing whereabouts	Every _____ mins. When changing whereabouts	Every _____ mins. When changing whereabouts
Communication	Talk calmly and truthfully throughout day	Talk calmly and truthfully throughout day, maintain ___ mins. conversation, and _____ _____.	Talk calmly throughout day, maintain ___ min. conversation, and _____ _____.
Chores	Record desired chores in "Record of Chores" form	Record desired chores in "Record of Chores" form.	Record desired chores in "Record of Chores" form
Work	_____ hours worked/ day or efforts to gain job	_____ hours worked/day, and/or efforts to gain job	_____hours worked/ day, and/or effort to gain job
School	_____ classes need to be attended/day, with ___ classes needing satisfactory conduct and achievement "OR" demonstrated efforts to gain an education	_____ classes need to be attended/day, with ___ classes needing satisfactory conduct and achievement	_____ classes need to be attended/day, with ___ classes needing satisfactory conduct and achievement
Other:			

Exhibit 6.4. Level System Recording Form.

LEVEL SYSTEM RECORDING FORM

Level: _____

Goals	Date	Date	Date	Date	Date	Date	Date	Date	Date	Date	Date	Date	Date
Good conduct													
Substance free													
Made curfew													
Told whereabouts													
Good com.													
Did chores													
Worked													
Good at school													

Daily Rewards													
	NA												
	NA												
	NA												
	NA												
	NA												
	NA												
	NA												
	NA												
	NA												
	NA												

Bonus Rewards

Reward = ____ _____ # of days= ____	NA														
Reward = ____ _____ # of days= ____	NA														
Reward = ____ _____ # of days= ____	NA														
Reward = ____ _____ # of days= ____	NA														
Reward = ____ _____ # of days= ____	NA														

I promise to provide my child all listed daily rewards the day after all goals are accomplished, and to restrict my child from getting any daily reward that are listed the day after 1 or more daily rewards are not accomplished. I may permit my child to "**make up**" missed goals. I will provide bonus rewards only when my child is able to demonstrate the specified number of consecutive days of performing all goals.

Caregiver Signature: _____ **Date:** _____

I agree to bring this form to my caregiver by _____ P.M. for review. Reinforcers will be provided the next day (if earned).

Youth Signature: _____ **Date:** _____

Exhibit 6.5. Record of Chores.

RECORD OF CHORES

Chores for Level 1 Week   **Chores for Level 2**

Chores	Monday	Tuesday	Wednesday	Thursday	Friday	Saturday	Sunday	Chores	Monday	Tuesday	Wednesday	Thursday	Friday	Saturday	Sunday

Chores for Level 3

Chores	Monday	Tuesday	Wednesday	Thursday	Friday	Saturday	Sunday

Exhibit 6.6. Daily School Progress Report.

DAILY SCHOOL PROGRESS REPORT

Daily School Progress Report   Date: _____

Course	Conduct and Achievement (Satisfactory/Unsatisfactory)	Signature

Dear Teachers:

Please refer to the **class** in which you are this youth's teacher (e.g., Social Studies), and indicate if this youth attended class, and if this youth's conduct and achievement were **"satisfactory"** or **"unsatisfactory"** for the day. Please also record your **signature**.

*NOTES: _____
_____
_____
_____
_____
_____
_____
_____
_____
_____

Exhibit 6.7. Level System Therapist Prompting Checklist Future Sessions.

LEVEL SYSTEM
THERAPIST PROMPTING CHECKLIST
FUTURE SESSIONS

Client ID#: _____   Clinician: _____   Session #: _____   Date of Session: _____

Begin Time:

Reviewing Level System Daily Review (Youth and Adult Significant Others)

___ 1. Instruct family to provide completed Level System Recording form.
___ 2. Descriptively praise youth for outstanding efforts to complete goals.
___ 3. Descriptively praise caregiver for monitoring goal completion.
     • Use problem solving to learn methods of monitoring goal completion.
___ 4. Descriptively praise caregiver for assuring that earned reinforcers were available to youth.
     • Encourage caregiver to provide rewards if not provided as agreed upon.
___ 5. Descriptively praise caregiver for restricting youth from accessing unearned rewards.
     • Problem-solve methods of making sure youth doesn't have access to unearned rewards.
___ 6. Query if level system should be modified, & modify LS, if desired.
     • Modify system if necessary.

Conducting Ratings

___ a. Disclose therapist's rating of client's compliance on 7-point scale (**7** = extremely compliant, **6** = very compliant, **5** = somewhat compliant, **4** = neutral, **3** = somewhat noncompliant, **2** = very noncompliant, **1** = extremely noncompliant).   Therapist's Rating: ____
     • Factors that contribute to compliance ratings are:
       1. Attendance
       2. Participation & conduct in session
       3. Homework completion
___ b. Explain how rating was derived, and methods of improving performance in future.
___ c. Solicit client's rating of helpfulness on the following 7-point scale after stating client should not feel obligated to provide high scores, as an honest assessment helps therapist better address client needs.
(**7** = extremely helpful, **6** = very helpful, **5** = somewhat helpful, **4** = not sure, **3** = somewhat unhelpful, **2** = very unhelpful, **1** = extremely unhelpful).   Client's Rating: _____.
___ d. Solicit how rating was derived & methods of improving intervention in future.

End Time: _____   **Reviewer notes:**

CHAPTER 7

Developing a Successful Treatment Plan

Overview

As reviewed earlier, there are three preparatory interventions that are implemented prior to developing the Treatment Plan. The formalized Orientation assists the family in preparing for treatment, and the Consequence Review and Level System are both designed to increase youth motivation to achieve therapeutic goals. In Treatment Planning, motivation is further instilled because the youth and caregivers determine the extent to which five skill-based treatments will be emphasized in therapy. Specifically, the youth and caregiver are provided a brief summary of Stimulus Control (also referred to as Environmental Control, Chapter 10), Self–Control (Chapter 11), Reciprocity Awareness (Chapter 8), Positive Request (Chapter 9), and Job-Getting Skills Training (Chapter 12), utilizing the Intervention Summary Worksheet for Adolescents. The youth and caregiver are both instructed to rank these interventions according to their priority in treatment. The treatment provider (TP) subsequently averages their rankings, and introduces the intervention components in therapy according to the pooled ranking. For instance, if the Stimulus Control component were ranked as the top priority, it would be the first skill-based treatment to be implemented and therefore reviewed more often than the other treatments since treatments are usually reviewed during most of the remaining treatment sessions if they appear to be effective (albeit to a progressively lesser extent as therapy progresses). The Treatment Plan usually takes less than 25 minutes to complete.

Goal for Intervention

➤ To assist the family in determining which treatments to emphasize during treatment

Materials Needed

➤ Treatment Plan for Adolescents Therapist Prompting Checklist (Exhibit 7.1)

➤ Intervention Summary Worksheet for Adolescents (Exhibit 7.2)

➤ Intervention Priority Worksheet for Adolescents (Exhibit 7.3)

Procedural Steps for Implementation

Providing Rationale (Youth and Adult Significant Others)

Utilizing the Treatment Plan for Adolescents Therapist Prompting Checklist (Exhibit 7.1) to guide intervention implementation, the TP explains Treatment Planning involves the youth and primary caregiver determining the order and extent to which the remaining interventions will be emphasized from a list of options. The TP then solicits why it is important for the family to determine which treatments to emphasize. Although family members are usually able to respond quite quickly to this query, when family members struggle to come up with viable reasons, the TP may indicate that other family members have suggested that intervention choice increases motivation. The TP concludes by answering any questions the family members may have about Treatment Planning. The following dialogue exemplifies the provision of a rationale for Treatment Planning.

TP: The next intervention involves you both briefly learning about the treatments we have available. I'll summarize what I will attempt to accomplish with each treatment, and you'll each rank them in your order of preference. This will permit me to average each of your rankings so I can start to implement or deliver the ones you're both most interested in experiencing. I think it will be important for you both to have a say in what we do in the upcoming weeks because you're both very bright and have good insights. Please tell me why you each think it will be important to have a say in the treatments we review.

Mom: I'm not sure it does. How is Ashley going to know what's going to work with her when she can't even see it's important to go to school?

Ashley: See, she never let's me choose what I want.

TP: Well first it is important to remind ourselves that Ashley did say she is willing to give school a try, and therefore must think school is important to some extent. If she doesn't think school is important, and she's willing to start attempting to go to school this speaks volumes about her respect for you to give it a shot anyways. Ashley, why do you think it will be important to involve you in the decision process.

Ashley: I'm not going to do anything I don't approve of, clear and simple!

TP: So, like other youth we've treated, this exercise will increase your motivation to participate in treatment. How do you think it will benefit you, Mom?

Determining the Order and Extent to Which Treatments Will Be Implemented in Therapy (Youth and Adult Significant Others)

The TP shows the Intervention Summary Worksheet for Adolescents (ISWA) to the youth and caregiver, and after each intervention description is read, the TP solicits how the respective treatment will be helpful. Most caregivers readily answer these questions, whereas youth are often quiet and reserved. When this happens, it may be helpful to prompt the youth and the youth's caregivers to take turns answering questions. If family members are unable to identify how a particular treatment is helpful, it is important to assist them in brainstorming potential benefits. If a family member repeatedly indicates that a particular intervention is not going to be helpful, the TP should emphasize that there will soon be an opportunity to rank the intervention as a low priority in treatment. Later, it may be decided to skip this intervention in treatment planning.

The TP then shows a copy of the IPWA and has the youth and caregivers separately rank the intervention components according to expected benefit. That is, the first intervention that is ranked is the top priority in treatment, and so on. Rankings can be determined with client and adult significant others separately. However, it is usually more efficient to obtain their rankings together. The TP records the youth rankings in the Youth Priority Rank column, and the caregiver's rankings are recorded in the Parent Priority Rank column. An effective engagement strategy is to instruct family members to report how their rankings were derived, and subsequently indicate how their rationales may have been similar. The rankings for each intervention are summarized, and the resulting dividend is recorded in the Sum of Youth and Caregiver's Rankings column. For instance, if the youth ranked the Positive Request a 4 and the caregiver ranked this intervention a 2, this intervention component would be summarized in the Sum of Youth and Caregiver's Rankings column as 6. The summary rankings are prioritized in the last column (i.e., Priority Rank), and the family is informed that each of the therapies will be implemented for the first time in this priority rank order. Priority rankings are almost always determined according to the pooled rank order. However, TPs may adjust priority rankings based on therapeutic factors. For instance, the TP may believe the positive request intervention needs to be ranked higher because poor communication skills may interfere with the implementation of other treatment components. The TP also has discretion to discuss rankings with family, and to negotiate changes in the order to which treatments will be implemented in therapy. Finally, the family should be informed that the order of treatment implementation can be changed in future sessions once all interventions are attempted.

Concluding Remarks

The Treatment Plan is a quick and easy consumer-driven method designed to determine which intervention components will be emphasized in therapy. It offers several advantages over existing methods, including therapeutic choice for both youth and youth caregivers, and family preferences are directly tied to treatment implementation. This treatment planning method also assists TPs in rapidly assessing therapeutic interests of family members, thus permitting TPs to customize the standardized interventions that are offered to address expressed needs. Although untested, we believe there is substantial information elsewhere to suggest this flexible approach to treatment planning may assist in preventing premature termination from therapy.

Supporting Materials for Chapter 7: Developing a Successful Treatment Plan

Exhibit 7.1. Treatment Plan for Adolescents Therapist Prompting Checklist.

TREATMENT PLAN FOR ADOLESCENTS
THERAPIST PROMPTING CHECKLIST
INITIAL SESSION

Reviewer: _____ Date of Review:_____

Client ID# _____Clinician: _____Session #: _____Date of Session: _____

MATERIALS REQUIRED

- Intervention Summary Worksheet for Adolescents (ISWA)
- Intervention Priority Worksheet for Adolescents (IPWA)

Begin Time: _____

Rationale (Youth and Adult Significant Others)

___a. Explain Treatment Planning involves youth and caregivers determining therapeutic interventions to emphasize.

___b. Solicit why it's good for family to choose order & extent to which interventions are implemented.

___c. Solicit & answer questions.

Determination of Treatment Order (Youth and Adult Significant Others)

___a. Show ISWA.

___b. Disclose what each treatment targets as per worksheet, & solicit how each treatment might be helpful.
  - If family can't identify how a particular tx. is helpful, assist in explaining how it might help.

___c. Show IPWA.

___d. State preferred order of treatment implementation will be based on avg. ranking of client & adult sig. others.

___e. Instruct client & adult significant others to each rank treatments in order of priority/ importance.
  - Rankings can be determined w/youth & adult sig. others separately, but usually together.

___f. Instruct client and adult sig. others to disclose rationale for rankings.

___g. Disclose order of treatments according to the following guidelines:
  - Lowest avg. rankings for youth & adult significant others are implemented first.
  - Therapist has discretion to adjust order of implementation.

___h. State order of treatments can be changed in future sessions once all interventions are attempted.

Conduct Ratings

___a.   Disclose therapist's rating of client's compliance on 7-point scale (**7** = extremely compliant, **6** = very compliant, **5** = somewhat compliant, **4** = neutral, **3** = somewhat noncompliant, **2** = very noncompliant, **1** = extremely noncompliant).   Therapist's Rating: ____
   • Factors that contribute to compliance ratings are:
   1. Attendance
   2. Participation and conduct in session
   3. Homework completion

___b.   Explain how rating was derived, and methods of improving performance in future.

___c.   Solicit client's rating of helpfulness for Treatment Planning on 7-point scale after stating client should not feel obligated to provide high scores, as an honest assessment helps therapists better address client needs.
   (**7** = extremely helpful, **6** = very helpful, **5** = somewhat helpful, **4** = not sure, **3** = somewhat unhelpful, **2** = very unhelpful, **1** = extremely unhelpful).   Client's Rating: ____.

___d.   Solicit how rating was derived and methods of improving intervention in future.

End Time: _____   **Note: Reviewer notes can be written on the back of this page.**

Exhibit 7.2. Intervention Summary Worksheet for Adolescents.

> # INTERVENTION SUMMARY
> # WORKSHEET FOR ADOLESCENTS
>
> ___I.   **Managing the Environment to be Substance and Trouble Free (Environmental Control)**
> Restructuring the environment to avoid people, places, and situations that increase risk of using drugs and getting into trouble, and spending more time with people, places and situations that do not involve drug use or trouble.
> How might this intervention be helpful?
>
> ___II. **Managing Self to Stay Free of Drugs and Trouble (Self-Control)**
> Redirecting impulses, urges, & thoughts that may lead to substance use or trouble into those that are incompatible or compete w/substance use and trouble.
> How might this intervention be helpful?
>
> ___III. **Improving Family Relationships (Reciprocity Awareness)**
> Family members exchange what is appreciated about each other.
> How might this intervention be helpful?
>
> ___IV. **Improving Communication (Positive Request)**
> Making positive requests so people are more likely to do what asked, and disagreements are settled.
> How might this intervention be helpful?
>
> ___V.   **Job-Getting Skills Training**
> Learning strategies to gain satisfying jobs at higher wages.
> How might this intervention be helpful?

Exhibit 7.3. Intervention Priority Worksheet for Adolescents.

INTERVENTION PRIORITY WORKSHEET FOR ADOLESCENTS

Client ID#: _____   Clinician: _____   Session #: _____   Date of Session: _____

Adolescent FBT Interventions	Priority Rank (Youth)	Priority Rank (Caregiver)	Sum of the Youth and Caregiver's Ranking	Priority Rank (Lowest to Highest)
Managing the Environment to be Substance and Trouble Free (Stimulus Control)				
Managing Self to Stay Free of Drugs and Trouble (Self-Control)				
Improving Family Relationships (Reciprocity Awareness)				
Improving Communication Skills (Positive Request)				
Job-Getting Skills Training				

Reviewing Past Appreciations to Improve Current Relationships

Overview

Adolescents who have been indicated to abuse illicit drugs and alcohol often evidence poor relationships with their family members. Of course, problems in family relationships are associated with negative emotional states, resentment, and low distribution of reinforcement among its members. Therefore, as a first step in repairing family relationships, the Reciprocity Awareness (RA) component is utilized by treatment providers (TPs) to teach family members to recognize and acknowledge family members when desired behavior occurs. During this intervention, each participating family member is prompted by the TP to disclose actions that have been appreciated by the other family members in the past and present. Family members are instructed to reciprocate these positive statements with expressions of appreciation and reassurance that the acknowledged behaviors will continue to occur. In this way, family members feel appreciated for the things they do and are more likely to spontaneously reciprocate desired behaviors in the future. RA includes therapy assignments to practice these skills at home between therapy sessions, and these prescribed interactions are occasionally reviewed during subsequent treatment sessions. Because RA is focused on non–problem behavior, all family members, including young children, are usually encouraged to participate in this intervention. RA usually requires up to 40 minutes to complete the first time, and about 20 minutes in subsequent sessions. RA is implemented several times throughout the course of treatment. RA is usually implemented early in Family Behavior Therapy (FBT) treatment to create a positive atmosphere in the family and encourage family members to work together in addressing the substance use of the client.

Goals for Intervention

➤ Increase the quality and frequency of appreciative statements within the family, thereby increasing the exchange of future reinforcement among family members.

Materials Needed

➤ Reciprocity Awareness Therapist Prompting Checklist for Initial Session (Exhibit 8.1)

➤ Reciprocity Awareness Therapist Prompting Checklist for Future Sessions (Exhibit 8.2)

➤ Things I Appreciate About My Family Worksheet (Exhibit 8.3)

➤ Things I Appreciate About My Family Assignment Sheet (Exhibit 8.4)

Procedural Steps for Implementation
Initial Session

Providing Rationale (Youth and All Family Members)   The TP implements RA utilizing the Reciprocity Awareness Therapist Prompting Checklist for Initial Session (Exhibit 8.1) to guide intervention implementation. The rationale for RA must be simple, positive, and quick because children are encouraged to participate in this intervention, and their attention may be limited. TPs explain that family members like to be appreciated when they do things for other family members. The family is also told that family members are more likely to continue to do positive things for one another when they are appreciated. Therefore, the family will learn to express their appreciation for one another. TPs are also encouraged to state why they believe RA is expected to be effective with the family, and the family is asked to indicate how the intervention will be helpful or fun. The following dialogue provides an example of a rationale for RA with a family that takes generosity for granted.

TP: I'm so excited to do this next intervention because family members like to feel appreciated for the things they do for one another, and this family is going to share things that are appreciated with one another. In this way you will all be more motivated to do things for one another. I think it is just what your family needs because some of you have expressed wanting to feel more appreciated. How do you all think this will be helpful?

Mother: I think it will feel good to be appreciated by my daughter for a change.

Chelsey: Yeah, that goes both ways, mom.

TP: Both of you raise good points. The importance of expressing appreciation is often overlooked, and very important for all family members.

Positive Statement Exchange (Youth and All Family Members) The family should be assembled in a circle to engage in the exercise. Each family member is provided a copy of the Things I Appreciate About My Family Worksheet (Exhibit 8.3). The TP instructs or assists the family in recording the names of participating family members in the worksheet, and then instructs each person to record at least one behavior that is performed by each of the other family members that is appreciated. Younger children often have a difficult time understanding the directions, whereas adults and older children may evidence long-term resentment for other family members that restricts responding. Therefore, the TP usually walks around the room assisting small children in recording pictures that represent positive behaviors (e.g., What does mommy do for you that you like?), and pointing out how busy everyone is in recording their responses (e.g., Wow! Dad you should see what Nick wrote about you.). The latter strategy assists in prompting people to write more information on their papers because they want to make sure they have just as many positive things on their papers as the others. TPs prompt additional responses by telling family members what parents and children in other families have reported. It is important to instruct family members to keep the number of appreciation statements the same between all family members (i.e., record one statement of appreciation for each family member prior to recording a second appreciation statement for someone). This prevents hurt feelings from family members who may otherwise receive relatively fewer appreciations. When all family members have recorded two or three responses for each family member, one of the family members (usually the caregiver) is instructed to disclose an appreciated behavior from the list that someone in the family does. The one who receives the compliment is instructed to respond as follows: (a) express how it felt to hear the positive statement; (b) express that the comment was appreciated; and (c) express that an attempt will be made to continue the desired behavior. Early in the process, the TP can prompt the family members in what types of things to say, and it is sometimes necessary to prompt family members in how to respond.

The dialogue below provides an example of the positive statement exchange between a father and his son, Kevin.

TP: Here's a copy of a worksheet for you all to record things you appreciate about the people in this room. As you look at this form, the top row has a space available where you can write the name of each person here today. After you record each name, please write one thing you appreciate about each of the persons under their names in the second row. When you are finished writing one thing you appreciate about each person, go on and do the same thing in the next row. Kevin (*who is not writing*), adolescents often appreciate when their parents permit them to do things with their friends, do activities with them, or help them with things.

Father: I'm ready.

TP: That's unusually quick, Dad. Let's give Kevin a few more minutes.

Kevin: I'm done.

TP: Great! Dad, since you finished first, tell me something Kevin does that you appreciate.

Father: I appreciate it when he does the lawn. He does it perfect, although he hardly ever does the lawn anymore.

Kevin: See, he can't even tell me what he appreciates without trying to cut me down with a backhanded compliment.

TP: So you appreciate it when Kevin does the lawn. Great! Go ahead and tell him what you appreciate about that chore. The key is to only indicate what you appreciate about his effort while ignoring things that you don't like.

Father: I really do appreciate when you do the lawn. Nobody else, including me, can get the lines straight like you can do.

TP: Absolutely perfect, Dad. You highlighted the specifics about what you liked, while not mentioning any negative aspects. This is a great approach to motivate Kevin to do the lawn more often. Now, Kevin, the ball is in your court. Tell your father how it felt to be appreciated.

Kevin: It did feel good to hear you say that because you never tell me the things you like about me.

TP: I like how you told him that you appreciated hearing him say that. Remember, however, that you should only include what you like, so you would not tell him that he doesn't tell you things he likes about you. At least at this time. Now, let him know you appreciated what he said and that you will try to mow the lawn more often.

Kevin: I appreciate it, Dad. I will try to do it more often.

Father: I'll believe that when I see the lawn mowed.

TP: Dad, we set the lawn mowing as one of his chores that will be rewarded in the Level System, so we have to believe that he is sincere in what he says and support him with encouragement.

Father: I'm sorry, I was just kidding. I'm looking forward to seeing you do the lawn, and believe what you're saying.

Kevin: Thanks. I understand where you're coming from and will get it done.

TP: Nicely done for both of you. Dad, how do you think kidding can lead to miscommunication?

Homework Assignment (Youth and All Family Members)   When assigning homework, the TP provides each family member with a copy of the "Things I Appreciate About My Family Assignment Sheet" (Exhibit 8.4), and assists each person in recording the participating family members' names in the left column. The TP then assigns each person to tell each family member something that was appreciated during the upcoming week. If necessary, the TP may assign adults or older children to assist in the recording process for younger children. Of course, each family member should be instructed to record at least one statement of appreciation in the assignment sheet for each of the other family members, and remind family members to respond positively when statements of appreciation are provided (e.g., thank you, statement of appreciation or that the behavior will continue to occur).

Future Sessions

Homework Review (Youth and All Family Members)   The Reciprocity Awareness Therapist Prompting Checklist for Future Sessions (Exhibit 8.4) is used to guide TPs during the review of homework for RA. The TP initiates the homework reviews by first collecting the completed assignment sheets from each participating family member. The review of homework involves the TP descriptively praising family members for their efforts in providing statements of appreciation. TPs instruct family members to describe how it felt to be appreciated and whether they were able to reciprocate statements of appreciation. TPs have discretion in choosing which of the recorded responses to review and for whom. After therapy assignments are reviewed, based on clinical impressions and the treatment plan, TPs decide when, and if, future RA assignments will occur. However, in general, these reviews are usually best implemented only two or three times throughout the course of therapy to maintain novelty in the provision of statements of appreciation. That is, doing the prescribed exercises relatively often appears to desensitize some family members to the positive effects of appreciations (i.e., the prescribed statements lose their reinforcing value). This does not appear to occur at home when statements are provided spontaneously. The following dialogue shows how therapy assignments are reviewed when the recording forms are left at home.

TP: Go ahead and turn in your completed worksheets. I can't wait to review them.

Mom: *We* did them, but I forgot them at home *(appears uncomfortable).*

TP: Well, I'm so glad you found the time to do the assignment. What would make it easier to bring the assignments to counseling?

Mom: I just forgot them. Maybe from now on, I could keep them by the bathroom in the hallway.

TP: Krisann, is there anything that you can do to assure you guys are able to remember to bring them to therapy?

Krisann: Well, I think putting them on the refrigerator would be better. I can also grab them before we go if she forgets.

Mom: That sounds better. We can do that.

TP: Fantastic. Since we don't have them this week, let's do the assignment in retrospect. Go ahead and fill out as many appreciations as you both can remember on these blank forms. I know your responses won't be as accurate, but it will help so we don't lose ground.

Mom: I have a few that I wrote down. Can I go first?

TP: Sure, tell me what you have.

Mom: I told Krisann that I appreciated her hard work studying for a math exam.

TP: That's absolutely wonderful! Krisann, how did you respond?

Krisann: I told her thanks for noticing.

TP: Were you able to tell her that you'd keep up the good work?

Krisann: She knows I will do this.

TP: She probably does, but just so we can use this wonderful interaction as a practice opportunity, please let her know how you will make this happen in the future. I'd like to see her reaction.

Krisann: Thanks again, Mom. I'm going to try to do my homework as soon as I get home to get it out of the way.

Mom: I love you, Krisann.

TP: Beautiful. I love this therapy. Krisann, tell me something that you appreciated this week about your mother.

Concluding Remarks

We have found that RA is a comforting intervention to address deep-rooted feelings of resentment and anger. Indeed, emphasizing the solicitation of positive behaviors is in sharp contrast to traditional therapy. Family members sincerely enjoy RA, frequently commenting that they appreciate the structured approach to positive communication. It is also therapeutically powerful when family members spontaneously exchange hugs, statements of affection, tears, and encouragement. For most family members, it has been a long time since others in the family have focused on their positive behaviors, and to do so brings about a sense of family unity. If during the exchange of appreciations, family members indicate they are not appreciative, they can be instructed to conduct Positive Requests (see Chapter 9) to encourage appreciation in the future. For instance, "Dad, if you didn't appreciate how your son mowed the lawn, please use your Positive Request handout and let him know what would make his performance of this behavior perfect for you. Your son will have a chance to make his own Positive Request after your request is on the table, and we'll continue until a successful compromise is achieved." In this way, RA may be utilized to enhance communication through the establishment of reciprocally reinforcing relationships.

Supporting Materials for Chapter 8: Reviewing Past Appreciations to Improve Current Relationships

Exhibit 8.1. Reciprocity Awareness Therapist Prompting Checklist for Initial Session.

RECIPROCITY AWARENESS
THERAPIST PROMPTING CHECKLIST
INITIAL SESSION

Client ID#: _____ Clinician: _____ Session #: _____ Date of Session: _____

MATERIALS REQUIRED

- Things I Appreciate About My Family Worksheet
- Things I Appreciate About My Family Assignment Sheet

Begin Time: _____

Rationale (youth and all family members):

- State (or solicit) the following:

___a. Family members who express their appreciation to one another are more likely to have good relationships.

___b. Reciprocity Awareness (RA) helps family members express their appreciation for one another.

___c. State why RA is expected to be effective with the family.

___d. Solicit why family thinks RA will be helpful.

___e. Solicit questions.

Positive Statement Exchange (youth and all family members):

- Give each family member a copy of "Things I Appreciate About My Family Worksheet."

___a. Instruct/assist each person to record all family names on the worksheet.

___b. Instruct/assist each person to write at least one thing that is appreciated about all other family members.

___c. Instruct each family member to state one thing that is appreciated about the other family members, and after each statement, instruct the recipient to respond to the appreciation w/the following:

    ___1. How it felt to hear the positive statement.

    ___2. Appreciation or thanks.

    ___3. State that an attempt will be made to continue the desired behavior.

Homework Assignment (youth and all family members):

- Give each family member a copy of "Things I Appreciate About My Family Assignment Sheet."

___a.   Instruct/assist each in recording every family member's name in the left column of assignment sheet, except their own.

___b.   Inform family that at least 1 positive statement should be made for each person by next session.

___c.   Instruct family to record each positive statement on the day it occurred.

___d.   Remind family that each positive statement should be reciprocated.

Conduct Ratings

___a.   Disclose therapist's rating of client's compliance on 7-point scale (**7** = extremely compliant, **6** = very compliant, **5** = somewhat compliant, **4** = neutral, **3** = somewhat noncompliant, **2** = very noncompliant, **1** = extremely noncompliant).   Therapist's Rating: _____

- Factors that contribute to compliance ratings are:
  - Attendance
  - Participation & conduct in session
  - Homework completion

___b.   Explain how rating was derived, and methods of improving performance in future.

___c.   Solicit client's rating of helpfulness for Reciprocity Awareness on 7-point scale after stating client should not feel obligated to provide high scores, as an honest assessment helps therapists better address client needs.

(**7** = extremely helpful, **6** = very helpful, **5** = somewhat helpful, **4** = not sure, **3** = somewhat unhelpful, **2** = very unhelpful, **1** = extremely unhelpful).   Client's Rating: _____.

___d.   Solicit how rating was derived and methods of improving intervention in future.

End Time: _____   **Reviewer notes:**

Exhibit 8.2. Reciprocity Awareness Therapist Prompting Checklist for Future Sessions.

RECIPROCITY AWARENESS
THERAPIST PROMPTING CHECKLIST
FUTURE SESSIONS

Client ID#: _____ Clinician: _____ Session #: _____ Date of Session: _____

MATERIALS REQUIRED

- Things I Appreciate About My Family Assignment Sheet

Begin Time: _____

Homework Review (youth and all family members)

___a. Solicit completed assignment sheet & praise for homework completion or instruct family to complete in retrospect.

___b. Solicit what efforts were done to make statements of appreciation.

___c. Praise efforts to provide appreciation statements and solicit how it felt to experience appreciation.

___d. Provide each person with a new copy of the Things I Appreciate About My Family Assignment Sheet.

___e. Assign each person to provide at least one appreciation statement for each family member prior to next session.

Conduct Ratings

___a. Disclose therapist's rating of client's compliance on 7-point scale (**7** = extremely compliant, **6** = very compliant, **5** = somewhat compliant, **4** = neutral, **3** = somewhat noncompliant, **2** = very noncompliant, **1** = extremely noncompliant).   Therapist's Rating: _____

- Factors that contribute to compliance ratings are:
  - Attendance
  - Participation and conduct in session
  - Homework completion

___b. Explain how rating was derived, and methods of improving performance in future.

___c. Solicit client's rating of helpfulness for Reciprocity Awareness on 7-point scale after stating client should not feel obligated to provide high scores, as an honest assessment helps therapists better address client needs.

(**7** = extremely helpful, **6** = very helpful, **5** = somewhat helpful, **4** = not sure, **3** = somewhat unhelpful, **2** = very unhelpful, **1** = extremely unhelpful).   Client's Rating: _____.

___d. Solicit how rating was derived and methods of improving intervention in future.

End Time: _____   **Reviewer notes:**

Exhibit 8.3. Things I Appreciate About My Family Worksheet.

THINGS I APPRECIATE ABOUT MY FAMILY WORKSHEET

Client ID#: _____ Clinician: _____ Session #: _____ Date of Session: _____

In the top row of the form, list the names of each of your family members (1 family member should be listed in each column). For each family member that is listed, write something that family member does for you that you appreciate. Do one row at a time.

Family Member 1	Family Member 2	Family Member 3	Family Member 4	Family Member 5	Family Member 6

Exhibit 8.4. Things I Appreciate About My Family Assignment Sheet.

THINGS I APPRECIATE
ABOUT MY FAMILY
ASSIGNMENT SHEET

Client ID#: _____Clinician: _____Session #: _____Date of Session:_____

Write the name of each member of your family in the far left column. At least one statement of appreciation should be made for each person each week. Each statement should be recorded under the day it occurred.

Family Member	Monday	Tuesday	Wednesday	Thursday	Friday	Saturday	Sunday

CHAPTER 9

Improving Communication With Positive Requests

Overview

Adolescents who abuse substances and engage in troublesome behavior (as well as their family members) are likely to evidence communication skill deficits, particularly as relevant to positive and negative assertion. Positive assertion involves the solicitation of positive reinforcers, such as asking to use the family car, extend curfew, or attend a drug-incompatible activity. Negative assertion involves the management of potential problems, such as responding to teasing, refusing an offer to use illicit drugs, or responding to a derogatory comment. Poor assertion skills influence problem behaviors in a number of ways. For instance, when requests are rejected in anger and without compromise, youth may experience upset or anxiety and engage in clandestine undesired actions to attain what was originally requested. The Positive Request intervention component (PR) is designed to improve positive and negative assertion among family members, thereby assisting in the prevention of substance abuse and other problem behaviors. The PR involves teaching family members to effectively request reinforcement, and respond to the requests of others. Through modeling and behavioral rehearsal, participants are taught to diplomatically resolve differences of opinion, resulting in perceived equity of reinforcement among family members. Specific communication skills include politely requesting specific actions (i.e., when, what, where), reporting benefits that are likely to occur if requests are completed, stating why requested actions might be difficult or inconvenient to perform, offering to assist in accomplishing what is being requested, offering to reciprocate reinforcement if the request is accomplished, and suggesting alternative actions. The procedure also involves learning to effectively respond to the requests of others. After positive requests are effectively performed in simulated scenarios, family members are assigned to practice positive requests at home, and these assignments are reviewed during subsequent treatment sessions. The PR is usually restricted to adolescents and adults because the content that is reviewed often focuses on responses to illicit situations that are not appropriate for children, and because concepts reviewed in PR are developmentally advanced. However, treatment providers (TPs) are encouraged to involve children in this intervention when the requests are expected to be irrelevant to problem behavior, and the requests are developmentally simplified. The PR usually requires 30 to 40 minutes to implement the first time, and about 20 to 40 minutes to implement thereafter.

Goals for Intervention

➤ Increase positive reinforcement between family members.

➤ Improve positive and negative assertion skills of family.

➤ Improve conflict resolution skills of family.

Materials Required

➤ Positive Request Therapist Prompting Checklist for Initial Session (Exhibit 9.1)

➤ Positive Request Handout (Exhibit 9.2)

➤ Positive Request Practice Assignment Worksheet (Exhibit 9.3)

➤ Positive Request Therapist Prompting Checklist for Future Sessions (Exhibit 9.4)

Procedural Steps for Treatment Implementation
Initial Session

Rationale (Youth, Adult and Adolescent Significant Others, When Appropriate) The TP utilizes the Positive Request Therapist Prompting Checklist for Initial Session (Exhibit 9.1) as a guide the first time PR is implemented. For the PR rationale the TP states people who are skilled in requesting things from others are likely to get what they want without arguments. Therefore, the PR assists family members in making requests, and assists in learning to effectively compromise when disagreements occur in responding to requests. Of course, the family is told specific reasons the PR is expected to be successful for them, and questions are solicited and answered as appropriate. The following dialogue demonstrates a rationale for the PR with a family that has experienced significant arguments in the recent past.

TP: I'm very excited to review the next intervention with your family, but before I do I wanted to emphasize that people who are skilled in requesting things from others are more likely to get what they want without arguments than people who lack such social skills. The PR assists family members in making requests that are likely to be successful. It's also a great technique to use when someone makes a request of you, and you don't want to do what is being requested. I think it will be especially effective with this family because you have all expressed an interest in learning to avoid arguments, which have been happening quite often lately. Does anyone have any questions?

Mother: I'm all for this, but my daughter will have to talk, and she just shuts down and doesn't respond to us.

Marilyn: Of course I keep my mouth shut! What am I supposed to do? You don't listen to what I have to say.

TP: That's the beauty of the Positive Request. It is set up to improve communication for all parties. Do either of you have any questions?

Marilyn: Yea, are you going to tell my parents that they have to listen to what I have to say?

TP: Yes. I'm going to make you all listen to each other (TP smiles).

Modeling PR (Youth, Adult and Adolescent Significant Others, When Appropriate) After providing the rationale and obtaining feedback from the family, TPs distribute a copy of the Positive Request Handout to all participating family members (Exhibit 9.2). The TP states that the Positive Request Handout is used to remind family members how to make positive requests whenever things are desired, whether at home or during treatment sessions. The TP brings copies of the Positive Request Handout to subsequent therapy sessions to assist family in positively resolving arguments if or when they spontaneously occur. Prior to modeling a positive request, the TP explains that all steps will be practiced in the order listed in the Positive Request Handout, but that in real-life situations it is not neces-sary to state all steps in the listed order. Moreover, it is unnecessary to state all steps in real-life situations. However, during sessions, all steps are performed so family members can practice all of them. The TP usu-ally solicits an example of something that is desired by one of the family members in order to demonstrate the steps that are listed in the Positive Request Handout. However, when communication skills are especially poor in families, or the solicited scenarios have been associated with upset, TPs should probably model superficial requests and progress to more difficult scenarios. Utilizing superficial requests makes it easier for family members to focus on learning the steps. The following demon-strates how to introduce the PR:

TP: Here is a handout that reveals the steps that are involved in making a Positive Request. I want each of you to use this handout when prob-lems are encountered in your home throughout the week. I will also like you to use this handout to make requests during our sessions, especially when we identify an important difference of opinion. If you notice, it is a good way to request what you want, not what you don't want. In real-life situations, you don't have to say all the steps, and you don't have to say them in the order that is listed in your handout. However, we will practice all of these steps in the order that is listed so that it will be easier for you to learn them.

The TP then solicits an example of something desired by one of the fam-ily members. If the TP determines that the request has a poor likelihood of being accepted because it is unrealistic, or that the request is associated with strong negative emotions, the TP may instead initiate a hypothetical or non–emotionally laden request to facilitate learning. The TP then role-plays the steps listed in the Positive Request Handout. In the role-play, the person who provided the request usually serves as the recipient of the request. This per-son is instructed to listen to the entire request prior to responding. The steps modeled in the role-play include the following:

1. Request a specific action using "please," and specify when the action is desired.

2. State how it would be difficult for the recipient do the action.

3. State how it would be good for the recipient if the request were performed.

4. State how it would be good for the person making the request if the request were performed.

5. Offer to help the person get the action done.

6. Offer to do something for the recipient.

7. Tell the recipient you would appreciate the action being done.

8. Suggest something that would be acceptable as an alternative action.

9. Ask the recipient to suggest an alternative in case the action can't be done.

The following dialogue exemplifies the TP modeling PR after a real-life scenario is obtained.

TP: Who has a request for one of the members in your family?

Father: Well, I would like Jennifer to come home for her curfew this Saturday night.

TP: That sounds like a great request, so I am now going to model the PR for the request you just provided me. Since you made the request, you will be the one who gets asked to come home for curfew on time. While requesting this action, I am going to attempt all the steps in the Positive Request Handout. Okay, here I go. (1) Please remember to come home for your curfew this Saturday at 11:30 p.m. (2) I know it will be difficult to come home at this time because we just changed your curfew time; (3) but I also know you don't want to make me nervous, and coming home on time will make me more likely to increase your curfew time in the future. (4) It will also make it easier for you to get up early in the morning to take out the trash. (5) I could give you a reminder call at 11:00 p.m. if you think this would make it easier to come home on time. (6) If you come home on time I will make sure you are able to use the car to go to your friend's house for dinner Sunday. (7) I would very much appreciate your coming home on time. (8) If you can't make it home at 11:30 p.m., give me a call an hour before your curfew to explain why and I might be able to give you an extra half-hour. (9) If you would like to provide me an alternative to what I requested, I'd be interested in hearing about it.

After the scenario is modeled by the TP, the recipient of the offer should be instructed to first indicate what was liked about the request, and then either indicate that the requested behavior will be performed, or request an alternative behavior that might be acceptable using the Positive Request Handout (i.e., counter request). The following dialogue is a continuance of the latter role-play, and exemplifies this procedure.

TP: I would like you all to respond to positive requests by first indicating what you liked about the request itself, and then either indicate that you will do what was requested, or make your own request as a counter request. That is, maybe the person who made the request would consider an alternative action. O.K., so Mr. Jones, stay in the role-play and answer my request. Remember that you will need to use the Positive Request Handout to make a counter request if you decide not to do what I requested.

Father: I really liked the way you presented me options. I will be home at 11:30 P.M.

TP: Well, you made that one easy for me, Mr. Jones. Nice job.

Consistent with all role-plays, the TP would subsequently solicit things that were liked about the modeled performance, and solicit things the family might do differently to perform the request in their own style while keeping the content relatively intact.

Role-Playing of PR by Family Members (Youth, Adult and Adolescent Significant Others, When Appropriate) Participating family member should all be encouraged to practice at least one positive request. The first person to attempt a request is usually the person who enacted the role of confederate in the modeled performance (i.e., person who volunteered to be the recipient). However, it is also appropriate for the TP to query the family for another volunteer. If the TP thinks the selected family member is willing and capable of performing the PR with integrity, it is appropriate to instruct this person to make a request for something that is genuinely desired. If not, the TP may instruct the family member to perform a hypothetical request that is simple, and perhaps silly, such as a request to move a pencil from one end of the desk to the other. The person making the request in the role-play scenario should be prompted to perform one step at a time utilizing the Positive Request Handout while the recipient of the request (TP or family volunteer) listens. During the role-play, the TP provides descriptive praise throughout and provides assistance, as necessary. The following dialogue shows how a TP might solicit an adolescent client to attempt a request for the first time.

TP: I'd like you guys to practice the request now. Who would like to make a request first? Usually, this is the person who is the recipient of the request I model.

Suzanne: I'll give it a try.

TP: Fantastic! Very briefly, what is it that you'd like?

Suzanne: I'd like to be able to borrow the car Saturday night.

TP: O.K., normally I recommend doing something simple the first time. However, you've been doing great, Suzanne. You've also demonstrated during the past couple of weeks how you can be calm with your father. So use your PR Handout as a guide in making this request with your father. After you do each step, look at your handout to see what you need to say for the next step. I'll help you if you get stuck. Dad, I'd like you to listen to her attempt all the steps. Any questions?

Suzanne: No.

TP: Great! Go ahead and do the first step in asking your father to borrow the car Saturday night. Remember to use "please" and state what exactly you want, and when, very briefly.

The TP helps the person who volunteers to conduct the role-play by prompting the volunteer to respond in a manner that is similar to the Positive Request Handout and offering praise for those steps that are completed effectively. The following dialogue shows how a TP is able to assist an adolescent client during her attempt to request, from her mother, more time watching television together. The example dialogue is specific to the PR step in which recipients are told how performance of requested actions will be beneficial to them. In this role-play, the adolescent, Rhiannon, is perplexed as to how her mother will benefit from their watching more television together when performing this PR step.

Rhiannon: Being able to watch television together will be good for me because I can learn more about real estate on the home network. This will be good for you because . . . (after a few seconds) O.K., I need to step outside the role-play for a minute. I'm not sure how my being able to watch more television with my mother will be good for her.

TP: Well, if you think you will learn about real estate, and your mom's a realtor, I wonder if watching this channel together will help you both communicate better.

Rhiannon: Got it. Mom, if you watch the home network with me, I will learn more about real estate and we could have something to talk about. That will be good for you because I can help you answer phones at work better.

After the last step in the PR Handout (i.e., "Ask what was liked about your request, and ask person to suggest an acceptable alternative if the person can't do the request") is performed, the TP instructs the recipient to first acknowledge what was liked about the request, and then either accept to do what was requested or respond with a compromising request. In doing so, the recipient will utilize the PR Handout to make a request in the spirit of compromise. For instance, if a parent requested her son to go to a company barbecue, and the youth didn't want to attend the barbecue, the youth could make a request to perhaps spend an hour at the barbecue. The parent would accept the youth's counter request or make another request. This process would continue until someone's counter request was accepted.

Assigning Homework (Youth, Adult and Adolescent Significant Others, When Appropriate)   To assist in skill acquisition, family members are assigned to practice the newly acquired PR skills at home prior to the next session. In doing so, each person is coached to utilize the Positive Request Practice Assignment Worksheet (Exhibit 9.3) to record one of the requests. The family is provided at least one Positive Request Handout to guide them in correct responding, at least until the steps are memorized. To enhance spontaneity, the family should not be assigned to perform specific a priori requests, but rather to refer to the steps in the handout anytime something is desired. As therapy progresses and communication skills improve, the necessity of recording positive request efforts is diminished. However, family members are told to practice positive requests throughout therapy when difficult interpersonally based problems are experienced. To facilitate skill acquisition, the family should be challenged to manage positive requests together. For instance, the requestor can notify the recipient of the request prior to making it so the requestor can be especially motivated to listen attentively while the request is being made. It is also helpful to encourage recipients to think of alternatives that would be acceptable and consistent with compromise rather than refusing requests outright.

Future Sessions

Reviewing Homework (in Future Sessions; Youth, Adult and Adolescent Significant Others, When Appropriate) All PR future sessions follow guidelines specified in the PR Therapist Prompting Checklist for Future Sessions (Exhibit 9.4). TPs initiate the future PR sessions by gathering the completed Positive Request Practice Assignment worksheets from all participating family members. In reviewing Positive Request Practice Assignment worksheets, TPs descriptively praise effort and success in achieving mutually satisfying communication. They also provide encouragement to all family members when requests are unsuccessful. Indeed, it is usually a good idea to instruct family members to repeat unsuccessful requests using their Positive Request Handouts to guide them while the TP provides assistance. The PR is usually reviewed in approximately two or three future sessions. However, when youth and their caregivers evidence long-standing communication problems, it may be necessary to review this intervention more frequently throughout therapy. The Positive Request Handout may be helpful when reviewing communication problems that occur during other interventions. For instance, during the review of Stimulus Control an adolescent client might be encouraged to use the Positive Request Handout to assist in asking her father to accept the boyfriend of her child as a member of the family. In such cases, the Positive Request Handout may assist both the adolescent and her father in being calm and determining what acceptance involves.

Concluding Remarks

The PR is the basis for communication skills training within FBT. It may be utilized to quell arguments during sessions, or may be implemented as a prescribed therapy to address underlying communication skill deficits.

When used spontaneously to circumvent arguments, the TP can usually skip the rationale and TP's modeling. In doing so, the TP, upon first recognition of upset (i.e., a father raises his voice), should pass the Positive Request Handout to the person who is upset, and instruct this person to make a request one step at a time. During spontaneous positive requests, the TP must be careful to quell undesired statements early in the process using Communication Guideline procedures that were reviewed during the Orientation section of Chapter 1. Using the Positive Request Handout usually assists in decreasing anger because the focus of conversation shifts to very manageable solution-oriented tasks that are listed on the paper. The recipient of the request is instructed to either accept the request outright or use the Positive Request Handout to make a compromising request. This process continues until the issue is successfully negotiated.

Supporting Materials for Chapter 9: Improving Communication With Positive Requests

Exhibit 9.1. Positive Request Therapist Prompting Checklist for Initial Session.

POSITIVE REQUEST
THERAPIST PROMPTING CHECKLIST
INITIAL SESSION

Client ID#:_____ Clinician: _____ Session #: _____ Date of Session: _____

Materials Required

- Positive Request Handout
- Positive Request Practice Assignment Worksheet

Begin Time: _____

Rationale (Youth, Adult and Adolescent Significant Others, When Appropriate)

State each of the following:
___a. People who are skilled in asking for things usually get what they want without arguments.
___b. PR designed to improve the way requests are made in the family.
___c. PR designed to teach family members to compromise without arguments.
___d. Disclose why PR is likely to be particularly good for the family.
___e. Solicit questions and provide answers.

Modeling Positive Request (Youth, Adult and Adolescent Significant Others, When Appropriate)

- Distribute copies of PR handout to family members.
___a. Instruct family to use PR steps in handout when things are desired from others at home or in tx. sessions.
___b. Explain all steps will be practiced in sessions as listed, but at home it may be unnecessary to do them all.
___c. Solicit example of something that is desired by a family member.
- Model PR for the solicited example, utilizing each of the following steps w/person who gave example.
  ___ 1. Request specific action using "please" and saying when action is desired.
  ___ 2. State how it might be difficult for other person to do the request.
  ___ 3. State how it might be good for the person if the request gets done.
  ___ 4. State how it might be good for you if the request gets done.
  ___ 5. State how you can help the person get the request done.

___ 6. State how you will reward the other person if the requested action gets done.

___ 7. Tell other person you'd appreciate the request getting done.

___ 8. Suggest something as an acceptable alternative.

___ 9. Ask person to state what was liked about how request was made, and suggest an alternative action if request can't be done.

___d. State that if the request is denied by recipient, the recipient should do a PR as a compromise.

- When motivation is low, to increase client "buy-in" query why each step is important prior to modeling.

Role-playing of Positive Request by Family Members (Youth, Adult and Adolescent Significant Others, When Appropriate)

___a. Solicit someone to practice PR w/TP (usually person who participated in the modeled role-play).

___b. Solicit from the volunteer an example of something desired.

- Usually best to make a hypothetical, silly request (moving pen to other side of the table).
- Recipient of request shouldn't respond until all steps are finished.

___d. Instruct volunteer to initiate PR using PR Handout.

___e. Instruct recipient to either accept request or attempt compromise using PR Handout as a guide.

- Assist all family members in practicing PRs, as appropriate.

Assigning Homework (Youth, Adult and Adolescent Significant Others, When Appropriate)

___a. Distribute PR Practice Assignment Worksheets.

___b. Instruct family to do at least 1 PR prior to next session, & record in PR Practice Assignment Worksheet.

___c. Review how to complete PR Practice Assignment Worksheet.

Conduct Ratings

___a. Disclose therapist's rating of client's compliance on 7-point scale (**7** = extremely compliant, **6** = very compliant, **5** = somewhat compliant, **4** = neutral, **3** = somewhat noncompliant, **2** = very noncompliant, **1** = extremely noncompliant).   Therapist's Rating: ____

- Factors that contribute to compliance ratings are:
1. Attendance
2. Participation and conduct in session
3. Homework completion

___b. Explain how rating was derived, and methods of improving performance in future.

___c. Solicit client's rating of helpfulness on the following 7-point scale after stating client should not feel obligated to provide high scores, as an honest assessment helps therapists better address client needs.

(**7** = extremely helpful, **6** = very helpful, **5** = somewhat helpful, **4** = not sure, **3** = somewhat unhelpful, **2** = very unhelpful, **1** = extremely unhelpful).   Client's Rating: _____.

___d. Solicit how rating was derived and methods of improving intervention in future.

End Time: _____   Notes: _____

Exhibit 9.2. Positive Request Handout.

POSITIVE REQUEST HANDOUT

1. Briefly state **what exactly is wanted and when** it is wanted (use "please").

2. State how you think it **might be difficult for the person to do** the request.

3. State how it might be **good for other person** if the request gets done.

4. State how it would be **good for you** if the request gets done.

5. Tell **how you could help** the other person to do the request.

6. Tell how you will **reward the person** if the request gets done.

7. Tell the person you'd **appreciate the request being done.**

8. **Suggest an acceptable alternative** if the person can't do what is being asked.

9. **Ask what was liked about your request,** and ask person to suggest an **acceptable alternative** if the person can't do request.

Exhibit 9.3. Positive Request Practice Assignment Worksheet.

POSITIVE REQUEST PRACTICE ASSIGNMENT WORKSHEET

Client ID#: _____ Clinician: _____ Session #: _____ Date of Session: _____

Write a description of what was requested and how you used each step of Positive Request.

What was requested:	_____ _____ _____
Was the request specific? (check one)	☐ Yes ☐ No
Did you say please? (check one)	☐ Yes ☐ No
Did you state when the action was desired? (check one)	☐ Yes ☐ No
Write what you said was difficult for the person to do:	_____ _____ _____
Write how you said it might it be good for the other person if the request was done:	_____ _____ _____
Write how you said it might be good for you if request was done:	_____ _____ _____
Write how you offered to help the other person do the request:	_____ _____ _____
Write what you offered to do for the other person if the request was performed:	_____ _____ _____
Did you tell the other person you would appreciate the action being done?	☐ Yes ☐ No
Write what you suggested as an alternative action:	_____ _____
Write how you asked the other person to provide an alternative to your request:	_____ _____
Write what was the result of your request:	_____ _____

Exhibit 9.4. Positive Request Therapist Prompting Checklist for Future Sessions.

POSITIVE REQUEST THERAPIST
PROMPTING CHECKLIST
FUTURE SESSIONS

Begin Time: _____

Client ID#: _____ Clinician: _____ Session #: _____ Date of Session: _____

Materials Required

- Positive Request Handout
- Positive Request Practice Assignment Worksheet

Begin Time: _____

Reviewing Homework (Youth, Adult and Adolescent Significant Others, When Appropriate)

- Distribute PR Handout
___a. Solicit completed PR Practice Assignment Worksheets.
   - If incomplete, instruct to complete retrospectively.
___b1. Review homework & instruct family to demonstrate how PR was performed.
   OR
___b2. If PR was not used, instruct family to role play PR using hypothetical situation following PR handout.
___c. Instruct family to attempt 1 PR prior to next session and distribute new PR Practice Assignment Worksheet.

Conduct Ratings

___a. Disclose therapist's rating of client's compliance on the following 7-point scale
   (**7** = extremely compliant, **6** = very compliant, **5** = somewhat compliant, **4** = neutral,
   3 = somewhat noncompliant, **2** = very noncompliant, **1** = extremely noncompliant).
   Therapist's Rating: ____
   - Factors that contribute to compliance ratings are:
   1. Attendance
   2. Participation and conduct in session
   3. Homework completion
___b. Explain how rating was derived, and methods of improving performance in future.
___c. Solicit client's rating of helpfulness on the following 7-point scale after stating client should not feel obligated to provide high scores, as an honest assessment helps therapists better address client needs.
   (**7** = extremely helpful, **6** = very helpful, **5** = somewhat helpful, **4** = not sure, **3** = somewhat unhelpful, **2** = very unhelpful, **1** = extremely unhelpful). Client's Rating: _____.
___d. Solicit how rating was derived and methods of improving intervention in future.

End Time: _____   **Notes:** _____

10

Restructuring the Environment to Facilitate a Drug–Free Lifestyle

Overview

There are things in the environment that make substance use more, or less, likely to occur. These things are referred to as antecedent stimuli or, more commonly, *triggers*. Triggers may include any environmental stimuli that can be heard, seen, smelled, touched, or tasted, such as people who are known to use substances, and specific locations, activities, events, and situations in which substance use has occurred (e.g., unattended homes, ill health, pain, celebrations, watching a television program involving drug use, receiving a poor report card, getting reprimanded by a teacher, having cash immediately after payday, being offered alcohol). Similarly, there are environmental stimuli that increase the likelihood of other problem behaviors, such as stealing (e.g., visiting a store that has very little security and valued items), arguments (e.g., irritability due to being teased at school), violence (e.g., being spit on), contracting HIV (e.g., unprotected sex with a sexually promiscuous stranger), and so on. Triggers lead to thoughts, physiological sensations, and/or emotions that are relevant to excitation or anticipation of the reinforcing aspects of substance use or other problem behaviors. For instance, an adolescent boy smells marijuana at a party, which reminds him how wonderful it felt the last time he was high, which leads to his smoking marijuana. Other triggers lead to aversive emotions, physical sensations, and/or thoughts that are negatively reinforced by substance use or other problem behavior. For instance, an adolescent girl gets teased by kids in her classroom, which leads her to experience thoughts of harming herself, which consequently leads her to ingest Valium so she no longer experiences aversive thoughts.

Conversely, there are "safe" stimuli that decrease the likelihood of substance use, such as abstinent peers and family members, and locations, activities, and situations in which substance use has yet to occur. These stimuli may include sports, exercise, performing homework, employment, going to a place of worship, and attending school. Safe stimuli that act to prevent other problem behaviors include, for example, not leaving "taboo" foods on the counter to prevent binge eating, communicating things that are desired in a positive manner to prevent arguments in the family, employment to prevent shoplifting, and monogamous sexual partners to prevent risk of HIV.

The aim of Stimulus Control is to identify, monitor, and eliminate or control stimuli that have influenced drug use or problem behaviors to occur in the past, and assist youths in spending more time with drug-incompatible "safe" stimuli doing "safe" activities. In doing so, it is important to teach skills that will assist youth to avoid or escape from at-risk stimuli and plan ways to spend more time with safe stimuli. Given that at-risk stimuli often occur unexpectedly, youths are taught to identify where and when at-risk stimuli are likely to occur, and to develop plans for managing such stimuli when avoidance is impossible.

In conducting Stimulus Control, the treatment provider (TP) first assists the youth and adult significant others in creating a comprehensive list of behavioral stimuli that decrease the likelihood of drug use and other problem behaviors (safe list). Later, a list of behavioral stimuli that increase the youth's likelihood of drug use and other problem behaviors is developed (at-risk list). Once the lists are obtained, the identified youth, participating significant others, and TP review the amount of time spent with safe and at-risk stimuli. In this review, the TP attempts to identify behaviors the youth demonstrated that increased time spent with safe stimuli, encourages those behaviors, and further assists the youth in spending more time with safe stimuli. The TP also attempts to identify behaviors that were performed to avoid or escape from at-risk stimuli. TPs then utilize various specified behavioral interventions to encourage and teach youths and significant others repertoires to spend more time with safe stimuli, and to avoid or escape from at-risk stimuli. These interventions include descriptive praise, behavioral rehearsal, self-control, job interviewing skills training, and communication skills training. While reviewing the safe and at-risk lists, TPs may spontaneously add goals to the Level System, and a family activity is scheduled to occur in "safe" environments and subsequently reviewed during the next session. Although children are not involved in most aspects of Stimulus Control, they are involved in the scheduling and review of family activities.

Goals for Intervention

➤ Assist youth and participating adult significant others in the identification and avoidance of at-risk stimuli that increase the youth's risk of using illicit substances and other problem behaviors.

➤ Assist youth and participating adult significant others in the identification, and participation with, safe stimuli that are incompatible with using illicit substances and other problem behaviors.

Materials Required

➤ Stimulus Control Therapist Prompting Checklist for Initial Session (Exhibit 10.1)

➤ Stimulus Control Therapist Prompting Checklist for Future Sessions (Exhibit 10.2)

➤ Safe and At-Risk Associations List (Exhibit 10.3)

➤ Things to Do and Places I Like to Visit Worksheet (two copies; Exhibit 10.4)

➤ Things That May Lead to Drug Use and Other Problem Behaviors (two copies; Exhibit 10.5)

➤ Family Invitation for Fun (Exhibit 10.6)

Procedural Steps for Treatment Implementation

Initial Session

Providing Rationale (Youth and Adolescent and Adult Significant Others, Whenever Appropriate)

Treatment providers (TPs) use the Stimulus Control Therapist Prompting Checklist for Initial Session (Exhibit 10.1) as a guide in treatment implementation. The rationale for Stimulus Control begins by explaining to youth and significant others that there are things in the environment that influence drug use and other problem behaviors to be more likely and less likely to occur. The family is informed that they will be assisted in developing a list of people, places, and situations that have involved drug use and other problem behaviors (an "at-risk" list) and another list of people, places, and situations that have not involved drug use and other problem behaviors (a "safe" list). If specific problem behaviors have been identified (e.g., stealing, unemployment), these behaviors can be included as potential targets in this intervention. However, it is also appropriate to target "troublesome behaviors," in addition or in lieu of, specific behavior problems. This strategy is particularly important when multiple behavior problems are present. It is further explained that items in these lists will be extensively reviewed so that appropriate interventions may be planned and implemented. As usual, the TP underscores the effectiveness of this intervention, and provides the youth with an explicit reason the intervention is expected to be effective. Perhaps more so than adults, youth appear to have more difficulty appreciating how environmental events may influence them to use substances or get into trouble. Thus, it sometimes helps to provide examples in which environmental stimuli increase substance use. The following dialogue exemplifies a Stimulus Control rationale with a youth, who evidenced drug dependence and school truancy as problem behaviors.

TP: There are people, places, and situations that make it easier to stay clean from drugs and attend school, which are both target behaviors your mother indicated in the Level System. Of course, there are also people, places, and situations that make it more difficult to stay clean from drugs and attend school. Together, you will both help me construct a list of people, places, and situations that have been associated with Leah's drug use and truancy in the past. We'll refer to this as an "at-risk" list. During separate interviews, you will each help me develop this at-risk list of people, places, and situations that have been associated with Leah's drug use and other problem behaviors, such as truancy. You will also both help me to develop a "safe" list for Leah that includes people, places, and situations that decrease the chances that she will engage in drug use, truancy, or other troublesome behaviors. These lists will be reviewed in future sessions to assist in developing skills that will help Leah spend more time with things that are listed in the safe list and less time with things in the at-risk list. In reviewing these lists, we'll also have opportunities to set new goals that will help Leah eliminate drug use and find school attendance enjoyable. This intervention has shown great success with others, and I think it will be especially effective with you, Leah, because your mother would walk across fire for you. Do either of you have any questions before we begin?

Obtaining "Safe" Associations (Youth and Adolescent and Adult Significant Others, Whenever Appropriate)

After the rationale is provided, the TP, in a neutral and nonjudgmental manner, prompts the youth and adult significant others to report all people, situations, and activities (stimuli) that the youth has enjoyed and not used drugs or alcohol. These stimuli are recorded in the Safe column of the Safe and At-Risk Associations List (Exhibit 10.3). If other problem behaviors are being targeted (e.g., stealing, truancy, vandalism), the TP should additionally ensure that the obtained stimuli have not influenced these target behaviors. Thus, stimuli in the safe list are likely to bring about healthy goal-directed behavior. TPs may need to query about stimuli that have not been a part of the youth's recent life in developing this list. For instance, the youth may have had old friends who were abstinent from substances, but who have not spent recent time with the youth. Another strategy in obtaining safe stimuli is to assess abstinent people (and activities) that youth think would be enjoyable but have yet to experience, for instance, meeting a new youth in school who earns outstanding grades.

While attempting to generate safe stimuli, youth and significant others may mention that a stimulus has preceded or has been associated with past substance use or other targeted behaviors. When this occurs, the stimulus is usually listed in the At-Risk column of the youth's at-risk associations list unless the substance use was primarily influenced by others and/or appeared to be an isolated event. In such cases, the respective item should be listed with an asterisk.

After the TP has exhausted all possibilities, the Things to Do and Places I Like to Visit Worksheet is provided to the youth to prompt additional safe associations (Exhibit 10.4). This worksheet contains commonly reported safe associations that are helpful to prompt youth when developing their safe lists. It is advisable to check to ensure that all generated stimuli have never been associated with drug use or other target behaviors. It is appropriate to separate risk factors from safe stimuli. For instance, if a youth indicated that she argued with her mother only when she didn't get what she wanted, "arguing with mother" could be recorded as an at-risk item, whereas "mother" could remain on the safe list.

If time permits, it is always good to solicit things that are liked and disliked about safe stimuli to facilitate an understanding of potential obstacles the youth may face in spending more time with safe situations, and determine things that are most valued about the safe items so these things can be emphasized in subsequent sessions. Knowing what is not liked about safe stimuli provides TPs opportunities to assist youth in eliminating these things. For instance, if a youth indicated that she didn't like how her father nags her for eating too much, effective solutions could be generated, such as requesting the father to make supportive comments when weight goals were accomplished, involving the father in her weight loss program, and so on. Eliminating this communication problem would likely enhance the client/father relationship, making it more likely the client would be willing to spend time with her father and thus reducing risk of using illicit drugs. In situations where the youth and participating adult significant others disagree about which list to put a person into, the person should conservatively be moved to the at-risk list, or if left in the safe list, an asterisk may be put next to the respective stimulus to ensure that the stimulus is reviewed with enhanced sensitivity. The following example dialogue with Leah and her older adult sister, Heather, illustrates how to generate a list of safe stimuli relating to Leah's goals of eliminating drug use and improving grades in school.

TP: Who are some people who do not use drugs and help you do better in school, raising your grades?

Leah: Well, there is my brother, Jim, and my best friend, Jessica.

Heather: What about Mom? She always asks if she can help with your schoolwork.

Leah: Mom is too critical. She stresses me out when we do my homework.

TP: Are they all clean from drugs, and do they help you with your homework?

Leah: Yes, Jim gets straight A's, and Jessica wants to do well but is not that smart. We like to do our homework together. They're all clean.

And are you kidding about my mom? She doesn't even drink alcohol, but, like I said, she doesn't know how to help me.

Heather: But what about Jessica? She just stopped smoking pot a few weeks ago, when you did.

TP: That is a good point, Heather. Let's put your mom and Jim in the Safe column of the Safe and At-Risk Associations List. We'll put Jessica in the At-Risk column of the Safe and At-Risk Associations List. Leah, it may be that Jessica doesn't use drugs anymore, but I want to put her there so we can be more ready to manage risky situations that may occur when you spend time with her alone since she is early in her attempts to eliminate substance use. We should also put Mom being critical during homework in the At-Risk column. This will permit us to remember to assess your interactions with Mom during homework, and maybe role-play some strategies that will help your mom present information to you in a noncritical way while you learn strategies to assist you in accepting her feedback without stress. (*The TP would continue to attempt to solicit more persons.*) Now, let's generate some positive activities or places you like to visit that do not involve drug use and problem behavior and make it easier for you to improve your grades.

Leah: I like to ride horses.

Heather: When I used to come over more, we played board games. I also love to ride horses.

Leah: Yeah, Heather always wins. I think she cheats (*laughs*).

TP: I like how you provided me some good things that you both can do together that do not involve drug use. You'll just need to make sure you get your homework done first, right? Just to be sure, Leah, have you ever used drugs in these situations?

Leah: Well, after I rode horses with Jessica, we'd usually smoke pot, but it's been a while. I never would smoke before or during my riding, and I've never used with anyone else after riding.

TP: I'm glad you're sensitive to these concerns. I think horseback riding should be put in the safe list because it seems like it was Jessica's influence. However, you smoked after riding so many times it is possible that horseback riding may bring back memories of smoking pot, which may increase your risk of using in the future. Let's put horseback riding with a clean person in the Safe list, but put a small asterisk next to her name just in case. I'd like to get a few items that will help improve grades. What are some things that can be done to improve grades?

Leah: I could do my homework as soon as I got home from school. Maybe start at 3:30.

TP: Outstanding. I'll write that down. (*The TP would continue to solicit activities and places.*)

Table 10.1 presents an example of a Safe and At-Risk Associations List that is completed based on the dialogue reviewed thus far. The table includes the safe people, activities, and places in the Safe column, including Jim, her mom, Heather, and board games. Because at-risk associations came up during the dialogue (her friend Jessica, her mom being critical, homework starting at 3:30 p.m.), these were listed in the At-Risk column. Horseback riding was included in the safe column, although with an asterisk.

The following dialogue demonstrates how the TP is able to use the Things to Do and Places I Like to Visit Worksheet (Exhibit 10.3) with Leah and Heather after they no longer are able to generate safe people, activities, and places.

TP: You both were able to come up with a lot of safe items. Here is a list of things to do and places to visit that are usually not associated with drug use or problem behaviors (*hands the worksheet to youth and significant other*). Read this list and check off which ones you'd enjoy and that have never been associated with drug use or other problem behaviors.

Leah: I like going to movies and restaurants and playing with my dog.

TP: Great, Leah, I just recorded those in your safe list. (*The therapist would continue to generate safe items from this list in a similar manner.*) We were able to get a lot of safe items quickly, and so, Leah, tell me a few things that you like and do not like about some of the stimuli we recorded. This will assist me in getting a better understanding of some of the things you enjoy and don't enjoy in life. Let's start with your mom.

Table 10.1. Example of Partially Completed Safe and At-Risk Associations List for Leah.

SAFE AND AT-RISK ASSOCIATIONS LIST

Instructions: Please indicate each day you spent time with each item on your safe list and at-risk list over the past week.

Safe List	Mon	Tues	Wed	Thur	Fri	Sat	Sun	At-Risk List	Mon	Tues	Wed	Thur	Fri	Sat	Sun
Jim (brother)								Jessica							
Mom								Mom being critical							
Heather															
Riding horses w / clean people*															
Board games															
Homework by 3:30 P.M.															

179

Leah: I love that I can trust my mom, but I don't like when she starts pushing me too much.

TP: That is great that she can be trusted. What other things do you like about her?

Leah: She loves me and means well. She'll always bail me out.

TP: Fabulous. It's so hard to find people, even relatives that have those qualities. (*The TP goes on to review things that are liked and disliked about other generated safe stimuli.*)

Table 10.2 presents a partially completed Things to Do and Places I Like to Visit Worksheet in which Leah endorsed "Going to restaurants," "Going to movies or attending plays," and "Playing/Walking with a pet" (see "X"). Once completed, the TP transfers these safe list items to the Safe and At-Risk Associations List Worksheet.

Table 10.2. Sampling of "Safe" Items from the Things to Do and Places I Like to Visit Worksheet.

Things to Do and Places I Like to Visit

Instructions: Put an "X" next to each thing you like to do and place you like to visit that does not involve drug use and benefits your family.

Leisure Activities

☐ Going to parks
  • Fishing in the local ponds
  • Feeding the ducks
  • Playing tennis/volleyball
☒ Going to restaurants
☐ Visiting museum/historical landmarks
☐ Visiting Visitor Center for local lakes or state or federal parks
  • Kids can become Jr. Rangers and earn badges.
  • Nature walks/hikes.
  • Guided tours or learning workshops.
☒ Going to the movies or attending plays
  • Free movies at local libraries
  • Inexpensive plays at schools/universities
☐ Gardening
☒ Playing/Walking with a pet
  • Doing arts/crafts

"At-Risk" Associations Rationale—Optional (Youth and Adolescent and Adult Significant Others, Whenever Appropriate)

Although not necessary, it is often helpful to provide a rationale relevant to transitioning from the generation of safe stimuli to the generation of at-risk stimuli. For instance, the TP may alleviate potential defensiveness by blaming the youth's past time with at-risk stimuli on environmental circumstances that may have been out of the youth's control. It is also important to let the youth and participating adult significant others know that outcomes are usually best when significant others are involved in developing, and subsequently reviewing, the at-risk list. Along these lines, they are told that the TP usually meets with the youth and adult significant others separately to gather at-risk items. While TPs strongly encourage youth and significant others to be forthright with each other throughout the process, it is explained that each will be asked while alone if there is any information to keep confidential. TPs explain that they will attempt to identify methods of discussing confidential information to the extent possible.

It is almost always the case that youth will agree to these procedures, but in some cases youth or their significant others request that they develop the lists together. In such cases, we recommend that they develop the lists separately to facilitate candid responses, but also to facilitate effective brainstorming that is not biased by input from the other. Youth also sometimes request that their friends join them in developing at-risk items. This is usually a good sign and results in the generation of additional at-risk stimuli. TPs may use the following dialogue as a model to transition from generation of safe stimuli to generation of at-risk stimuli with Leah, who has also listed stealing as one of her problem behaviors.

TP: Now, we will compile an at-risk list that will help me to identify all the people, places, and situations that put you at risk to use drugs, and increase the chances of your stealing something. Leah, you were exposed to other drug users who approved of stealing, and this exposure was initially out of your control. Of course, it is extremely hard to sever these relationships, but I'm so happy with your commitment to talk about some of these influences with me. We've found best results when youth and their significant others are involved in the development of the at-risk list. However, I'd like to work with each of you individually in developing these at-risk lists. We have found that we can identify more at-risk items when we do this separately because you don't bias each other's reports.

Obtaining "At-Risk" Associations (Youth)

TPs begin generating at-risk associations with youth. In a neutral and non-judgmental manner, TPs prompts youth to provide a list of people with whom they have used drugs and may have future contact, or who in some way influence drug use or other problems indirectly, such as by increasing stress or other negative emotional states. A similar at-risk list is generated for other problem behaviors. These stimuli are recorded in the At-Risk column of the Safe and At-Risk Associations List. In some cases, youth may indicate that they do not want to put people on the at-risk list due to fears that parents or TPs will prevent them from spending time with these persons once their names are disclosed. In such cases, it should be explained that these persons may elicit cravings or desires for drug use. TPs should also emphasize that these persons are not considered "bad" people and may, in fact, benefit them in some ways. If youth decide to spend time with these persons, it is explained that they are at risk to use drugs or troublesome behavior, so they should take precautions to prevent these things from happening when spending time with these at-risk individuals. It is also important to let them know that parents usually provide more trust in their youth when they see youth being open about things that cause them risk of substance use or other problem behaviors. Examples of preventative measures might include having at least one safe person present in activities involving at-risk persons, and limiting contacts to safe places. Youth are also told that persons who have an extended history and commitment to drug abstinence and healthy living (e.g., sponsor of Alcoholics Anonymous) may be recorded in the safe list if there is no history of past drug use with the youth. When youth do not want to mention names of at-risk persons because they are concerned these people will get into trouble, TPs may replace their names with unique, and ideally derogatory, characteristics that describe them (e.g., backstabbing Martha), or include at-risk persons in safe lists with asterisks next to their names. During the generation of at-risk items, TPs may also suggest goals for therapy.

After youth respond with all the at-risk people, places, and situations they can think of, TPs provide them with the Things That May Lead to Drug Use and Other Problem Behaviors List, which is included at the end of this chapter (Exhibit 10.5). This list may prove useful to assist youth in identifying other at-risk items that either they forgot to mention or that they had not previously associated with drug use or other problem behavior. TPs ask youth to indicate items from this list that have been found to be associated with drug use or other problem behaviors in the past. TPs subsequently query how these stimuli put youth at risk, and summarize these circumstances in the At-Risk column of the Safe and At-Risk Associations List. Whenever time permits, youth are queried to discuss the things that are liked and disliked about the at-risk items to identify potential reinforcers that may be stressed during reviews of "safe" stimuli. That is, if a youth indicates he likes hanging out with one of his at-risk friends because this friend makes him laugh, the TP can point out when persons on his safe list are humorous and assist the youth in finding safe friends with a good sense of humor. TPs provide empathy when youth report things that are disliked about at-risk stimuli and attempt to solicit things in the safe list that might help to replace or satisfy desired aspects of at-risk stimuli.

The following dialogue depicts implementation of the at-risk list generation with Leah, who is resistant to disclosing the identity of an at-risk person.

TP: Leah, who are all the people in your life with whom you have used drugs, or who have influenced you to use drugs?

Leah: Z, Kat, and Tiffany. Some of my family members use, like my dad drinks alcohol pretty bad. Then, of course, the guy who gets me my drugs, but I can't tell you his name. I guess there are also all those people I meet when I go out partying, but I don't know half their names anyway.

TP: That's a great start. I'm proud of you for being so candid. Can you tell me how you think your father influences you to use?

Leah: Because he stresses me out when he's drunk.

TP: I'd like to record specific things that stress you out about your father.

Leah: Okay, so like whenever I go over to his house, he drinks and gets stupid. He slurs his voice and yells a lot. He looks like a pathetic old man.

TP: I'll record these specific stressors in your at-risk list. Later, we'll practice strategies to help cope with them. I thought Tiffany didn't use. Why is she on the list?

Leah: You know I love Tiffany and love to have her around, but we argue too much. I often end up smoking pot afterwards to try to relax.

TP: That's great. I'll put "Argue with Tiffany" in your at-risk list. Now, I remember that you did not want to identify your drug dealer. Like I said before, everything is confidential if you want it to be. However, I wonder if you would permit me to record a code name or some characteristic to describe this person. Many kids like to put characters that are not so good to make it easier for them to remember bad things about these people. This way I can discuss important issues that put you at risk, while maintaining confidentiality.

Leah: Just put down Sam.

TP: Great, I'll put Sam on your at-risk list. Now, let's identify some other people for your at-risk list.

The TP would continue to identify at-risk items in a similar manner. The following dialogue shows how the TP shifts to using the worksheet to identify more items.

TP: Outstanding job! This is a great list so far. Now, look at the Things That May Lead to Drug Use and Other Problem Behaviors form and try to use it to think of additional at-risk stimuli.

Leah: Here are two things I didn't think of—being alone or lonely and being bored. When that happens, I start thinking about using drugs. If I'm shopping and this happens, I also think about stealing as a challenge.

TP: Great, now let's talk about what you like and dislike about each of these stimuli. First, what do you like and dislike about Tiffany?

Leah: I like that she will fight for me if I ever get in a fight or something. She is loyal and cares about me. Bad things . . . I guess she has a short temper and never lets things go. Like, she has to be the person in the right all the time.

TP: It is just like you to recognize the positive qualities in others. It also shows how loyalty and anger management is important to you. I'm sorry to learn she has a bad temper and feels she has to be in the right. Flexibility is so important. I'll make sure we hit these things in therapy.

The TP would continue to discuss things the youth liked and disliked about at-risk stimuli that were provided as time permitted. It is very rare to assess likes and dislikes for all stimuli. Therefore, TPs should select for review the stimuli that are perceived to be most relevant and important. A useful strategy is to permit youth to determine which stimuli are reviewed. Generally, youth will choose to review the stimuli that are most important to them.

Youth are next queried to report if any information that was disclosed about risk items should remain confidential. It is reported that most youth do not have any problems with such disclosure. However, sometimes youth prefer to keep information confidential. In such cases, the TP should first assess why the youth feels the information should remain confidential. Most youth don't want to disclose information because they are concerned they, or others, will get into trouble. The TP should immediately empathize with such concerns and assist the youth in generating methods of disclosing such information. Indeed, the TP may indicate that the information will likely come out eventually, and that it is usually best to bring it up in the presence of the TP. It is also important to indicate that information can be modified or partly discussed.

Obtaining "At-Risk" Stimuli (Adult Significant Others)

After the TP completes the at-risk list with the youth, the youth is then excused, and the adult significant other is asked to come into the room. All at-risk stimuli are reported to the significant other, with the exception of stimuli that were requested to be confidential by the youth. The significant other is then asked to list additional persons, places, and situations that have been associated with the youth's drug use or other problem behaviors. The methods of soliciting, recording, and reviewing these stimuli are the same as those utilized with the youth.

Reviewing "At-Risk" and "Safe" Associations List (Youth and Adolescent and Adult Significant Others, Whenever Appropriate)

After completing the at-risk list with the significant other, the youth is instructed to come back into the room, and both the youth and significant other are descriptively praised for their work in developing the lists, including their honesty. The TP solicits how they can increase more enjoyable time with safe stimuli. In this regard, it is very important that TPs solicit specific details involved in these strategies. Whenever possible, goals are recorded in the Level System as target behaviors (see Family Supported Contingency Management, Chapter 6), and TPs provide solutions to assist the practical implementation of time spent with safe stimuli. For the at-risk list, TPs spend time discussing how more time can be spent avoiding or managing at-risk stimuli, and goals are recorded in the Level System, whenever possible. The following dialogue contains an excerpt of a typical review of items on the at-risk and safe lists.

TP: You were both fabulous in developing a lot of safe and at-risk stimuli. As far as I can tell, you were both honest and very straightforward. This will go a long way in the upcoming sessions involving this intervention. What can you both do so Leah can spend more time with safe stimuli in upcoming week?

Leah: We could try to avoid arguments.

TP: That is a great idea. How will you two avoid arguments?

Leah: I could try to use the handout you gave us. The Positive Request Handout.

TP: I'm so proud of you. What other things can you do to stay clean and problem free?

The TP would continue to review additional safe items, and then do the same for the at-risk list, as indicated in the following dialogue:

TP: Let's review some things you can both do to avoid or manage at-risk stimuli.

Heather: We could take the dog for a walk after dinner together. I could also help her with her homework on Wednesdays when I go over to the house.

TP: That's tremendous. What a big help that will be. I like that one because you will help Leah accomplish two goals, homework completion and staying clean. What will you do to control your impulses if you spontaneously decide to change your plans?

The TP would continue to assist the youth and her significant other in the identification of strategies to decrease time with at-risk stimuli for the upcoming week. To the extent possible, TPs should problem-solve with youth and significant others for "hypothetical" situations that might arise. This is particularly important if the TP suspects, based on information gained from the session, that some situations might prove particularly challenging in the upcoming week. For example, while Leah and Heather have set a goal of walking after dinner, Leah often visits her friends when she first gets home from school. Given this knowledge, the TP would problem-solve these potential difficulties with Leah and Heather to help ensure that they meet Leah's goals.

Planning a Family Activity (Youth and All Family Members)

The last part of the initial session of Stimulus Control involves scheduling a pleasant family activity that is relatively novel. All family members, including small children and infants, are encouraged to attend. When children are available, they are usually very excited to participate, and should be chiefly involved in generating the activity. It is helpful to emphasize activities that are inexpensive, fun, interactive, educational, and involve physical activity. Families can use the Things to Do and Places I Like to Visit Worksheet to help generate activities. It is also important to encourage youth to bring their friends to some of the family activities. In this way, family members can establish relationships with the client's friends, permitting them to be monitored and comfortable spending more time in the youth's home where youth can be reinforced for desired behavior. Once an activity is identified, the Family Invitation for Fun Worksheet (Exhibit 10.6) is completed to increase the likelihood that the activity will be performed as prescribed. This form requires family members to record what the activity will involve, when it will occur, and who will participate. It is important to let the family members know the activity will be reviewed during the next session to promote accountability.

Future Sessions
Reviewing Safe and At-Risk Associations List (Youth and Adolescent and Adult Significant Others, Whenever Appropriate)

As indicated in the Stimulus Control Therapist Prompting Checklist for Future Sessions (Exhibit 10.2), all future sessions involving Stimulus Control involve first instructing youth to complete the Safe and At-Risk Associations worksheet. Youth are instructed to record a check mark in the column and row corresponding to each safe and at-risk stimulus in which time was spent since the last session. Thus, if a youth spent time with her "safe" brother, Jim, on Saturday, a check is recorded in the column marked Saturday and the row that includes the name of the brother. Prior to completing the form, it is critical for TPs to explicitly state that they will focus their discussions on youths' strengths and positive behaviors (rather than on weaknesses or negative behaviors). With this assurance, youth feel less defensive about potential negative events and behaviors that occurred during the prior week, such as substance use, and so are more willing to candidly report and discuss these matters. TPs typically review all endorsed safe stimuli prior to reviewing endorsed at-risk stimuli. However, TPs are free to alternate in their review of safe and at-risk stimuli based on priority or preference. For instance, a TP may wish to review all endorsed at-risk items first, and finish with a review of safe items to end on a positive note. Regardless of the approach used for review, for each endorsed item, TPs first solicit actions that were performed to avoid drug use or other problem behaviors (in reviews of at-risk and safe stimuli), and then descriptively praise performance of these actions. If drug use or other problem behavior is indicated, youth are asked to indicate how they intended or attempted to stay drug free or problem free. Again, the responses of youth are descriptively praised, and they are encouraged to make, and assisted in making, plans to stay clean and avoid behavior problems in the future. Therefore, mistakes and efforts to use drugs or engage in other problem behaviors are essentially ignored. Rather, youth are encouraged to report plans that are relevant to spending more time with safe stimuli in the future.

Family Behavior Therapy (FBT) interventions are initiated during the review whenever appropriate to assist in solving problems that are likely to occur in the future. For instance, TPs may encourage or facilitate the generation of goals for inclusion in the Level System, teach youth to prepare and do well in a job interview (see Job-Getting Skills Training, Chapter 12), practice a Positive Request (see Positive Request Procedure, Chapter 9), or manage a negative impulse or urge to use drugs (see Self-Control, Chapter 11). Therefore, the focus of the review is on the prevention of future undesired behaviors through encouragement and practice of desired behaviors or skills. The number of items reviewed in any session is ultimately determined by the youth, family and TP, and guided by practical considerations, such as time constraints, experiencing a contemporaneous drug urge, and so on. Significant others are prompted for assistance and support throughout the review, as indicated in the following dialogue:

TP: Last week we obtained lists of items that either increase or decrease your likelihood of maintaining abstinence from substances, attending your classes, and staying out of trouble. We put them on this form (*provides a copy of the Safe and At-Risk Associations List* worksheet). If you spent time with one of the people, places, or situations listed, I want you to put a check in the row that includes that item and the column that represents the day you spent time with the item. Do the same for the remaining items. It is important for you to know that when we review your responses, I will emphasize your strengths and things you do that are positive. Together, we will generate solutions to problems you may have experienced in staying clean from drugs and free from other troubles.

After the TP permits the youth to complete the form, the TP may either select items to review that are important and/or permit the youth and significant others to determine items to emphasize in the review.

TP: Tell me something that is listed in your safe list that you would like to review first. I'm particularly interested in knowing what you did to stay clean from drugs, do your homework, and stay out of trouble.

Leah: I spent a lot more time with Heather and got more exercise than I had in a long time because of our walks after dinner. Mom joined us, as well.

TP: That's wonderful! Exercise is so incompatible with drug use, and you'll start losing weight and getting into shape.

Leah: Well, I don't think I exercised that hard, but I really enjoyed playing with my puppy.

TP: Heather, way to go! You guys are starting to really work as a team. I wonder if you guys could lift some weights at home like you had wanted to do. Is there a way to make that happen?

Heather: I'd like to work out with Leah. I could help with her homework, than we could take our walk with the dog and work out before we go to bed.

Leah: I don't think it is realistic, although it would be great to do this together.

> *TP:* Leah, remember you both agreed you'd encourage each other. I have another way I'd like you both to resolve this dilemma. Two weeks ago you both practiced Positive Request. Leah, I'd like you to please make a request of your sister to exercise. Let me get out my Positive Request Worksheets from my files. . . .

In the preceding example, the TP goes on to implement the Positive Request Procedure. The TP puts aside the Safe and At-Risk Associations List and takes out all materials necessary to implement the Positive Request Procedure. After this intervention is completed, the TP again takes out the Safe and At-Risk Associations List and resumes the review of this form.

While the review focuses on the strengths and positive behaviors of the youth and significant others, it is often the case that negative behaviors occur between sessions, and TPs need to address these in the review process. The following dialogue demonstrates the review of a common negative behavior in which the youth used drugs when spending time with Jessica, a person on her at-risk list.

> *TP:* I absolutely love how you tried to invite your sister to be around when you hung out with Jessica. How did your actions keep you clean from using drugs?

> *Leah:* I just kept suggesting we go to the restaurant, and when Jessica brought up drugs I used the broken record technique to say I didn't use anymore. I also told my sister to never let her get us to go downtown. I knew she respected my sister too much to go against her.

> *TP:* I'm really proud of you. Did you get any urges to use, and if so, how did you handle these?

> *Leah:* Well (*looking embarrassed and sad*), I did get them. In fact, I should mention that behind my sister's back I told Jessica to meet me outside the house. Later, we smoked a couple of joints.

> *Heather:* I knew you used! What a fool I was to believe your lies again!

> *TP:* I can see how both of you are very upset. First, Leah, I'd like to say I'm glad you had the courage to tell us you used, and I know you must be disappointed you won't be able to take advantage of the reward trip to the play that Heather planned for next week in celebration of being clean for your first month in over 2 years. However,

the important thing is that you learn to respond better to urges in the future. Although it wasn't selected in your treatment plan until much later, I think practicing the Self-Control intervention will help you manage your urges. We'll do that in a few minutes. However, this experience shows that Jessica is too big a trigger to spend time with, even with trusted, safe people. Last week, Heather told you she thought Jessica was a problem, and her instincts were correct. Are there any ways Jessica can be eliminated from your life?

Heather: Leah is like putty in Jessica's hands. I've got no problem letting Jessica know she's not welcome here anymore.

TP: I think that's a good idea for now. Your family needs you now more than ever. However, Leah, you will eventually have to learn to be more assertive with people like her. Leah, let's do the Self-Control intervention now for the situation with Jessica. This intervention will give you a chance to brainstorm options to do instead of spending time with Jessica for the scenario you just mentioned. One of the options you might think about during this trial might be assertively telling Jessica you can't spend time with her. This might be an option we can do on the phone in our session after the Self-Control. I know severing relationships with drug-using friends is difficult, but maybe we should make it one of your goals.

Leah: I think you are right. Thanks.

Reviewing Family Activity (Youth and All Family Members)

Each review of the Stimulus Control ends with a review of the family activity that was prescribed during the past session. The TP invites all family members into the room and asks the family to provide a copy of the completed Family Invitation for Fun form. Family members are encouraged to discuss what they liked about the activity they performed, and they are descriptively praised and encouraged to do similar activities in the future. When the prescribed activity is not performed, TPs discuss methods of ensuring prescribed family activities will occur in the future. This discussion typically includes a review of solutions to potential obstacles. The family is then provided another copy of the Family Invitation for Fun form, and a new activity is scheduled for the next week, including what it will be, when it will occur, and who will participate. All family members are invited to indicate what they can do to ensure that the activity is performed, and they are informed that the activity will be reviewed during the next session.

Concluding Remarks

Stimulus Control is often conceptualized as the control center of FBT, as all interventions may be initiated during its review. For instance, if an TP recognized a skill deficit while reviewing Stimulus Control, all forms that are relevant to the Stimulus Control intervention might be temporarily put on hold, and another skill-based FBT component could be implemented immediately (e.g., Job-Getting Skills Training could be implemented to assist in gaining employment if a job interviewing skill deficit was recognized while reviewing "employment" in Safe List). Upon completion of the skill-based intervention, the TP would terminate the other FBT component as prescribed, and return to Stimulus Control if sufficient time remained in the session. Stimulus Control would resume where the therapist left off.

Supporting Materials for Chapter 10: Restructuring the Environment to Facilitate a Drug–Free Lifestyle

Exhibit 10.1. Stimulus Control Therapist Prompting Checklist for Initial Session.

Youth ID:_____ Clinician: _____ Session #: _____ Session Date: _____

Materials Required

- Safe and At-Risk Associations List (SARAL)
- Things I Like to Do and Places I Like to Visit List (TILDPLVL)
- Things That May Lead to Drug Use and Other Problem Behaviors (TLDUOPB)
- Family Invitation for Fun Form (FIFF)

Begin Time:_____

Presenting Rationale (youth & adol. & adult sig. others)

- State the following:

___a. Things in environment make drug use & problem behaviors more or less likely to occur.

___b. Youth & sig. other will together develop safe list of people, places, and situations that increase likelihood of staying clean from drugs & avoiding problem behavior.

___c. Youth & sig. others will separately develop at-risk list of people, places, and situations that decrease likelihood of staying clean from drugs and avoiding problem behavior.

___d. Lists will be reviewed each session to discover how to enjoy more time w/safe items & avoid risky items.

___e. Intervention has been successful w/other youth.

___f. Indicate how intervention is expected to be successful w/youth.

___g. Solicit & answer questions.

Obtaining "Safe" Associations (youth & adult sig. others)

___a. Solicit enjoyable people who do not use drugs/do problem behavior.

___b. Solicit enjoyable <u>activities/places</u> that do not involve drugs or problem behavior.

___c. Solicit enjoyable activities that have not involved drug use or problem behavior from TILDPLVL.

- Record solicited safe stimuli in the Safe column of the SARAL.

___d. Assure all generated items have not involved drug use or problems.

If time permits, solicit things liked about safe items.

Obtaining "At-Risk" Associations (youth)

___a. Solicit people who increase youth's drug use and problem behavior.

___b. Solicit <u>activities/places</u> that have involved drug use or problem behavior.

___c. Solicit activities/places that have involved drug use or problem behavior from TILDPLVL.

- Record solicited at-risk stimuli in the At-Risk column of the SARAL.

___d.   Query if information in at-risk lists should remain confidential, & modify future reviews accordingly.
   • If time permits, solicit things liked and disliked about at-risk items.

Obtaining "At-Risk" Associations (adult significant others)

___a.   Solicit people who increase youth's drug use and problem behavior.
___b.   Solicit activities/places that have involved drug use or problem behavior.
___c.   Solicit activities/places that have involved drug use or problem behavior from TLDUOPB.
   • Record solicited at-risk stimuli in the At-Risk column of the SARAL.
___d.   Query if information in at-risk lists should remain confidential, & modify future reviews accordingly.
   • If time permits, solicit things liked and disliked about at-risk items.

Reviewing Safe and At-Risk Associations List (youth and adol. & adult significant others)

___a.   Praise youth and sig. other in developing lists and being honest.
___b.   Review how youth & sig. others can each increase youth's time & enjoyment w/safe stimuli.
___c.   Review how youth & sig. others can decrease youth's time & risk w/at-risk stimuli.
   • Assist in developing goals to include in Level System.
   • Suggest solutions that may help increase time spent in safe situations.
   • Descriptively praise suggestions that assist youth in spending more time w/safe stimuli.
   • Descriptively praise suggestions that assist youth in spending less time w/at-risk stimuli.

Planning a Family Activity (youth and all family members)

___a.   Solicit one family activity.
___b.   Record information about family activity in FIFF.
___c.   Assign family to conduct the family activity.

Youth's Assessment of Helpfulness of the Intervention

___a.   After stating youth should not feel obligated to provide high scores, as an honest assessment helps better address youth needs, solicit how helpful youth thought intervention was using 7-point scale:
   7 = extremely helpful, **6** = very helpful, **5** = somewhat helpful, **4** = not sure, **3** = somewhat unhelpful, **2** = very unhelpful, **1** = extremely unhelpful
   • Record Youth's Rating Here:
___b.   Solicit how rating was derived, and methods of improving intervention in future.

Therapist's Rating of Youth's Compliance with Intervention

___a.   Disclose therapist's rating of youth's compliance using the following 7-point scale:
   7 = extremely compliant, **6** = very compliant, **5** = somewhat compliant, **4** = neutral,
   3 = somewhat noncompliant, **2** = very noncompliant, **1** = extremely noncompliant
   • Factors that contribute to compliance ratings are:
   • Attendance
   • Participation and conduct in session

- Homework completion
- Record Therapist's Rating of Youth's Compliance Here:_____
___b.   Disclose youth's compliance rating.
___c.   Explain how rating was derived, and methods of improving performance in future.

End Time: _____   **Notes:** _____

Exhibit 10.2. Stimulus Control Therapist Prompting Checklist for Future Sessions.

STIMULUS CONTROL

THERAPIST PROMPING CHECKLIST

FUTURE SESSIONS

Youth ID:_____ Clinician:_____ Session #:_____ Session Date: _____

Materials Required

- Safe and At-Risk Associations List (SARAL)
- Family Invitation for Fun Form (FIFF)

Begin Time:_____

Reviewing Safe and At-Risk Associations Recording Sheet (youth and adol. & adult sig. others)

___a. Provide SARAL.
___b. Instruct youth to put checks in boxes for days in which time was spent w/stimuli.
___c. Review completed SARAL, including:
    ___1. Solicit actions performed w/stimuli to stay clean and free of problems.
    ___2. Encourage/descriptively praise actions consistent w/staying clean & free of problems.
    ___3. Encourage/assist in plans to stay clean & free of problems.
    ___4. Integrate other FBT interventions, including:
        • Adding goals to Family Supported Contingency Management.
        • Soliciting & performing job interviews (Job-Getting Skills Training).
        • Practicing requests (Positive Request Procedure).
        • Developing impulse control & problem-solving skills (Self-Control).
        • Enhancing overall tone in family relationship (Reciprocity Awareness).

Reviewing Family Activity (youth and all family members)

___a. Solicit completed copy of Family Invitation for Fun Form (FIFF).
    • If not complete, instruct to complete in retrospect or discuss what would have been enjoyed if assignment were performed.
___b. Instruct family to discuss what they liked about the activity they performed.
___c. Descriptively praise family for positive experiences, and encourage future family activities.
___d. Provide Family Invitation for Fun Form, & schedule new activity.

Youth's Assessment of Helpfulness of the Intervention

___a. After stating youth should not feel obligated to provide high scores, as an honest assessment helps better address youth needs, solicit how helpful youth thought intervention was using 7-point scale:
7 = extremely helpful, **6** = very helpful, **5** = somewhat helpful, **4** = not sure, **3** = somewhat unhelpful, **2** = very unhelpful, **1** = extremely unhelpful
    • Record Youth's Rating Here:_____
___b. Solicit how rating was derived, and methods of improving intervention in future.

Therapist's Rating of Youth's Compliance with Intervention

___a. Disclose therapist's rating of youth's compliance using the following 7-point scale:
7 = extremely compliant, **6** = very compliant, **5** = somewhat compliant, **4** = neutral,
3 = somewhat noncompliant, **2** = very noncompliant, **1** = extremely noncompliant
  • Factors that contribute to compliance ratings are:
  • Attendance
  • Participation and conduct in session
  • Homework completion
  • Record Therapist's Rating of Youth's Compliance Here:_____
___b. Disclose youth's compliance rating.
___c. Explain how rating was derived, and methods of improving performance in future.

End Time:_____   Notes:_____

Exhibit 10.3. Safe and At-Risk Associations List.

SAFE AND AT-RISK ASSOCIATIONS LIST

Instructions: Please indicate each day you spent time with each item on your safe list and at-risk list over the past week.

Safe List	Mon	Tues	Wed	Thur	Fri	Sat	Sun	At-Risk List	Mon	Tues	Wed	Thur	Fri	Sat	Sun

Exhibit 10.4. Things I Like to Do and Places I Like to Visit List.

THINGS I LIKE TO DO AND PLACES I LIKE TO VISIT LIST

Instructions: Put an "X" next to each thing you like to do and place you like to visit that does not involve drug use and/or benefits your family.

- ☐ Attending sporting events, football, baseball, hockey, etc.
- ☐ Community center activities
- ☐ City-sponsored activities, visit museum or historical site
- ☐ Read paper for community events or jobs
- ☐ Attending school/clubs (choir, band, sport leagues, bowling, yoga, photography, sewing/knitting, school clubs)
- ☐ Participating in outdoor events (hiking, picnicking, swimming, camping, skiing/sledding, fishing, hunting, gardening)
- ☐ Attending church, temple, mosque, etc.
- ☐ Computer games
- ☐ Practicing a musical instrument, dancing
- ☐ Playing board and card games
- ☐ Talking on the phone
- ☐ Cooking
- ☐ Write/videotape a play
- ☐ Volunteer at the animal shelter or charitable organization
- ☐ Read stories to/entertain children
- ☐ Start a club (book club, poetry club/party)
- ☐ Keep a journal and write every week
- ☐ Work on photo album, writing stories about the pictures
- ☐ Painting/artwork, drawing
- ☐ Doing repair work (carpentry, landscaping, fixing car)
- ☐ Family gatherings (invite friends to spend time w/family)
- ☐ Organize a family reunion
- ☐ Employment/work
- ☐ Volunteering for community or school
- ☐ Libraries (check out books, movies, games)

Exhibit 10.5. Things That May Lead to Drug Use and Other Problem Behaviors.

THINGS THAT MAY LEAD TO DRUG USE AND OTHER PROBLEM BEHAVIORS

Instructions: If you have used illicit drugs/alcohol, or gotten in trouble with any of the following risk factors, please indicate this with a check.

People

- ☐ Friends/Peers/Acquaintance
- ☐ Coworkers
- ☐ Family

Places and Situations

- ☐ Attending parties or get-togethers
- ☐ Smoking cigarettes
- ☐ Drinking alcohol
- ☐ Being angry or sad
- ☐ Stress
- ☐ Being bored
- ☐ Being alone
- ☐ Experiencing tension
- ☐ Having lots of cash available
- ☐ Car
- ☐ Specific times of day
- ☐ Excitement/anxiety
- ☐ Celebrations
- ☐ Being in places where you have used before (e.g., parks, casinos, people's homes)

Exhibit 10.6. Family Invitation for Fun.

Family Invitation for Fun

What are we going to do?

_____

_____

_____

_____

_____

_____

When are we going to do the fun activity?

_____

_____

_____

_____

_____

_____

Who is going to attend the fun activity?

_____

_____

_____

_____

_____

_____

We can't wait to have fun!

11

Using Self-Control to Manage Negative Behaviors, Thoughts, and Feelings

Overview

As reviewed in Chapter 10, chronic substance use inevitably becomes associated with stimuli that can be sensed in the environment, such as particular places (e.g., back patio, parties without adult supervision), persons (e.g., friends who use drugs), sounds (e.g., crackling sound of burning "crack" cocaine), smells (e.g., burning pot), or events (e.g., birthday parties, weddings, sporting events). These stimuli often become conditioned to elicit pleasant physiological cravings, images, and thoughts about the reinforcing aspects of substance use. With continued exposure these things often intensify, which in turn increases motivation to use substances. Of course, it is best to plan and implement strategies that facilitate avoidance of substance use triggers, such as the stimulus control strategies that were reviewed in the last chapter. However, when youth are unexpectedly exposed to substance use triggers, it is important to (a) recognize the triggers when they first occur and are less intense; and (b) consequently engage in thoughts, images, and actions that are incompatible with substance use. A similar process occurs when unexpectedly confronted with troublesome problem behaviors.

Self-Control targets drug use and various undesired impulsive behaviors, such as risk behaviors associated with sexually transmitted diseases (i.e., sex without condom use), school truancy, symptoms associated with mental health disorders, aggression, and arguments, among others. In the Self-Control intervention, youths are taught to recognize the triggers, or "antecedent" stimuli, to substance use and other problem behaviors early in the response chain, before cravings intensify. After stimulus recognition, they are taught to engage in the following cognitive and behavioral skill sets that are incompatible with drug use and other problem behaviors:

1. Interrupting the association by thinking or shouting, "Stop!"

2. Thinking or stating at least one negative consequence for self and one negative consequence for others that could occur if drug use or other problem behavior is permitted to occur.

3. Relaxing by scanning and relaxing muscles while taking a few deep breaths.

4. Thinking or stating four prosocial alternatives to drug use or other problem behavior for the respective situation.

5. Choosing one or more of the generated alternative behaviors, and imagining out loud or doing the chosen behaviors.

6. Thinking (or telling) a friend or loved one how the respective drug or problem behavior was avoided, and imagining the person responding positively.

7. Thinking or stating at least two positive consequences that are likely to result from the avoidance of the respective drug or problem behavior.

The treatment provider (TP) provides descriptive praise and assistance as the youth responds correctly throughout practice trials. The number of practice trials in any given session depends on the extent of problem behaviors that were evidenced since last contact in therapy. For instance, if drug use were indicated during the past week, four or five Self-Control trials might be performed, whereas no drug use since the last session might require one or two practice trials. Consistent with other Family Behavior Therapy (FBT) interventions, a therapy assignment is prescribed to assist in practicing Self-Control during *real-life* situations that occur between sessions.

Goals for Intervention

➤ Teach youth to recognize antecedent stimuli that act to trigger drug use or other problem behaviors (i.e., triggers).

➤ Teach youth to interrupt intensity of triggers with thoughts and behaviors that are incompatible with drug use or problem behavior.

Materials Required

➤ Self-Control Therapist Prompting Checklist for Initial Session (Exhibit 11.1)

➤ Self-Control Rating Form (one copy for youth, one copy for therapist; Exhibit 11.2)

➤ Self-Control Therapist Prompting Checklist for Future Sessions (Exhibit 11.3)

Procedural Steps for Treatment Implementation

Initial Session

Presenting Rationale (Youth and Adult Significant Others)   The TP utilizes the Self-Control Therapist Prompting Checklist for Initial Session (Exhibit 11.1) to guide intervention implementation. The intervention begins with a rationale that is presented to the youth and adult significant others. The treatment provider (TP) explains that Self-Control is a skill set the youth can use to assist in decreasing the frequency of drug use and other problem behaviors. TPs often point out stimuli that have triggered drug use and other problem behaviors for youth in the past to make the rationale more meaningful. It is explained that Self-Control teaches people to recognize cues or triggers that act to signal drug use and other problem behaviors. It is further explained that Self-Control helps youths to generate actions that are incompatible with drug use or other problem behaviors. While learning Self-Control, these actions are practiced out loud during trials while the TP provides feedback. TPs conclude the rationale by explaining how the therapy is expected to help the youth from the TP's perspective, and soliciting from youths how Self-Control will be useful from their perspective. The following sections provide an example of a TP implementing this rationale.

TP: Chelsey, you're now going to learn a skill that you can use when you experience triggers that often act to signal drug use and other problem behaviors. For instance, you indicated that arguments with your mother get you thinking about how pot can relax you, which increases your likelihood of using drugs.

Chelsey: I really don't want to talk about those things, because it will bring up bad thoughts and feelings again.

TP: That is a good sign because it means the associations between drug use and various things in your environment are now relatively weak, probably because you have some clean time under your belt. However, your urine test was positive for marijuana 3 weeks ago, and it will be important for you to learn how to manage triggers in case you experience them in the future. You'll learn this Self-Control procedure during our sessions. We'll imagine you being exposed to various triggers when they are first recognized in your imagination. You will subsequently learn to terminate triggers and refocus on behaviors that are inconsistent with drug use. How does that sound?

Chelsey: Sure.

TP: Just like with drug use, there are also cues that may lead to other problem behaviors. For instance, you indicated that kissing may lead to unprotected sex because kissing gets you thinking about the good aspects of sex, while ignoring negative consequences associated with the absence of condom use. Self-Control has been very successful in helping youth recognize triggers to problem behaviors early, so they can instead focus on doing behaviors that will keep them healthy and free of problems. I think this is going to be especially good for you because, although these associations may be weak, you became anxious when I mentioned that I was going to talk about things that have been associated with your drug use in the past, and this intervention has a relaxation component. How do you think this intervention might help you?

Chelsey: I think it would help improve my confidence when I have to face drug triggers since I know that will happen.

TP: Great, do you have any questions?

Identification of At-Risk Situation for Drug Use (Usually Youth Alone)   After presenting the rationale with the youth alone, the TP uses brainstorming with the youth to identify triggers to drug use and other problem behaviors.

It is explained that it is easier to stop drug use (as well as other undesired behaviors) when triggers are first recognized, or before thoughts and images are permitted to intensify. The TP then instructs the youth to disclose a recent situation in which drug use occurred. If the youth is unable to think of one, the TP can choose something from the Stimulus Control At-Risk List (see Chapter 10) or provide something that was a trigger for another youth. Some youth may feel apprehensive in disclosing such information because they think they are admitting to drug use that could get them into trouble. Such youth are usually early in their recovery or are mandated to treatment by someone from legal or school systems. In such cases, it is best to simply indicate that the treatment sessions will focus on prevention, and make an attempt to gather scenarios that may have occurred in the distant past, or perhaps ones that are based on hypothetical information. Such scenarios might include being at a party where marijuana was present, or being offered drugs during a car ride. It is often the case that apprehensive youth will indicate that they are providing a hypothetical situation, but in truth are providing a genuinely experienced scenario.

Once a drug use scenario is obtained, the TP instructs the youth to identify the first thought that occurred in the drug use situation. The TP uses a *backward chaining* procedure to prompt the very "first" thought or image that is relevant to using drugs in the obtained situation, which is illustrated in the following dialogue:

TP: Tell me about a recent situation in which you used cocaine, or any other drug. I'm especially interested in knowing about the first thought or image that you had before you used drugs.

Chelsey: This weekend a couple of my friends and me were hanging out, and one of them asked if I wanted to do a few lines.

TP: What was the first thought or image you can remember that happened as soon as you were offered cocaine?

Chelsey: I don't know what you mean. I just told her I'd do it with her.

TP: Yes, it's not easy. If you think about it, our minds usually motivate us to do the things we do. In that situation, I wonder if there was something you said to yourself, or thought about, just before you indicated that you'd do a line.

Chelsey: Well, I usually have an image in my head of getting high. When she offered, I kind of flash to that situation.

TP: Very good. Now you know what I'm talking about. Now I want you to think even harder. Did you have any thought or image that brought you to where you guys were hanging out? It sounds like you've used in this sort of situation before so there may have been a signal that this could happen again.

Chelsey: When my friend asked me if I wanted to go behind the softball field, I knew what she wanted.

TP: Good, now go back further. Before she asked you, did you know this situation might happen?

Chelsey: When she met me after school, I had a feeling she'd want to do that because it was Friday, and we do it a lot on Fridays together.

TP: You're doing so well. I'm so impressed with your insight. Any thoughts or images before that?

Chelsey: No. I was going to go shopping with my mom that night, so I wasn't even thinking that would happen.

TP: Great, when you saw your friend in school for the first time, that's when you'd do the Self-Control.

As evident from the aforementioned dialogue, Chelsey believed her first trigger for cocaine use occurred when she was offered cocaine. However, the first trigger actually occurred much earlier, when she was approached by her friend to go to the softball field. The TP was able to solicit the first trigger by using the backward chaining procedure. This method is based on the idea that drug use and other problem behavior consist of behavioral chains that are interconnected by thoughts or images of the reinforcing aspects of drug use. Desire to use substances or engage in other problem behavior usually intensifies as the behavioral chain of events approaches the reinforcer (e.g., immediate positive effects of drug use, possession of stolen object). Therefore, it is easier to terminate the behavioral chain upon first recognition of the trigger. Once this first thought is identified, it is important for the youth to appreciate that thoughts, desires (or physiological responses) to environmental triggers generally intensify as the reinforcing aspects of drug use are permitted to occur. To assist in this demonstration, it usually is best to identify the point immediately prior to drug use and query if it would be easier to avoid drug use at this point or the point at which the first thought or image of drug use occurred. Usually, the youth will indicate the first drug use thought or image. In this case, Chelsey would find it much easier to avoid drug use by denying her friend's initial offer to go to the softball field, rather than at the point of being offered to use cocaine.

Sometimes, youth indicate that the outcome of drug use is not dependent on catching the thought or image early. Of course, it is possible that the trigger results in a reflexive impulse to use, usually due to chronic and severe use of very physiologically addictive substances. However, it is more likely the case that the identified trigger is, indeed, not the first one for the respective situation. In such scenarios, TPs need to reinstate backward chaining for the respective scenario to identify the "true" first thought or image. When youth cannot identify earlier thoughts in response chains, TPs state that increased awareness will occur with continued practice, as illustrated in the following dialogue:

TP: Let me ask you this. Would it be easier for you to avoid drug use when you were first approached by your friend, or when you were asked to do a line?

Chelsey: Probably when I was asked to go over there, but it didn't matter 'cause I can do whatever I want to do.

TP: That's right. If you have it in front of you, it is far more difficult, as you indicated. However, it sounds like you had already made your mind up when she asked you. That means it's going to be tougher for you than perhaps other youth because you've done it so many times you have a habitual response to accept her offer. In such cases we need to go back even further in the behavioral response chain. This might be hard, but did you know your friend might hook up with you that day?

Chelsey: I had a feeling she might be there after school.

TP: Great. At that point, you'd need to make an effort to avoid running into her. If you didn't want to use drugs that would be the best time to make it easiest to avoid drug use because you wouldn't have to have any confrontation in your mind, or with her.

Chelsey: True.

TP: Sounds like you've got it.

Modeling Self-Control Procedure for Identified Drug Use Situation (Usually Youth and Adult Significant Others)   Once the trigger is identified with the youth, each of the nine steps in the Self-Control Rating Form (Exhibit 11.2) is modeled in sequence by the TP for the identified drug use situation from the point at which the first trigger was identified. The TP and youth should each have a copy of this rating form. The TP explains that the steps will be modeled thinking "out loud" while doing the practice trials during sessions so thinking patterns can be better understood. However, it is explained that in *real-life* situations, the youth will imagine the steps. In most situations, adult significant others may be included during the modeling of Self-Control if the youth talks about drug use openly. If not, significant others should not be present. During the modeling, if significant others are present, it is important to explain how open and honest the youth was in generating ideas. If youth wish to keep the reviewed scenario confidential, the TP should model the steps using a similar hypothetical scenario. Each step of the Self-Control process is outlined in the following exchanges between youth and TP:

TP: I am going to teach you the Self-Control Procedure in a series of practice trials here in the office, where you will imagine being confronted with triggers for drug use. Later, I'll do the Self-Control in response to other problem behaviors. I'll first model these skills. I'll then have you do them while I help guide you. These trials will permit you to practice getting out of drug use situations by managing the feeling and thoughts that result when you encounter triggers for drug use. During these trials we will state our thoughts "out loud" so we will each know what the other is thinking, and so I can know how this technique is working for you. However, at home in real-life situations, you will do the steps in your head or imagination.

As indicated in the recording form, the first step to model is the termination of the first thought, image (or physiological feeling) associated with drug use in the identified situation, by loudly and forcefully stating, "Stop," as soon as the trigger is recognized. All muscles should be tense during this time (e.g., tight fists).

TP: The first thing to do when trying to prevent drug use is to firmly yell "Stop!" as soon as you recognize the drug use trigger. During this time, other youths have told me that it helps to tighten their fists, arms, and other muscles to simulate the tension. I'm going to show you how to do this for the drug use situation you just told me about. I will say two or three things about the situation, and as soon as I recognize a drug thought, I will state, "Stop!" Okay, here I go. I'm at school and I start to think that my friend will probably try to meet me after school . . . "Stop!"

For the second and third steps, the youth describes at least one negative consequence of drug use for self, and at least one negative consequence for friends or loved ones who are respected. For instance, if the youth was upset that an addiction to drug use might develop in adulthood, the youth could indicate fear of losing control of self and making things bad for a future spouse. During modeling, the TP should state negative consequences with affect reflecting sadness, anger, disgust, or despair, as appropriate. Muscles should remain tense throughout the trial (e.g., clenched fists). Consequences may be rotated (or added) as trials progress. TPs should provide details regarding these negative consequences. In the following example, the TP intentionally elaborates on the details of the negative consequences, to make them more real, and to better appreciate their negative ramifications. Youths sometimes gloss over these details, and in these cases, TPs should assist in developing these details.

TP: The second and third steps are to describe at least one negative consequence resulting from drug use for you, and at least one negative consequence for your friends and loved ones, or any other individuals who are affected by your behavior. For example, a negative consequence for me if I were to use drugs is that I could get expelled from school and end up working in a low-paying job for the rest of my life. A negative consequence for others is that it makes my mother sad and she blames herself for my behavior.

The fourth step is to perform deep, rhythmic breathing and conduct a body scan for sensations of tension in major muscle groups to eliminate any tension that is present. Major muscles should be reviewed from head to toe. During this review, if a major muscle is relaxed (e.g., shoulders), the person should state that the muscle is relaxed, calm, and so on. If a muscle is tense, the person should state several relaxing cue words until the muscle is no longer tense; for example, "My arms are getting more and more relaxed. I am imagining a band of relaxation around my arms. They feel relaxed, calm . . . more and more relaxed." Deep, rhythmic breaths should occur throughout the rest of the trial. Statements referring to the relaxed state of the body are acceptable throughout the relaxation period; for example, "I feel so relaxed and comfortable, I feel like I'm floating away." The brief relaxation period should continue until all muscle groups feel relaxed. Although the relaxation period will only last 5 to 10 seconds when it is eventually mastered, this phase of the Self-Control intervention may initially last several minutes. Indeed, if stress is present or there was a delay in recognizing the drug use trigger, the TP may need to allow more time for the relaxation phase. Adolescents usually require less time relaxing than adults due to the nature of their substance use patterns. However, the modeling of this step should be comprehensive, particularly for those youth who abuse downers (e.g., benzodiazepine, barbiturates). It may be explained that thinking about relaxation helps to focus thoughts away from the reinforcing aspects of substances and other problem behaviors. An example of a TP's doing this step follows:

TP: The fourth step is to relax your body. Although this relaxation process may last up to a few minutes if I'm stressed or I didn't recognize the trigger, this phase of the trial usually will eventually last only a few seconds once you've mastered the technique. So let me take a few seconds to breathe deeply and focus on my muscles to make sure I'm not tense, upset, or angry. *(While breathing slowly)* I'm letting my shoulders get more and more relaxed. Okay, my shoulders feel loose and relaxed. I'm breathing in relaxation, and exhaling calmness. . . . My legs, toes, and whole body feel completely relaxed now.

The fifth and sixth steps are to review four or more prosocial alternative behaviors that do not involve drugs, including potential pros and cons of each of these alternative behaviors. Trials include stating several alternatives that do not include drug use, briefly checking to make sure the response is unlikely to bring about drug use, and reviewing positive and negative consequences for self and others that are likely to occur. To implement steps 5 and 6, the TP might say:

TP: The fifth and sixth steps are to review potential solutions or behaviors that do not involve drugs, and then think about the good and bad things about each generated solution. For example, some things that I could do to avoid drugs are to go home right after work or I could go to the movies with my sister. I could tell my mom to pick me up so we could go shopping, or I could ask my mom to take me skating. I go home right after school. If I call my sister, I might have a great time and wouldn't use with her. However, my mom may not like this idea because I promised to go shopping with her. If I went with skating, my mom wouldn't be able to skate, but we'd have a great time afterwards. I can't think of any negative consequences for going out with her shopping.

During the youth's trial after the TP models the Self-Control steps, the TP may utilize prompts to teach the youth the fifth and sixth steps. These prompts include:

1. *Additional alternative behaviors;* for example, "If your mom changed her mind and didn't want to go to the mall, what could you do?"

2. *How self and others would be positively affected* by alternative behaviors; for example, "What good things would happen in your relationship with your sister if you gave her a call instead of meeting your friend who uses? How would your mom feel if you walked away?"

3. *What others would do for the youth* if alternative behaviors were performed; for example, "What do you think your father would do for you if he found out that you came home?"

4. *Quickly disclosing negative consequences* when behaviors are stated that lead to drug use; for example, "What negative things might happen if you did that?"

Step 7 is to imagine doing, or do for real if performed in vivo, one or more of the drug-incompatible behaviors and imagining positive things happening as a result of these behaviors. The behavioral experience should be described in a first-person narrative in the *present tense*.

TP: Step 7 is to imagine doing one or more of the behaviors that were reviewed that are incompatible with drug use. I will tell a story describing myself doing these actions in the first person, as if it were happening to me right now. Okay, here I go. I think the best thing to do is to call my mom and ask her to pick me up to go to the mall. I'm giving her a call, and she answers pleasantly. I ask her to pick me up to go to the mall and tell her that it would be good to go to the movie afterwards if she is up to doing this. She tells me how proud she is of me and how much she is looking forward to the evening. She tells me she'll be right over to pick me up. I feel fantastic and know I made the right move.

When the youth performs step 7, the TP should provide prompts to elicit detail; for example, "Describe how your mom's face looks. I'll bet she's very happy." It may be necessary to instruct the youth to role-play potentially difficult interpersonal situations and subsequently provide feedback regarding correct responding; for example, "Show me how you would tell your friend you had to go home. I'll be her." Efforts to engage in the chosen alternative behavior(s) should be presented with positive outcome(s); for example, "I want you to describe your friend agreeing that it is the best thing for you to be with your mom."

Step 8 is to imagine telling a friend or family member who does not use drugs about having performed the behavior that is incompatible with drug use. Again, the youth should use first person and present tense when describing this interaction. The friend or family member should respond in a favorable manner and share positive feelings. The following scenario demonstrates these points:

TP: The next step is to imagine telling at least one family member or friend who does not use drugs what I did to avoid using drugs. I imagine how I'd feel, and what I'd say. It is important to also imagine the other person responding positively to reinforce you for doing things to get away from drugs or problem behaviors. So, I'm imagining telling my sister that I could have gone to the softball field and used drugs after school, but instead I called our mom and went to the mall. As soon as I tell her, she looks at me and smiles. She tells me how proud she is of me.

The ninth step is to state several positive consequences that might result due to performance of the drug-free behavior. This step is performed to reinforce the participant for having performed the previous steps. An example follows:

TP: The final step is to state several positive consequences that might result from my drug-free behavior. For example, I'm really proud of myself for deciding to spend the evening with my mom. That says a lot about the kind of person I am and what a great relationship I'm building with my mom. My sister is proud of me, too. Life is good!

After the TP models the steps, it is helpful to model the entire nine steps in sequence, without interruption or feedback as to what is being performed. That is, the TP performs the steps without stopping to explain what is being performed. In this way, the youth is able to appreciate the natural flow of Self-Control through observation. This step may be unnecessary, however, when youth are especially bright and appear to understand the steps.

Evaluation of TP's Performance for First Drug Use Trial (Usually Youth and Adult Significant Others)   After modeling, the youth and the TP evaluate the TP's performance using the Self-Control Rating Form. This evaluation teaches the youth how to correctly complete the form, as each of the nine steps is reviewed. In evaluating the TP's performance, the TP should ask the youth what was generally liked about the modeled performance, and respond with enthusiasm and general agreement, whenever possible.

To complete the Self-Control Rating Form, the date and a cue word describing the modeled situation (e.g., "bleachers") are recorded in the appropriate places on both the youth and TP copies of the form. The youth is instructed to grade each step the TP performed on the youth's Self-Control Rating Form using a 0% to 100% scale of correctness (0% = forgot to do the step, 100% = did the step perfectly). Youth record their scores on their copy of the rating form, and TPs score their performance on their copy of the rating form. The youth and TPs then compare their scores. The procedure for this starts with the TP asking the youth to report the score that was indicated for the first step. Then, the TP's score is disclosed. The TP asks how the youth's score was derived and provides descriptive praise for accurate responses and enthusiasm. The TP then states how the scores are consistent and asks what the youth might do differently if performing the step. The TP then points out methods to improve performance in the future. If one of the youth's scores is more than 20 percentage points different than the TP's score, feedback should be given regarding the discrepancy so that the youth understands the rationale underlying the rating, and future scores are more accurate. If scores are within 20 percentage points, the TP praises the youth for accurate responses. With practice, the TP may phase out feedback for each step of the youth's performance until feedback is provided only for the step that helped the youth the most as indicated by the youth.

An example dialogue is provided for completion of the first of the nine Self-Control steps.

TP: What score did you give me for the first step?

Chelsey: I gave you a 100.

TP: Wow, 100! That is quite impressive. Did you record that in your rating form?

Chelsey: Yes, I recorded all of my ratings here (pointing to the appropriate areas on the form).

TP: Great. I also gave myself a high score. I gave myself a 90%. How did you come to give me 100%?

Chelsey: Well, you said "STOP" in a really loud voice, so I thought you should get a 100.

TP: I also thought our scores were similar, and I thought I was loud and stated it soon after I recognized I was at risk. I think I could have done a little better in stating it sooner because I actually waited until the image of drug use was in my head. Next time, I'll try to knock it off earlier. Would you do anything differently to put this step into your own style?

Chelsey: I think I would yell "screw it" instead of "stop" because I think it will work better for me.

TP: That's great. Anything that will work for you is good.

After reviewing all nine steps in this manner, the TP then reports a self-rating for likelihood of using drugs immediately prior to stating "stop," and another self-rating for the likelihood of using drugs after the trial was complete. Ratings are based on a 0 to 100% scale. Zero means the person who conducted the trial is not even thinking or imagining anything associated with drug use, whereas a 100 means the person is using drugs. The TP provides a rationale to the youth after each rating is disclosed, and then describes how the rating was derived. Risk of drug use increases as scores increase. Therefore, the ideal pre-likelihood rating will be less than 10 percentage points. If the pre-score is below 10, the post-rating will usually be 0. However, if the pre-likelihood rating is relatively high (e.g., 30 or above), the post-likelihood of drug use score will be hard to bring down to 0. Lower ratings usually result when the drug-associated thought or image is terminated early in the sequence. TPs provide this information to youth when providing scores in the modeled performance. In this way, youths learn the importance of terminating drug-associated thoughts or images early in the process. These ratings are recorded in the "Pre-Likelihood Rating" and "Post-Likelihood Rating" rows on the Self-Control Rating Form corresponding to the first trial. The following example shows how this information would be disseminated to a client.

TP: The likelihood of my using drugs just before I yelled "stop" was about 5 percent on this 0 to 100% scale because I yelled "stop" as soon as the thought started to occur. I didn't even let myself finish the sentence; otherwise, I would be increasing my likelihood of drug use. The likelihood of my using drugs after I finished this trial was a 0 because I wasn't even thinking of using after I finished the last step. Now, if I didn't terminate the drug-associated image early, my pre-likelihood score would have been higher, and it would have been harder to get my post-likelihood score down to 0. In order to get the post-likelihood score down to 0, you usually have to identify the trigger immediately, when it is a 10 or so.

The TP concludes the critique by disclosing which of the nine steps helped decrease the likelihood of engaging in drug use the most during the trial, including a rationale as to why. The number corresponding to the most helpful step is recorded in the appropriate box of the Self-Control Rating Form. Youth are encouraged to emphasize the step that is perceived to be most helpful when conducting their own trials in the future.

TP: I thought the first step was most helpful for me in getting my post-likelihood rating down to 0. I loved how I caught it early, and even though
it could be improved, it was still pretty good. This self-feedback lets me
know I need to emphasize this in the future.

**Youth's First Self-Control Trial for Drug Use Situation (Usually Youth
Alone)**   After the TP has modeled the nine Self-Control steps and the performance is critiqued, the youth tries to apply the nine steps to a drug use
situation. Significant others should be excused, even when youth indicate
the presence of others is acceptable. In some situations, TPs may decide it
is appropriate for adult significant others to observe youth trials, but only
after they have perfected the relevant skill sets and the youth indicates preference to have the adult significant other in the room. Youth may also prefer
to have their friends observe their trials, or have the TP assist these youth
in their own trials. This is appropriate, but again, only after the youth has
mastered the Self-Control steps.

The youth should be instructed to perform Self-Control for the drug
use situation just modeled by the TP. The youth should be instructed to
utilize the Self-Control Rating Form to prompt correct responding, and
to do so using the "think aloud" strategy. TPs additionally prompt youth
to perform components initially; for example, "State one negative consequence for yourself"; "Imagine telling someone who cares about you
what you did to avoid drug use." As the youth becomes more skilled,
TPs fade out this assistance. For the first step, yelling "stop," it may be
necessary to state the situation and prompt the youth to yell "stop!"; for
example, "You're in the park. Bob unexpectedly comes up to you and asks
if you want to smoke reefer. You say . . . go on, yell 'stop!'"). In the latter
example, the TP might use hand signals to prompt the youth in immediately yelling "stop!"

**Evaluation of Youth's First Self-Control Trial for Drug Use Situation
(Usually Youth Alone)**   The TP initiates a review of the youth's Self-Control
trial by asking what was generally liked about the youth's performance. In
this initial session, the youth's first trial is recorded under Trial 2 of the Self-
Control Rating Form, on both the youth and TP copies. Like the first trial
modeled by the TP, the date and a cue word are recorded to describe the

situation (e.g., paycheck) on each of the Self-Control Rating Forms. The youth is instructed to grade each of the nine steps using the 0 to 100% scale of correctness (0% = forgot to do the respective step, 100% = did the respective step perfectly). Youth scores are recorded on the youth's copy of the rating form, and TP scores on the TP's copy of the form. Once completed, the TP asks the youth for personal scores, and after each score is reported, the following feedback is provided by the TP: (a) the TP's score, (b) how youth and TP scores were consistent, (c) asking how the youth might do the step differently if it were performed again, and (d) suggesting methods of improving performance in the future.

The youth is queried to provide a rating of the likelihood of using drugs immediately prior to stating "stop!" and a rating for after the trial is completed, as well as rationales as to what influenced derivation of the ratings (0 = not even thinking of drugs, 100 = using drugs). If the post-rating is above 10%, the TP should inform youth that it is easier to reduce urges when the pre-likelihood rating is low. Therefore, the youth will need to catch the drug-associated thought or image earlier in the response chain. The TP and youth then use backward chaining to identify the earliest thought of drug use, and up to three additional trials are performed until the post-likelihood rating is reported to be less than 5%. All likelihood ratings are recorded in the recording form. For instance:

TP: What was the likelihood of your using drugs just before you yelled "stop," and after you were done with the trial? It would be good to know why you scored yourself in this way?

Chelsey: My pre-urge was probably about 25% because I wasn't even thinking about using. My post-urge rating was a 15%.

TP: Interesting, a 0% means you're not even thinking about drug use, so 25% would mean you're already thinking about it a bit, although you may not have taken any steps to actually get the drug, which is good. It's much easier to control these urges when you are about a 5 on the 0 to 100% scale. If you allow the urge to get too high, you're more likely to use because it's harder to get the score down to 0%. This makes sense because although you were able to get your percentage score down to 15%, it's still on your mind. Let's go back and see if there was an even earlier time when you could have stopped yourself from thinking about drugs. For instance, when you very first recognized the trigger. After we identify an earlier time to stop the urge or desire to use, we can do another trial, and see if we can get the pre-likelihood rating down to 5 or 10%.

Additional Trials Targeting Behavior Problems (Usually Youth Alone)   Drug use Self-Control trials should be alternated with trials that are focused on other problem behaviors. The trials use essentially the same procedures as drug use trials. Target behaviors often include impulsive problem behaviors (e.g., physical fight). Interestingly, these problem behaviors are also sometimes antecedents or triggers to drug use. For instance, after a physical fight, an adolescent may attempt to use drugs to remove aversive consequences caused by the fight (e.g., pain, anxious thoughts). The backward chaining procedure is used to identify contributing factors that can be addressed in Self-Control trials. The number of trials should be mutually determined between the TP and youth. However, it is important to alternate between drug use and other problem behaviors. The TP may also implement Self-Control trials impromptu, while reviewing other interventions (e.g., Stimulus Control, Level System), or the trials may be prescribed based on past experiences.

Future Trials (Usually Youth and Adult Significant Others, if Appropriate)   TPs utilize the Self-Control Therapist Prompting Checklist for Future Sessions (Exhibit 11.3) to guide all future Self-Control trials. These trials usually include the youth modeling the sequence of steps for drug use or other problem behaviors while the significant other provides encouragement. If the youth appears apprehensive or expresses reservations with the significant other being present, the significant other should be excused. Future sessions usually include one trial for a drug use situation and one trial for another problem behavior. However, the number of trials is dependent on difficulties experienced by youth between therapy sessions. Substance use or urges since last contact warrant extended drug trials, whereas clinical problems warrant extended trials as indicated. In future sessions, the TP does not typically model trials in their entirety (i.e., all steps of Self-Control). Assistance during trials is faded as youth become more adept at Self-Control. Similarly, the amount of feedback TPs provide to youth about their performance decreases as youths become more adept in self-evaluation and enhance their performance. Youth are generally instructed to perform no more than three trials in drug use and three trials relevant to other problems during each session. Adult significant others and friends may become involved in future trials, as they may be encouraged by the TP to prompt appropriate responding and descriptively praise the efforts of youths.

Concluding Remarks

The Self-Control intervention is extremely robust, as it is capable of managing a wide array of problem behaviors and may be used to assist youths in determining moments when behavioral skills may be optimally implemented. It is also theoretically sound, easy to implement, and comprehensive. Being transportable, it may be used during Stimulus Control (Chapter 10) as a skill to assist in refusing drugs, managing urges, and solving problems that may occur when reviewing at-risk stimuli. It may also be used to manage anger prior to conducting the Positive Request Procedure (Chapter 9), and prevent impulsive undesired behaviors that may have occurred in the recent past (e.g., vandalism, unprotected sex, swearing at a teacher).

Supporting Material for Chapter 11: Using Self-Control to Manage Negative Behaviors, Thoughts, and Feelings

Exhibit 11.1. Self-Control Therapist Prompting Checklist for Initial Session.

SELF-CONTROL
THERAPIST PROMPTING CHECKLIST
INITIAL SESSION

Youth ID: _____   Clinician: _____   Session #: _____   Session Date: _____

Materials Required

• Self-Control Rating Form (SCRF), 1 copy for therapist, 1 copy for youth

Note: Although this checklist will be utilized to target drug use primarily, Self-Control (SeC) is robust, and may be utilized to ameliorate various impulsive/disruptive behaviors, such as HIV risk behaviors, school truancy, aggression, arguments, etc.

Begin Time:_____

Rationale (youth & adult sig. others)

> • Review the following:
___ a. SeC assists in decreasing drug use & other problem behaviors.
___ b. SeC improves recognition of cues that signal urges or desires to use drugs or do things that may lead to problems.
___ c. SeC assists in learning to generate effective alternatives.
___ d. Solicit how SeC will be useful.
___ e. Explain how SeC is expected to be useful.
___ f. Solicit & answer questions.

Identification of At-Risk Situation for Drug Use (usually youth alone)

> • Explain each of the following:
___ a. Things in environment that lead to drug use called triggers.
___ b. Brainstorm drug use triggers for the youth.
___ c. Easier to stop drug urges or desires when these triggers are 1st recognized, before they intensify.
___ d. Practice trials will be performed "thinking out loud" to assist in managing triggers to drug use.
___ e. Solicit recent situation in which drug urges or use occurred.
     If resistant, choose item from Stimulus Control At-Risk list & use hypothetical situation.
___ f. Assist youth in identifying first thought of drug use in solicited situation (use backward chaining).

Modeling SeC Procedure for Identified Drug Use Situation (usually youth & adult sig. others)

___ a. Provide SCRF to youth.
___ b. Model 9 steps in SeC Rating Form for earliest trigger in solicited situation, including:
    ___ 1. Stop!
    ___ 2. State 1 neg. consequence of drug use for self.
    ___ 3. State 1 neg. consequence for friends/loved ones.
    ___ 4. 5 to 10 seconds of deep, rhythmic breathing and/or a muscle relaxation.
    ___ 5. State 4 drug-incompatible behaviors.
    ___ 6. Briefly evaluate some of the pros & cons for significant incompatible behaviors.
    ___ 7. Imagine doing 1 or more of the drug-incompatible behaviors.
    ___ 8. Imagine telling loved one about drug-incompatible behavior & person responding positively.
    ___ 9. State several + consequences that might result from drug-incompatible behavior.

Evaluation of Therapist's Performance for 1st Drug Use Trial (usually youth & adult sig. others)

___ a. Record trial 1 & date in youth & therapist versions of SCRF.
    ___ 1. Record word to describe solicited situation in youth & therapist versions of SCRF.
        • Youth scores therapist's performance on youth's copy of this rating form.
___ b. Instruct youth to grade each step in SCRF using 0 to 100% correctness scale.
___ c. After soliciting youth scores for each SeC step, do each of the following:
    ___ 1. Disclose therapist's score.
    ___ 2. State how youth & therapist scores were consistent.
    ___ 3. Ask what youth liked about modeled step.
    ___ 4. Ask what youth would do differently, if anything.
    ___ 5. Agree w/areas of youth's critique, & suggest methods of improving in future.
___ d. State likelihood of using drugs immediately prior to stating stop in the trial (0 = not thinking about drugs, 100 = using drug).
    ___ 1. Show where to record this rating in SCRF.
___ e. State likelihood of using drugs immediately after the last step in the trial (0 = not thinking about drugs, 100 = using drugs).
    ___ 1. Show how to record this rating in SCRF.
___ f. Disclose which step helped decrease likelihood of drug use most.
    ___ 1. Record # of most helpful step in SCRF.

Youth's 1st SeC Trial for Drug Use Situation (usually youth alone)

___ a. For most recent drug use situation, instruct youth to do following 9 steps:
    ___ 1. Stop!
    ___ 2. State 1 neg. consequence of drug use for self.
    ___ 3. State 1 neg. consequence for friends/loved ones.
    ___ 4. 5 to 10 seconds of deep, rhythmic breathing and/or a muscle relaxation.
    ___ 5. State 4 drug-incompatible behaviors.
    ___ 6. Briefly evaluate some of the pros & cons for significant incompatible behaviors.
    ___ 7. Imagine doing 1 or more of the drug-incompatible behaviors.
    ___ 8. Imagine telling loved one about drug-incompatible behavior & person responding positively.
    ___ 9. State several positive consequences that might result from drug-incompatible behavior.

- Provide the following assistance throughout the trial:
  - ___ a. Prompt youth in performing steps, fading assistance w/improved performance.
  - ___ b. Make suggestions to better performance.

Evaluation of Youth's 1st SeC Trial for Drug Use Situation (usually youth alone)

___ a. Instruct youth to complete SCRF, assisting as necessary.
  - Therapist scores youth's performance on therapist's copy of this rating form.
___ b. Instruct youth to grade each step & record in SCRF using 0 to 100% correct sale.
___ c. Solicit youth's scores, & after each score is reported perform the following:
  - ___ 1. Disclose therapist's score.
  - ___ 2. State how youth & therapist scores were consistent.
  - ___ 3. Ask what youth would do differently in the implementation of the step.
  - ___ 4. Express areas of agreement w/youth's critique, & suggest ways to improve in future.
___ d. Solicit youth's rating of likelihood of using drugs immediately prior to stating "stop" in the trial.
___ e. Solicit youth's rating of likelihood to using drugs immediately after performing last step in trial.
___ f. Solicit which step helped decrease likelihood to engage in drug use the most.
  - ___ 1. Encourage youth to emphasize this step when practicing SeC.

Identification of At-Risk Situation for Problem Behavior (usually youth alone)

- Explain each of the following:
___ a. There are things in environment that lead to problems, called triggers.
___ b. Brainstorm triggers to problems experienced by youth.
___ c. Easier to stop problems when triggers are 1st recognized, before they intensify.
___ d. Practice trials will be performed "thinking out loud" to assist in managing triggers to problems.
___ e. Solicit recent situation in which a problem was experienced.
  If youth is resistant, choose item from Environmental Control At-Risk list & use hypothetical situation.
___ f. Assist youth in identifying 1st thought leading to problem in solicited situation (use backward chaining).

Modeling 1st SeC Trial for Problem Behavior (usually youth & adult sig. others)

___ a. Model 9 steps on SCRF to prevent earliest trigger in solicited situation, including:
  - ___ 1. Stop!
  - ___ 2. State 1 neg. consequence of problem behavior for self.
  - ___ 3. State 1 neg. consequence of problem behavior for friends/loved ones.
  - ___ 4. 5 to 10 seconds of deep, rhythmic breathing and/or a muscle relaxation.
  - ___ 5. State 4 behaviors that are incompatible w/problem behavior.
  - ___ 6. Briefly evaluate some of the pros & cons for incompatible behaviors.
  - ___ 7. Imagine doing one or more of the incompatible behaviors.
  - ___ 8. Imagine telling friend/family member about having done the alternative behaviors.
  - ___ 9. State several positive consequences that might result from the alternative behaviors.

Evaluation of 1st Trial for Problem Behavior (usually youth & adult sig. others)

___ a. Record trial 3 & date in SCRF for youth & therapist.
___ b. Record cue word to describe situation in SCRF.

___ c. Solicit each of the youth's scores, & do the following for each step:
    ___ 1. Disclose therapist's score.
    ___ 2. State how youth & therapist scores were consistent.
    ___ 3. Ask what youth liked about the therapist's performance.
    ___ 4. Ask what youth would do differently, if anything.
    ___ 5. Agree w/areas of youth's critique, & suggest methods of improving future performance.
___ d. Solicit youth's rating of likelihood of avoiding problem immediately prior to stating "stop" in the trial.
___ e. Solicit youth's rating of likelihood of avoiding problem immediately after performing last step in the trial.
___ f. Solicit which step helped decrease likelihood of engaging in problem behavior.
    ___ 1. Encourage youth to emphasize this step when practicing self-control.

Youth's 1st SeC Trial for Problem Situation (usually youth alone)

___ a. For most recent problem situation, instruct youth to do following 9 steps:
    ___ 1. Stop!
    ___ 2. State 1 neg. consequence of problem behavior for self.
    ___ 3. State 1 neg. consequence of problem behavior for friends/loved ones.
    ___ 4. 5 to 10 seconds of deep, rhythmic breathing and/or a muscle relaxation.
    ___ 5. State 4 behaviors that are incompatible w/problem behavior.
    ___ 6. Briefly evaluate some of the pros & cons for incompatible behaviors.
    ___ 7. Imagine doing one or more of the incompatible behaviors.
    ___ 8. Imagine telling friend/family member about having done the alternative behaviors.
    ___ 9. State several positive consequences that might result from the alternative behaviors.
  • Provide the following assistance throughout the trial:
    ___a. Prompt youth in performing steps, fading assistance w/improved performance.
    ___b. Make suggestions to better performance.

Evaluation of Youth's 1st SeC Trial for Problem Situation (usually youth alone)

___ a. Instruct youth to complete SCRF, assisting as necessary.
    Therapist scores youth's performance on therapist's copy of this rating form.
___ b. Solicit youth's scores, & after each score is reported perform the following:
    ___ 1. Disclose therapist's score.
    ___ 2. State how youth & therapist scores were consistent.
    ___ 3. Ask what youth liked about the performance.
    ___ 4. Ask what youth would do differently in the implementation of the step.
    ___ 5. Express areas of agreement w/youth's critique, & suggest ways of improving.
___ c. Solicit youth's rating of likelihood of doing problem behavior prior to stating "stop" in the trial.
___ d. Solicit youth's rating of likelihood of doing problem behavior after last step in the trial.
___ e. Solicit which step helped increase likelihood of avoiding problems.
    ___ 1. Encourage youth to emphasize this step when practicing self-control.
      • Additional trials are completed at discretion of therapist, but not recorded for adherence.
      • Situations for additional trials often come from at-risk list in Environmental Control or Behavioral Goals.
      • Can do additional trials w/adolescent or adult significant others at therapist's discretion (usually sig. others are faded into room).

Youth's Assessment of Helpfulness of the Intervention

___a.   After stating youth should not feel obligated to provide high scores, as an honest assessment helps better address youth needs, solicit how helpful youth thought intervention was using 7-point scale:
7 = extremely helpful, **6** = very helpful, **5** = somewhat helpful, **4** = not sure, **3** = somewhat unhelpful, **2** = very unhelpful, **1** = extremely unhelpful

Record Youth's Rating Here:_____

___ b.   Solicit how rating was derived & methods of improving intervention in future.

Therapist's Rating of Youth's Compliance With Intervention

___ a.   Disclose therapist's rating of youth's compliance using the following 7-point scale: **7** = extremely compliant, **6** = very compliant, **5** = somewhat compliant, **4** = neutral, **3** = somewhat noncompliant, **2** = very noncompliant, **1** = extremely noncompliant
• Factors that contribute to compliance ratings are:
    • Attendance
    • Participation & conduct in session
    • Homework completion

Record Therapist's Rating of Youth's Compliance Here:_____

___ b.   Disclose youth's compliance rating.
___ c.   Explain how rating was derived & methods of improving performance in future.

End Time: _____

Exhibit 11.2. Self-Control Rating Form.

SELF-CONTROL RATING FORM

	Record details to describe each step	Record details to describe each step	Record details to describe each step	Record details to describe each step
	Trial # 1	Trial # 2	Trial # 3	Trial # 4
	Date: _____	Date: _____	Date: _____	Date: _____
	Word to describe situation _____	Word to describe situation _____	Word to describe situation _____	Word to describe situation _____
1. Stop!	Forgot to Perfect (0 to 100) =	Forgot to Perfect (0 to 100) =	Forgot to Perfect (0 to 100) =	Forgot to Perfect (0 to 100) =
2. One bad thing for self	Forgot to Perfect (0 to 100) =	Forgot to Perfect (0 to 100) =	Forgot to Perfect (0 to 100) =	Forgot to Perfect (0 to 100) =
3. One bad thing for others	Forgot to Perfect (0 to 100) =	Forgot to Perfect (0 to 100) =	Forgot to Perfect (0 to 100) =	Forgot to Perfect (0 to 100) =
4. Relax	Forgot to Perfect (0 to 100) =	Forgot to Perfect (0 to 100) =	Forgot to Perfect (0 to 100) =	Forgot to Perfect (0 to 100) =
5. State 4 solutions	1. 2. 3. 4. Forgot to Perfect (0 to 100) =	1. 2. 3. 4. Forgot to Perfect (0 to 100) =	1. 2. 3. 4. Forgot to Perfect (0 to 100) =	1. 2. 3. 4. Forgot to Perfect (0 to 100) =
6. Briefly evaluate some of the pros & cons for significant incompatible behaviors	1. 2. 3. 4. Forgot to Perfect (0 to 100) =	1. 2. 3. 4. Forgot to Perfect (0 to 100) =	1. 2. 3. 4. Forgot to Perfect (0 to 100) =	1. 2. 3. 4. Forgot to Perfect (0 to 100) =
7. Imagine doing 1 or more solution(s)	Performance (0 to 100) =	Performance (0 to 100) =	Performance (0 to 100) =	Performance (0 to 100) =
8. Imagine telling someone about using the solution brainstormed	Performance (0 to 100) =	Performance (0 to 100) =	Performance (0 to 100) =	Performance (0 to 100) =

9. State positive things that will happen as a result of using the solution	Performance (0 to 100) =	Performance (0 to 100) =	Performance (0 to 100) =	Performance (0 to 100) =
Pre-Likelihood rating	Not aware to using or doing problem (0 to 100) =	Not aware to using or doing problem (0 to 100) =	Not aware to using or doing problem (0 to 100) =	Not aware to using or doing problem (0 to 100) =
Post-Likelihood rating	Not aware to using or doing problem (0 to 100) =	Not aware to using or doing problem (0 to 100) =	Not aware to using or doing problem (0 to 100) =	Not aware to using or doing problem (0 to 100) =
Step that helped the most & why it helped the most				

Exhibit 11.3. Self-Control Therapist Prompting Checklist for Future Sessions.

SELF-CONTROL

THERAPIST PROMPTING CHECKLIST

FUTURE SESSIONS

Youth ID: _____ Clinician: _____ Session #: _____ Session Date: _____

Materials Required

• Self-Control Rating Form (SCRF)

Note: Although this checklist will be utilized to target drug use primarily, Self-Control (SeC) is robust, & may be utilized to ameliorate various impulsive/disruptive behaviors, such as HIV risk behaviors, school truancy, symptoms associated w/mental health disorders, aggression, arguments, aversive thoughts associated w/traumatic experiences, etc.

Begin Time:_____

Reviewing Drug Use & Problem Behavior Trials (usually youth & sig. other)

___ a. Solicit a recent drug use or problem situation.

___ b. For most recent drug use or problem situation, instruct youth to do following 9 steps:

    ___ 1. Stop!

    ___ 2. State 1 neg. consequence of drug use or other problem behavior for self.

    ___ 3. State 1 neg. consequence of drug use or other problem behavior for friends/loved ones.

    ___ 4. 5 to 10 seconds of deep, rhythmic breathing and/or a muscle relaxation.

    ___ 5. State 4 behaviors that are incompatible w/drug use or other problem behavior.

    ___ 6. Briefly evaluate some of the pros & cons for incompatible behaviors.

    ___ 7. Imagine doing one or more of the incompatible behaviors.

    ___ 8. Imagine telling friend/family member about having done the alternative behaviors.

    ___ 9. State several positive consequences that might result from the alternative behaviors.

    • Provide the following assistance throughout the trial:

    ___ a. Prompt youth in performing steps, fading assistance w/improved performance.

    ___ b. Make suggestions to better performance.

    ___ c. Ask what was generally liked about youth's performance.

    ___ d. Instruct youth to complete SCRF (therapist completes own copy).

    ___ e. Solicit youth's scores, & after each score is reported, perform the following:

        ___ 1. Disclose therapist's score.

        ___ 2. State how youth & therapist scores were consistent.

        ___ 3. Ask what youth liked about the performance.

        ___ 4. Ask what youth would do to enhance scores.

        ___ 5. Express areas of agreement w/youth's critique, & suggest how to improve performance.

___ c. Solicit youth's rating of likelihood to perform undesired behavior immediately before stating stop in trial.

___ d. Solicit youth's rating of likelihood to perform undesired behavior after last step in trial.

___ e. Solicit which step decreased likelihood of engaging in undesired behavior the most.

Youth's Assessment of Helpfulness of the Intervention

___ a. After stating youth should not feel obligated to provide high scores, as an honest assessment helps better address youth needs, solicit how helpful youth thought intervention was using 7-point scale:

7 = extremely helpful, **6** = very helpful, **5** = somewhat helpful, **4** = not sure, **3** = somewhat unhelpful, **2** = very unhelpful, **1** = extremely unhelpful

Record Youth's Rating Here:_____

___ b. Solicit how rating was derived, & methods of improving intervention in future.

Therapist's Rating of Youth's Compliance with Intervention

___ a. Disclose therapist's rating of youth's compliance using 7-point scale:

7 = extremely compliant, **6** = very compliant, **5** = somewhat compliant, **4** = neutral, **3** = somewhat noncompliant, **2** = very noncompliant, **1** = extremely noncompliant

- Factors that contribute to compliance ratings are:
  - Attendance
  - Participation & conduct in session
  - Homework completion

Record Therapist's Rating of Youth's Compliance Here:_____

___ b. Disclose youth's compliance rating.
___ c. Explain how rating was derived & methods of improving performance in future.

End Time: _____

CHAPTER 12

Gaining Employment

Overview

It is often difficult for youth who have evidenced problems with illicit drugs or other problem behaviors to obtain jobs that pay well and are consistent with their treatment plan. Some are unable to obtain gainful employment because they have prematurely withdrawn from school, are immature, have poor social skills with adults, or have not obtained technical or job-specific skills. Because of these difficulties, many youth often end up unemployed or working in settings that contribute to their risk of using illicit drugs and alcohol, such as working side-by-side with unqualified adults who have substance abuse problems. Many youth remain underemployed because they establish a poor record of employment due to not showing up for scheduled shifts, performing poorly when working, or coming to work intoxicated or high. Research indicates that individuals who use cocaine or marijuana more often quit their current jobs than those who do not use these drugs (Hoffman, Dufur, & Huang, 2007). Many of the aforementioned problems are directly targeted in Family Behavior Therapy (FBT). However, in addition to these considerations, we have also found that youth have poor "job-getting skills." For instance, they do not know how to assertively seek employment and often lack the skills or confidence required to perform well during preemployment interviews. Being unemployed or underemployed contributes to low self-worth and makes it difficult for youth to financially support themselves or their family, particularly when youth have dropped out of school. Poor self-esteem contributes to stress and boredom, which are highly associated with drug use and other problem behaviors.

Therefore, Job-Getting Skills Training is an abbreviated application of Job Club, which is one of the most successful job-getting programs developed (Azrin, Philip, Thienes-Hontos, & Besalel, 1981). This intervention is designed to teach youth to effectively request job interviews with potential employers and prepare them for job interviews. Through modeling and behavior rehearsal, youth learn to be motivated to obtain employment and solicit job interviews. After job-getting skills are performed effectively in simulated scenarios, youth call potential employers and request interviews in the presence of their treatment providers (TPs). Youth also learn how to present themselves favorably during job interviews.

Goals for Intervention

> Motivate youth to pursue employment.

> Teach youth to effectively request job interviews from potential employers.

> Teach youth to obtain employment.

Materials Required

> Job-Getting Skills Training Therapist Prompting Checklist for Initial Session (Exhibit 12.1)

> Interviewing Skills Worksheet (Exhibit 12.2)

> Job-Getting Skills Training Therapist Prompting Checklist for Future Sessions (Exhibit 12.3)

Procedural Steps for Implementation

Initial Session

Rationale for Job Interview Solicitation (Youth and Adolescent and Adult Significant Others)   As indicated in the Job-Getting Skills Training Therapist Prompting Checklist for Initial Session (Exhibit 12.1), the youth is provided a rationale for the Job-Getting Skills Training by the TP. The rationale begins with a very brief assessment to determine if the youth is interested in getting a satisfying job. If so, the youth is asked to indicate how a satisfying job would be important, and the TP reinforces statements that suggest a job is important. It is often helpful to solicit components of a "dream job" or career, including the benefits of such a career. Youth are often only looking to gain temporary employment and are not interested in a "dream job." In these cases, it is important to inform such youth that temporary jobs are practice for ideal jobs. It is also helpful to inquire as to how dream jobs are acquired, including solutions to obstacles that might interfere with attainment of the dream job. These queries are designed to instill motivation to pursue employment, which is often lacking in youth who are referred for treatment. Youth are told Job Getting is designed to assist in preparing them for job interviews, including skills that are relevant to obtaining job interviews. It is helpful to remind youth that classified advertisements account for only a small percentage of the jobs that are available and that it is important to practice alternative job-getting strategies, such as telephone networking with potential employers. Youth are told that Job Getting has been successful in achieving employment for others, and they are asked to indicate how Job Getting would be helpful to them. The TP asks for questions from the youth and provides answers, as indicated in the following dialogue.

TP: Would you be interested in finding a satisfying job?

Jasmine: Yeah, I need some extra money, but I can't seem to get one 'cause they say I'm too young.

TP: You are young, but we can turn that into a strength. We'll talk about some ways to find jobs, but before we do that, tell me why a satisfying job would be important to you.

Jasmine: If I had a job, I could get my own apartment or at least my own car.

TP: So it seems like a job might get you extra mobility and independence. How else might it be helpful?

Jasmine: Lots of things. Like I could get my girlfriend nice things, and get enough money to take trips to places I want to visit.

TP: Fantastic! Additional income is always a big help, and travel is very important to growth. What other things would a satisfying job provide you?

Jasmine: Well, I could give my mom some money for rent until my apartment comes through.

Mom: Amen! I was waiting to see if she'd say that!

TP: That's great. I don't often hear kids look out for their mothers that way. You should be very proud of her. What would your dream job or career be like, Jasmine?

Jasmine: I always wanted to be a carpenter. My father left me a whole bunch of tools, but I never use them. It would be great to own my own business.

TP: He'd be very proud to hear that, I bet.

Mom: Her father really loved her so much, and used to tell me that he couldn't wait to some day take her out to job sites with him when she got older.

Jasmine: What would you need to do to make this a reality, Jasmine?

Jasmine: I think most people learn by doing and pass their proficiency test for the state. I don't really know anyone for that, but there are vocational schools where I could do that, too.

TP: Maybe you could do a little of both. We could find someone who would take you under his or her wing, while you attend classes. Maybe we could find someone who could pay your way through school.

Jasmine: They do that?

TP: Sure, it happens all the time. We just need to present this as a plan before you're hired. If you promise to work for a certain number of years, I can't see why the person wouldn't see that as not being an advantage.

Jasmine: That would be nice.

TP: I love your attitude. The first step in acquiring gainful employment is getting an interview with a potential employer. Many people do this by looking through the paper's classified advertisements. However, this represents only a small percentage of job positions available, as many employers don't advertise their positions in the paper, and many jobs are created only after an outstanding applicant comes to their attention. This Job-Getting Skills Training involves teaching individuals like you to obtain job interviews from potential employers. By getting a job interview, you are no longer likely to be treated like just another number. You have an opportunity to show off your skills. Job-Getting Skills Training also helps individuals learn how to best present themselves during interviews. This intervention has been successful with other people your age, and I think it will work really well for you because you have a strong work ethic. How do you think this intervention will be able to assist you?

Modeling Job Interview Solicitation (Youth and Adolescent and Adult Significant Others)   After discussing the potential benefits of Job Getting with the youth and answering any questions, the TP models how to ask for a job interview with a potential employer. Prior to modeling the solicitation of a job interview, the youth should be provided a copy of the Job Interviewing Skills Worksheet (Exhibit 12.2) to prompt correct responding during Job Getting role-plays. The Interviewing Skills Worksheet contains simple, step-by-step prompts that help youth prepare to ask for a job interview, and also assists them as they make the actual phone calls to request an interview. The TP then models how to ask for a job interview, instructing the youth to pretend to be an office manager or secretary answering the telephone for a potential employer. The potential employer may be an ex-employer of the youth or a business for which the youth is interested in working. This permits the TP an opportunity to manage potential problems that are enacted by the youth. TPs are usually able to manage such resistance with experience, practice, and preparation, which further assists in motivating youths to feel confident in Job Getting.

First, the TP calls the potential employer (i.e., youth in role-play) and provides basic salutary remarks. After an introduction, the TP solicits the name of the manager or supervisor. Once this is accomplished, the TP asks to speak with this person. The youth is told that if the person who answers the phone asks why the manager is desired, the response should be, "It's personal." Youth should not disclose that they are calling for a job interview to a secretary or other employee who first answers the phone because they may state that there are no jobs available, and the youth will not have an opportunity to talk directly with the supervisor or manager. Speaking directly with a supervisor or manager is critical because the youth will be in a better position to ask these persons about potential job opportunities that might be available at other companies. Sometimes it helps to explain to youth how getting a job is "personal," as youth sometimes feel insecure in not disclosing that they are looking for jobs. If the manager is unavailable, the youth should request a good time to call back, but not leave a message for the manager because these messages are often not returned.

The following dialogue demonstrates the TP calling for an interview, with the youth pretending to be a receptionist.

TP: Hello, my name is Jasmine. Who is the manager on shift today?

Jasmine: That's Kevin.

TP: And what is Kevin's last name?

Jasmine: His last name is Kevin, Kevin Kevin.

TP: Great, may I speak with Mr. Kevin, please?

Jasmine: Why do you want to talk with him?

TP: It's personal.

Jasmine: He is not in right now. Can I take a message?

TP: No, that's fine, thank you. Is there a good time that I can call back and speak with him?

If the manager is able to come to the phone, the TP provides an introduction and thanks the manager for accepting the call. The interviewer (TP) then lists a few personal strengths and/or qualifications, and requests an in-person interview to further discuss personal qualifications and strengths. Strengths that are often reported include something about having a strong work ethic, being trustworthy, being passionate about work, or being assertive. Two or three qualifications are usually drafted prior to the call and are specific to the job position or workplace. These might include outstanding math skills, ability to type quickly, physical strength, ability to operate basic relevant equipment, and so on. Thus, if done smoothly, a job interview is never requested. That is, the only thing that is requested is to meet in person to discuss the candidate's strengths and qualifications. Of course, most employers are able to recognize that the interviewee is attempting to gain employment, but in a sophisticated and unique manner. If the manager is not able to meet due to a lack of job opportunities, the interviewee attempts to schedule the meeting anyway in case a job opportunity should become available in the future. If the manager still cannot arrange an interview, the interviewee solicits potential employers who may be hiring. If the manager is aware of potential employers, the youth asks if it would be fine to indicate that the manager referred the interviewee to this employer (or business). It is sometimes important to inform youth that this is an example of networking, and that people usually like to have others indicate that they are being referred by them because it shows the persons they're referred to that the persons making the referral trust them. The youth would later call the referral and indicate that the respective manager referred the youth to call.

The following dialogue exemplifies the TP making it past the receptionist and getting an opportunity to speak with the manager of a carpentry business, Mr. Kevin.

TP: Hello, Mr. Kevin. My name is Jasmine. Thank you for taking the time to speak with me. I'm a very motivated, loyal, and hard-working person with some experience working in carpentry. I was hoping you could arrange to meet with me at your earliest convenience.

Jasmine: I am sorry to say that I'm not hiring anybody right now. That's why you're calling, right?

TP: Could I meet with you anyway, just in case something should open up later? I really think you'd find that I have a lot to offer. I'd also like to talk about my future and a few things I think I could do to help your company.

Jasmine: Right now is not a good time for me. I just don't have time to meet with you.

TP: Okay, I understand. May I ask, do you know of any other employers who may be interested in someone with my qualifications?

Jasmine: I have a friend who is looking for a young person like you to train. Maybe he could talk with you.

TP: Thank you. This is wonderful news. After I get his number, is it all right if I tell him that you referred me to him?

Youth Role-Play of Job Interview Solicitation (Youth and Adolescent and Adult Significant Others)   After the TP models how to request a job interview, the youth is instructed to attempt to ask for a job interview, with the TP playing an accommodating and compliant potential employer. It is important for the TP to be compliant during the role-play to build the youth's self-efficacy in requesting job opportunities. To assist in this endeavor, the youth should be instructed to utilize the Interviewing Skills Worksheet to prompt correct responding. It may be necessary to instruct the youth to make several attempts until the steps are executed with ease. The TP may also conduct further modeling throughout the process whenever indicated. Of course, the TP will gradually phase out assistance as the youth's performance improves. It is also very appropriate to instruct significant others to role-play the job interview solicitation.

TP:	I would now like you to go through the steps I just modeled in requesting a job interview. We'll pretend I'm the office manager answering the phone, and later I'll pretend to be a potential employer. Who do you want me to be?
Jasmine:	A carpenter.
TP:	Sure. Remember to refer to your Interviewing Skills Worksheet to help you go through the steps, and take your time, as you're not expected to memorize them. Even later, you'll always be able to use the worksheet you have in your hand, as the people on the other end of the telephone line won't know you have it there. You're going to be on the phone, so feel free to read it as you go. Let's write a couple of strengths and qualifications in the spaces by the fourth step so you're prepared to smoothly list them off when you get there in the phone interview.
Jasmine:	Like you said, I'm a hard worker and dependable, and my dad taught me to do some easy stuff.
TP:	Great, I wrote that stuff here. So, ring, ring. Hi, this is Larry from Joe's carpentry.
Jasmine:	Hello, this is Jasmine. Is Joe working there today?
TP:	Great stuff, Jasmine. Good recognizing that Joe is probably the boss. Let me get into the role. Yes, he is. Hold on a second. Yes, this is Joe. How can I help you?
Jasmine:	I'm a hard worker and dependable. I was looking for a job.
TP:	Remember to just ask if you can come in and talk with him about yourself. Go ahead from the top. Hi, I'm Joe.

Jasmine: Oh yeah. Hi, Joe. I'm a hard worker and very dependable. I was wondering if I could come in and talk to you more about myself. It would only take a few minutes.

TP: Are you wanting to get into carpentry?

Jasmine: Yes, I am.

TP: Excellent, Jasmine. Let me go back into the role. Sure. Do you know where I'm located?

The role-play would continue in this manner, with the TP praising the youth for doing the steps and assisting whenever indicated. It is important to consider potential nervousness of youth, as similar efforts may have resulted in rejection. Thus, the TP should avoid commentary about signs of nervousness and provide ample encouragement and praise throughout the role-play. It is important to completely avoid all critical remarks. Significant others are often instructed to praise efforts of youths and potentially attempt job-getting role-plays themselves, whenever appropriate.

Youth Job Interview Solicitation With Potential Employer (Youth and Adolescent and Adult Significant Others)   Once the youth and, potentially, the significant others have successfully solicited job interviews during two or three role-plays, it is important to instruct them to attempt such job solicitation interviews with potential employers utilizing the Job Interviewing Skills Worksheet. The TP provides verbal prompts in correct responding throughout the interview, and may also point to specific instructions in the Interviewing Skills Worksheet if the youth gets lost during the telephone interview.

Prior to making calls, youth should identify potential employers in telephone books or based on personal knowledge of businesses in their area that might be appropriate. It is best to start with employers who are geographically far away from the youth's residence to assist in gaining practice with less desirable jobs. Jobs that are particularly desired should be the last ones called. The youth will need to have a pen or pencil to record potential leads. Youth are often very nervous in making these calls; thus, it is particularly important to keep critique of these telephone interviews positive, avoiding suggestions unless specifically requested. If the youth hangs up due to nervousness or embarrassment during an interview, immediately reinforce positive actions and tell the youth the interview was good practice.

Preparation for Job Interview (Youth and Adolescent and Adult Significant Others)   It is important to prepare youth for job interviews. Along these lines, the TP first queries the youth's understanding of how to properly dress for a job interview. This provides an assessment of the youth's insights into dress codes, as well as the youth's receptivity to dressing formally (suit and/or tie for men, suit or dress for women), which is highly encouraged. They are encouraged to conservatively hide tattoos and take off nose rings, hats, and ill-fitting, baggy, or worn clothing. Conservative colors are also recommended, such as gray, black, and blue tones. Youth are also encouraged to avoid gaudy jewelry and makeup.

It is important to assess the youth's understanding of what to say during the interview. Generally, youths are encouraged to keep conversation focused on youth's strengths, being honest, expressing passion about various opportunities, and stating positive qualities about past employers and the potential employer. Youth are also advised to avoid derogatory aspersions about others. General interviewing strategies should be extensively and spontaneously role-played to assist the youth in being comfortable during the interviewing process. Responses to a prescribed list of common interview questions listed in the Prepare for Common Interview Questions section of the Interviewing Skills Worksheet are also role-played. Appropriate responses to interview questions should be reviewed prior to role-playing.

TPs should assign youth to practice job-interviewing skills with family members and seek job interviews until a job is obtained. They should be forewarned that the strategy of soliciting job interviews is likely to be successful only when a high number of calls are attempted.

Future Sessions (Youth and Adolescent and Adult Significant Others)   Future sessions that review this intervention follow the steps outlined in the Job-Getting Skills Training Therapist Prompting Checklist for Future Sessions (Exhibit 12.3). Job Getting may be utilized in future sessions to assess skills during calls to employers and improve skills through practice. It is also important to continuously review in-person job interviewing skills, including simulated job interviews.

Concluding Remarks

Job-Getting Skills Training is a skill-based intervention with demonstrated effectiveness in helping youth successfully obtain employment by providing them with strategies to assist in obtaining job interviews and performing well once interviews are obtained. Youth value these basic skills. Indeed, many gain a sense of self-confidence as they apply these skills to interviews. It is important, however, that youth practice making telephone calls to potential employers during their intervention sessions so TPs will have opportunities to descriptively praise them and support them through the process, as many will be nervous and give up quite easily without such encouragement. After the first call is made to a potential employer, it will be very important to avoid critique. That is, no suggestions should be offered regarding changes in behavior to raise self-efficacy to attempt more telephone calls, which is the key to eventual employment. If the youth gets nervous and hangs up, he or she should be praised for making an effort, and simply try with another potential employer.

Supporting Material for Chapter 12: Gaining Employment

Exhibit 12.1. Job-Getting Skills Training Therapist Prompting Checklist for Initial Session.

JOB-GETTING SKILLS TRAINING
THERAPIST PROMPTING CHECKLIST
INITIAL SESSION

Youth ID: _____ Clinician: _____ Session #:_____ Session Date:_____

Materials Required

  • Interviewing Skills Worksheet (ISW)

Begin Time:_____

Rationale for Job Interview Solicitation (youth & adol. & adult sig. others)

___a. Ensure youth is interested in obtaining a satisfying job.
___b. Query why a satisfying job would be important.
___c. Solicit components of a dream job or career.
___d. Solicit benefits of a dream job or career.
___e. Solicit methods of making the dream job or career happen.
___f. Determine solutions to obstacles involved in obtaining a "dream job."
  • Problem-solve if necessary.
___g. State JG is designed to obtain job interviews.
___h. State JG helps individuals learn how to present themselves well during interviews.
___i. State JG has been successful w/others.
___j. State why JG is expected to be particularly effective w/youth.
___k. Solicit questions and provide answers as indicated.

Modeling Solicitation of Job Interview (youth & adol. & adult sig. others)

  • Provide youth a copy of ISW.
  • Model the following telephone interviewing components:
___a. Introduce self.
___b. Solicit name of manager on shift.
___c. Ask to speak w/manager.
  ___ 1. If asked what it is regarding, state it is "personal."
  ___ 2. If unavailable, disclose that you will call back (do not leave a message to call back).
___d. When manager answers do the following:
  ___ 1. Introduce self.
  ___ 2. Thank manager for taking call.
  ___ 3. List a few qualifications or personal strengths.
  ___ 4. Solicit an in-person interview to discuss qualifications.

___e. If manager can't arrange interview, attempt to schedule later time.

___f. If not scheduled, solicit referral to other employers & verify it's O.K. to reference manager.

Youth Role-Play of Job Interview Solicitation (youth & adol. & adult sig. others)

___a. Instruct youth to solicit interview w/MHP pretending to be potential employer via phone using ISW.

___b. Prompt or descriptively praise youth for performing each of the following:

    ___ 1. Introduce self.

    ___ 2. Solicit manager on shift.

    ___ 3. Ask to speak w/ manager.

        ___a. If asked what it is regarding, state it is "personal."

        ___b. If unavailable, disclose that you will call back.

    ___ 4. When manager answers, do the following:

        ___a. Introduce self.

        ___b. Thank manager for taking call.

        ___c. List a few qualifications or personal strengths.

        ___d. Solicit an in-person interview.

            ___i.   If manager can't arrange interview, attempt to schedule later time.

            ___ii. If not scheduled, solicit referral to other similar employers.

Youth Job Interview Solicitation w/ Potential Employer (youth & adol. & adult sig. others)

___a. Instruct youth to solicit interview w/potential employer via phone using ISW.

___b. Prompt youth in performing each of the following steps, if not initiated by youth:

    ___ 1. Introduce self.

    ___ 2. Solicit manager on shift.

    ___ 3. Ask to speak w/ the manager.

        ___a. If asked what it is regarding, state it is "personal."

        ___b. If unavailable, disclose that you will call back.

    ___ 4. When manager answers do the following:

        ___a. Introduce self.

        ___b. Thank manager for taking call.

        ___c. List a few qualifications or personal strengths.

        ___d. Solicit an in-person interview.

            ___ i.   If manager can't arrange interview, attempt to schedule later time.

            ___ ii. If not scheduled, solicit referral to other similar employers.

___c. Descriptively praise youth after call is completed.

Preparation for Job Interview (youth & adol. & adult sig. others)

___a. Solicit youth's understanding of how to dress for job interview, & assist when appropriate.

___b. Indicate usually important to dress formally/conservatively (suit and/or tie for men, suit or dress for women).

___c. Indicate to hide tattoos; don't wear nose rings, hats, torn, ill-fitting, baggy, or worn clothing, or gaudy jewelry.

___d. Solicit youth's understanding of what to say during interview, and assist when appropriate.

    • Generally keep conversation focused on youth's strengths, being honest, being passionate about opportunities, stating positive qualities of employer and agency.

    • Don't speak derogatorily about other employers or other people.

___e.   Review responses to the following list of common interview questions w/youth, including potential solutions.

     ___ 1. Tell me about yourself.

     ___ 2. Why do you want to work here?

     ___ 3. What are some of your strengths and weaknesses?

     ___ 4. Why did you leave your last job?

     ___ 5. Why should we hire you?

       • State if offer is made youth should indicate happiness w/offer, but that hoping for more given personal strengths and qualifications.

Youth's Assessment of Helpfulness of the Intervention

___a.   After stating youth should not feel obligated to provide high scores, as an honest assessment helps better address youth needs, solicit how helpful youth thought intervention was using the following 7-point scale:

7 = extremely helpful, **6** = very helpful, **5** = somewhat helpful, **4** = not sure, **3** = somewhat unhelpful, **2** = very unhelpful, **1** = extremely unhelpful

     • **Record Youth's Rating Here:_____**

___b.   Solicit how rating was derived, and methods of improving intervention in future.

Therapist's Rating of Youth's Compliance With Intervention

___a.   Disclose therapist's rating of youth's compliance using the following 7-point scale: **7** = extremely compliant, **6** = very compliant, **5** = somewhat compliant, **4** = neutral, **3** = somewhat noncompliant, **2** = very noncompliant, **1** = extremely noncompliant

     • Factors that contribute to compliance ratings are:

     • Attendance

     • Participation and conduct in session

     • Homework completion

     • **Record Therapist's Rating of Youth's Compliance Here:_____**

___b.   Disclose youth's compliance rating.

___c.   Explain how rating was derived, and methods of improving performance in future.

End Time:_____

Exhibit 12.2. Job Interviewing Skills Worksheet.

JOB INTERVIEWING SKILLS WORKSHEET

Instructions: Follow these steps when attempting to set up an interview with an employer over the phone.

1. Introduce yourself.

2. Ask the name of the manager on shift.

3. Ask to speak with the manager.
If asked why or what call is regarding, answer "it's personal."
If manager is unavailable, state that "you'll call back."

4. **When manager answers, do the following:**
Introduce self.
Thank manager for taking call (& state if someone referred you).
State a few qualifications or personal strengths:

a. _____

b. _____

c. _____

Ask to schedule an interview to further discuss qualifications.
a. If scheduled: state you're looking forward to the interview.
b. If manager can't arrange interview: attempt to schedule a later time.
c. If manager can't schedule later time: ask for referral.

Prepare for Common Interview Questions

1. Tell me about yourself.

2. Why do you want to work here?

3. What are some of your strengths and weaknesses?

4. Why did you leave your last job?

5. Why should we hire you?

Exhibit 12.3. Job-Getting Skills Training Therapist Prompting Checklist for Future Sessions.

JOB-GETTING SKILLS TRAINING

THERAPIST PROMPTING CHECKLIST

FUTURE SESSIONS

Youth ID: _____ Clinician: _____ Session #:_____ Session Date:_____

Materials Required

- Interviewing Skills Worksheet (ISW)

Begin Time:_____

Youth Solicits Interview With Therapist's Assistance (youth & adol. & adult sig. others)

___a. Instruct youth to solicit an interview w/a potential employer over the telephone utilizing the ISW as a guide.

___b. Assist youth in performing each of the following:

    ___ 1. Introduce self.

    ___ 2. Solicit manager on shift.

    ___ 3. Ask to speak w/manager.

        ___a. If asked what it is regarding, state it is "personal."

        ___b. If unavailable, disclose that you will call back.

    ___ 4. When manager answers do the following:

        ___a. Introduce self.

        ___b. Thank manager for taking call.

        ___c. List a few qualifications or personal strengths.

        ___d. Solicit an in-person interview to further discuss qualifications.

            ___ i. If manager can't arrange interview, attempt to schedule later time.

            ___ ii. If not scheduled, solicit referral to other similar employer & verify it's O.K. to reference the manager.

___c. Review things to focus on during job interviews, as well as things to avoid during job interviews.

Youth's Assessment of Helpfulness of the Intervention

___a. After stating youth should not feel obligated to provide high scores, as an honest assessment helps better address youth needs, solicit how helpful youth thought intervention was using the following 7-point scale:

7 = extremely helpful, **6** = very helpful, **5** = somewhat helpful, **4** = not sure, **3** = somewhat unhelpful, **2** = very unhelpful, **1** = extremely unhelpful

- **Record Youth's Rating Here:_____**

___b. Solicit how rating was derived, and methods of improving intervention in future.

Therapist's Rating of Youth's Compliance With Intervention

___a. Disclose therapist's rating of youth's compliance using 7-point scale:
7 = extremely compliant, **6** = very compliant, **5** = somewhat compliant, **4** = neutral, **3** = somewhat noncompliant, **2** = very noncompliant, **1** = extremely noncompliant
 - Factors that contribute to compliance ratings are:
 - Attendance
 - Participation and conduct in session
 - Homework completion
 - **Record Therapist's Rating of Youth's Compliance Here:_____**

___b. Disclose youth's compliance rating.

___c. Explain how rating was derived, and methods of improving performance in future.

End Time:_____

CHAPTER 13

Concluding Treatment and Planning for Success

Overview

Family Behavior Therapy (FBT) usually lasts between 4 and 6 months, and its timing of termination is mutually determined between youth, the youth's parents, and treatment provider (TP). Treatment termination is ideally based on the youth's demonstration of positive results from various therapeutic progress indicators, such as negative urinalysis, decreased symptoms based on validated questionnaires, demonstrated skills during role-plays, and collateral reports of behavioral goal accomplishment.

In the last session, the TP queries family members to indicate how their personal strengths, particularly those addressed during therapy, may be utilized to maintain accomplishment of goals that were a focus in therapy. Thus, youth and their families are assisted in reviewing how treatment effects can be generalized to future endeavors. The session concludes with all family members communicating things they love, admire, and respect about each other. The emphasis on acquired skills is important because it reinforces self-efficacy in youth.

Goals for Intervention

➤ Identify family strengths that may be used to assist in generalizing treatment effects to future endeavors.

Materials Required

➤ Last Session: Concluding Treatment and Planning for Success Prompting Checklist (Exhibit 13.1)

Procedural Steps for Treatment Implementation

Initial Session

Reviewing Strengths (Youth and Adult Significant Others)   The first half of the last session involves the youth and adult significant others. As indicated in the Last Session: Concluding Treatment and Planning for Success Therapist Prompting Checklist (Exhibit 13.1), TPs initiate the session by instructing youth and their adult significant others to report how they will utilize their strengths and skills to assist the youth in avoiding drug and alcohol use, maintaining cohesive and functional family relationships, and personal achievement (e.g., employment, school graduation). For instance, youth may be asked, "What personal strengths and abilities will you use to help keep living a clean and healthy life?" Of course, TPs provide enthusiastic and descriptive praise for all positive responses and disallow statements that are consistent with self-deprecation, or statements that are consistent with potential future difficulties. It is, however, appropriate for TPs to solicit methods of managing potential obstacles. TPs may also implement FBT interventions and solicit discussion about methods of accomplishing future aspirations throughout the last session. The following dialogue shows a TP soliciting strengths during a final session.

TP: Well, what a great ride it's been, and I'm so proud of what this family has accomplished during the past few months. Today, we're going to go out talking about how your strengths are going to assist Sarah in maintaining her goals. Let's bring on the positive stuff. How are each of you going to use your strengths and abilities to keep Sarah living a clean and healthy life?

Mom: Well, I'm going to keep staying focused on letting her know how proud I am of her. I'm also going to continue to make good decisions in listening to her when she comes to me with problems and asks me for assistance. I love her so much and will never let anger get in the way of our relationship. I've learned the importance of appreciating her for who she is, and realize how important it is to set aside family time.

Sarah: Yeah, I think I'm most happy that my mom listens to me, and because she spends more time with me now we have good times together and have gotten very close. I don't ever want to hurt her again. Besides doing things together, I want to continue to use the Positive Request when I need things. I notice when this happens my mother is more patient and listens to what I have to say. Even when we disagree, she now throws out alternative things I can do.

TP: Fantastic! It sounds like you both respect each other quite a lot. Because your relationship is strong, it sounds like you are both being extra careful to keep each other happy. Sarah, how are you going to be able to use your skills to graduate high school? I'm particularly interested in knowing how your new social network can assist you in this goal.

The dialogue would continue with the TP's asking family members to indicate how newly acquired skills will be utilized. The following dialogue demonstrates a TP soliciting solutions to potential obstacles.

TP: I'm extremely impressed with the plans I'm hearing, and glad to learn you decided to work for your mom's boss, Sarah. How could you both work together to take advantage of this newly formed network?

Mom: I will be introducing her to people at work, and letting them know she's interested in selling houses later.

TP: That's wonderful, Mom. Sarah, you're so lucky to have her in your corner. What will you be able to do to show your assertiveness at work?

Sarah: I'm going to listen a lot at first. I'll learn a lot that way, and I'll practice complimenting people and showing my appreciation. Once people know me, I'll start asking around for greater responsibilities.

TP: What if people tell you that you're too young.

Sarah: I'll agree I have a lot to learn, but because I'm young I have a lot of positive energy, and can learn like a sponge! I will also be sure to point out my specific strengths and willingness to learn.

Family Exchange of Positive Remarks (All Family Members) When all strengths and obstacles are reviewed, usually after about 20 to 35 minutes, children in the family, if present, are invited into the room to participate. Without recording forms for the family, TPs instruct all family members to exchange things they love, admire, and respect about each other. Of course, this procedure is consistent with the guidelines established earlier when utilizing Reciprocity Awareness. However, the exercise is less formal, and the TP is involved in the role of an additional "family member." That is, family members are provided an opportunity to disclose things they appreciate about the TP. Similarly, the TP indicates things that are appreciated about each of the family members. The session usually ends with a group hug or other sign of affection.

TP: This is the last time you'll all be able to share things you appreciate about yourselves with me in the room so I thought I'd like to be part of the family this time if that's O.K.

Mom: I have something for you. I respect how you helped me get my daughter back. After my husband died, I wasn't sure if Sarah would ever listen to me again and you helped me realize how to be firm with consequences without being emotional. You also helped me to realize I could be flexible in my parenting, and she really responded well to that. So, thank you!

TP: Thank you. I really appreciate your saying that. It's those kinds of comments that keep me going. I also respect you for raising three daughters on your own, and working extra hours on the weekends to save money for them to get through college some day. Sarah, what did you have for your mom?

Concluding Remarks

The last session encourages family members to review the positive aspects of their efforts during the past few months, and assists them in looking to the future with optimism. The TP solicits positive affect, while emphasizing skill development. That is, when reviewing strengths and skills in family members, TPs provide descriptive praise. The review also assists family members in realizing the extent of their improvement, and competency in being able to manage potential obstacles. Indeed, the reviewed obstacles are typically identified during the previous treatment sessions, so family members are usually quite adept at generating viable solutions. It is also important to emphasize the importance of having the TP included in the exchange of positive remarks, as family members usually experience great joy in using this exercise to show their appreciation of the TP.

Exhibit 13.1. Last Session: Concluding Treatment and Planning for Success Prompting Checklist.

LAST SESSION: CONCLUDING TREATMENT AND PLANNING FOR SUCCESS

PROMPTING CHECKLIST

Youth ID:_____ Clinician: _____ Session #: _____ Session Date:_____

Materials Required

NA

Begin Time:_____

Reviewing Strengths (youth & adult sig. others)

Solicit/Provide strengths of family to assist youth in:
___a. having great family relationships.
___b. maintaining an effectively functioning family.
___c. personal achievement.
___d. other treatment goals.
     • Role-play FBT modules as needed if obstacles are reported.

Family Exchange of Positive Remarks (all family members)

___a. Instruct family in <u>exchanging what is appreciated </u>about each other, including therapist. Therapists exchange positive remarks w/ family, as well.

Youth's Assessment of Helpfulness of the Intervention

___a. After stating youth should not feel obligated to provide high scores, as an honest assessment helps better address youth needs, solicit how helpful youth thought intervention was using the following 7-point scale:
7 = extremely helpful, **6** = very helpful, **5** = somewhat helpful, **4** = not sure, **3** = somewhat unhelpful, **2** = very unhelpful, **1** = extremely unhelpful
     • **Record Youth's Rating Here:**_____
___b. Solicit how rating was derived and methods of improving intervention in future.

Therapist's Rating of Youth's Compliance with Intervention

___a. Disclose therapist's rating of youth's compliance using 7-point scale:
7 = extremely compliant, **6** = very compliant, **5** = somewhat compliant, **4** = neutral, **3** = somewhat noncompliant, **2** = very noncompliant, **1** = extremely noncompliant
     • Factors that contribute to compliance ratings are:
     • Attendance

- Participation and conduct in session
- Homework completion
- **Record Therapist's Rating of Youth's Compliance Here:_____**

___b. Disclose youth's compliance rating.

___c. Explain how rating was derived, and methods of improving performance in future.

End Time:_____   Notes:_____

References

Allen, D. N., Donohue, B., Sutton, G., Haderlie, M., & LaPota, H. (2009). Application of a standardized assessment methodology within the context of an evidence-based treatment for substance abuse and its associated problems. *Behavior Modification, 33*(5), 618–654.

Azrin, N. H., Acierno, R., Kogan, E. S., Donohue, B., Besalel, V., & McMahon, P. T. (1996). Follow-up results of supportive versus behavioral therapy for illicit drug use. *Behaviour Research and Therapy, 34,* 41–46.

Azrin, N. H., Donohue, B., Besalel, V. A., Kogan, E. S., & Acierno, R. (1994). Youth drug abuse treatment: A controlled outcome study. *Journal of Child & Adolescent Substance Abuse, 3*(3), 1–15.

Azrin, N. H., Donohue, B., Teichner, G., Crum, T., Howell, J., & DeCato, L. (2001). A controlled evaluation and description of individual-cognitive problem solving and family-behavioral therapies in conduct-disordered and substance dependent youth. *Journal of Child and Adolescent Substance Abuse, 11,* 1–43.

Azrin, N. H., Flores, T., & Kaplan, S. J. (1975). Job-finding club: A group-assisted program for obtaining employment. *Behavior Research & Therapy, 13,* 17–24.

Azrin, N. H., McMahon, P. T., Donohue, B., Besalel, V. A., Lapinski, K. J., Kogan, E. S., . . . Galloway, E. (1994). Behavior therapy for drug use: A controlled treatment outcome study. *Behavior Research and Therapy, 32*(8), 856–866.

Azrin, N. H., Philip, R. A., Thienes-Hontos, P., & Besalel, V. A. (1981). *Journal of Vocational Behavior, 18*(3), 253–254.

Azrin, N. H., Sisson, R. W., Meyers, R. J., & Godley, M. D. (1982). Alcoholism treatment by disulfiram and community reinforcement therapy. *Journal of Behavior Therapy and Experimental Psychiatry, 3*, 105–112.

Bartholomew, N. G., Joe, G. W., Rowan-Szal, G. A, & Simpson, D. D. (2007). Counselor assessments of training and adoption barriers. *Journal of Substance Abuse Treatment, 33*, 193–199.

Bender, K., Springer, D. W., & Kim, J. S. (2006). Treatment effectiveness with dually diagnosed adolescents: A systematic review. *Brief Treatment and Crisis Intervention, 6*(3), 177–205.

Bukstein, O. G., & Horner, M. S. (2010). Management of the adolescent with substance use disorders and comorbid psychopathology. *Child and Adolescent Psychiatric Clinics of North America, 19*, 609–623.

Burgard, J., Donohue, B., Azrin, N. H., & Teichner, G. (2000). Prevalence and treatment of substance abuse in the mentally retarded population: An empirical review. *Journal of Psychoactive Drugs, 32*, 293–298.

Carroll, K. M., & Onken, L. S. (2005). Behavioral therapies for drug abuse. *American Journal of Psychiatry, 162*, 1452–1460.

Carruth, A. K., Tate, U. S., Moffett, B. S., & Hill, K. (1997). Reciprocity, emotional well-being, and family functioning as determinants of family satisfaction in caregivers of elderly parents. *Nursing Research, 46*, 93–100.

Cautella, J. (1967). Covert sensitization. *Psychological Reports, 20*, 459–468.

DeCato, L., Donohue, B., Azrin, N. H., & Teichner, G. (2001). Satisfaction of conduct-disordered and substance abusing youth with their parents. *Behavior Modification, 25*, 44–61.

Del Boca, F. K., & Darkes, J. (2007). Enhancing the validity and utility of randomized clinical trials in addictions treatment research: I. Treatment implementation and research design. *Addiction, 102*, 1047–1056.

Dennis, M., Godley, S. H., Diamond, G., Tims, F. M., Babor, T., Donaldson, J., et al. (2004). The Cannabis Youth Treatment (CYT) study: Main findings from two randomized trials. *Journal of Substance Abuse, 27*(3), 197–213.

D'Zurilla, T. J., & Goldfried, M. R. (1971). Problem-solving and behavior modification. *Journal of Abnormal Psychology, 78*, 107–126.

Donohue, B., & Allen, D. A. (2011). *Treating adult substance abuse using Family Behavior Therapy: A step-by-step approach.* Hoboken, NJ: Wiley.

Donohue, B., Allen, D. N., Romero, V., Hill, H. H., Vasaeli, K., LaPota, H., et al. (2009). Description of a standardized treatment center that utilizes evidence-based clinic operations to facilitate implementation of an evidence-based treatment. *Behavior Modification, 33,* 411–436.

Donohue, B., Azrin, N. H., Lawson, H., Friedlander, J., Teichner, G., & Rindsberg, J. (1998). Improving initial session attendance of substance abuse and conduct disordered adolescents: A controlled study. *Journal of Child and Adolescent Substance Abuse, 8,* 1–13.

Donohue, B., Decato, L., Azrin, N. H., & Teichner, G. (2001). Satisfaction of parents with their substance abusing and conduct-disordered youth. *Behavior Modification, 25,* 21–43.

Donohue, B., Romero, V., Herdzik, K., LaPota, H., Abdel Al, R., Allen, D. N., et al. (2010). Concurrent treatment of substance abuse, child neglect, bipolar disorder, post-traumatic stress disorder, and domestic violence: A case examination involving family behavior therapy. *Clinical Case Studies, 9,* 106–124.

Donohue, B., Teichner, G., Azrin, N. H., Silver, N., Weintraub, N., Crum, T. A., & Decato, L. (2003). The initial reliability and validity of the Life Satisfaction Scale for Problem Youth in a sample of drug abusing and conduct disordered youth. *Journal of Child and Family Studies, 12,* 453–464.

Donohue, B., & Van Hasselt, V. B. (1999). Development of an ecobehavioral treatment program for child maltreatment. *Behavioral Interventions, 14,* 55–82.

Dutra, L., Stathopoulou, G., Basden, S. L., Leyro, T. M., Powers, M. B., & Otto, M. W. (2008). A meta-analytic review of psychosocial interventions for substance use disorders. *American Journal of Psychiatry, 165,* 179–187.

Forehand, R., & McMahon, R. J. (1981). Helping the noncompliant child: A clinician's guide to effective parent training. New York, NY: Guilford.

Godley, S. H., Garner, B., Smith, J. E., Meyers, R. J., & Godley, M. D. (2011). A large-scale dissemination and implementation model for evidence-based treatment and continuing care. *Clinical Psychology: Science and Practice, 18*(1), 67–83.

Godley, M. D., Godley, S. H., Dennis, M. L., Funk, R. R., & Passetti, L. L. (2007). The effect of assertive continuing care on continuing care linkage, adherence and abstinence following residential treatment for adolescents with substance use disorders. *Addiction, 102,* 81–93.

Higgins, S. T., Delaney, D. D., Budney, A. J., Bickel, W. K., Hughes, J. R., Foerg, F., & Fenwick, J. W. (1991). A behavioral approach to achieving initial cocaine abstinence. *American Journal of Psychiatry, 148,* 1218–1224.

Hoffman, J. P., Dufur, M., & Huang, L. (2007). Drug use and job quits: A longitudinal analysis. *Journal of Drug Issues, 37,* 569–596.

Hunt, G. M., & Azrin, N. H. (1973). A community reinforcement approach to alcoholism. *Behavior Research and Therapy, 13,* 1115–1123.

Macgowan, M. J., & Engle, B. (2010). Evidence for optimism: Behavior therapies and motivational interviewing in adolescent substance abuse treatment. *Child and Adolescent Psychiatric Clinics of North America, 19,* 527–545.

Madson, M. B., Campbell, T. C., Barrett, D. E., Brondino, M. J., & Melchert, T. P. (2005). Development of the Motivational Interviewing Supervision and Training Scale. *Psychology of Addictive Behaviors, 19,* 303–310.

Marlatt, G. A., & Gordon, J. R. (1985). *Relapse prevention: Maintenance strategies in the treatment of addictive behaviors.* New York, NY: Guilford Press.

Meyers, R. J., Miller, W. R., Smith, J. E., & Tonigan, J. S. (2002). A randomized trial of two methods for engaging treatment-refusing drug users through concerned significant others. *Journal of Consulting and Clinical Psychology, 70*(5), 1182–1185.

Miller, W. R. (1983). Motivational interviewing with problem drinkers. *Behavioural Psychotherapy, 11,* 147–172.

Miller, W. R., Meyers, R. J., & Tonigan, J. S. (1999). Engaging the unmotivated in treatment for alcohol problems: A comparison of three intervention strategies. *Journal of Consulting and Clinical Psychology, 67*(5), 688–697.

Morgan, M. M., & Sprenkle, D. H. (2007). Toward a common-factors approach to supervision. *Journal of Marital and Family Therapy, 33*(1), 1–17.

Moyer, A., Finney, J. W., & Swearingen, C. E. (2002). Methodological characteristics of quality of alcohol treatment outcome studies, 1970–98: An expanded evaluation. *Addiction, 97,* 253–263.

National Institute on Drug Abuse, National Institutes of Health. (1998, April). *Principles of drug addiction treatment: A research based guide* (Publication No. 99–4180). Retrieved August 25, 2008, from NIDA NIH Reports Online via: www.nida.nih.gov/PDF/PODAT/PODAT.pdf

National Institutes of Alcoholism and Alcohol Abuse. (2005). Adolescents and treatment of Alcohol Use Disorders. In *NIAAA: Social work education for the prevention and treatment of alcohol use disorders* (Module 10A). Retrieved December 27, 2008, from http://pubs.niaaa.nih.gov/publications/Social/Module10AAdolescents/Module10A.html

National Registry of Evidence-Based Programs and Practices (2008, June). *Anonymous reviews.* Retrieved July 14, 2008, from www.nrepp.samhsa.gov/

Patterson, G. R., Reid, J. B., Jones, R. R., & Conger, R. E. (1975). *A social learning approach to family intervention: Families with aggressive children* (Vol. 1). Eugene, OR: Castalia.

Power, T. J., Blom-Hoffman, J., Clarke, A. T., Riley-Tillman, T. C., Kelleher, C., & Manz, P. H. (2005). Reconceptualizing intervention integrity: A partnership-based framework for linking research with practice. *Psychology in the Schools, 42*(5), 495–507.

Romero, V., Donohue, B., & Allen, D. N., (2010). Treatment of concurrent substance dependence, child neglect and domestic violence: A single case examination involving family behavior therapy. *Journal of Family Violence, 25*(3), 287–295.

Romero, V., Donohue, B., Hill, H. H., Gorney, S., Van Hasselt, V., & Allen, D. N. (2010). Family Behavior Therapy for use in child welfare: Results of a case study involving an abused woman formally diagnosed with alcohol dependence, bipolar disorder, and several anxiety disorders. *Clinical Case Studies, 9,* 353–368.

Rowan-Szal, G. A., Greener, J. M., Joe, G. W., & Simpson, D. D. (2007). Assessing program needs and planning change. *Journal of Substance Abuse Treatment, 33,* 121–129.

Sheidow, A. J., Donohue, B., Hill, H. H., Henggeler, S. W., & Ford, J. D. (2008). Development of an audio-tape review system for supporting adherence to an evidence-based practice. *Professional Psychology Research & Practice, 39,* 553–560.

Sisson, R. W., & Azrin, N. H. (1989). The community reinforcement approach. In R. K. Reid & W. R. Miller (Eds.), *Handbook of alcoholism treatment approaches: Effective alternatives* (pp. 242–258). Elmsford, NY: Pergamon Press.

Slesnick, N., Prestopnik, J. L., Meyers, R. J., & Glassman, M. (2007). Treatment outcome for homeless, street-living youth. *Addictive Behaviors, 32,* 1237–1251.

Smith, J. E., & Meyers, R. J. (2004). *Motivating substance abusers to enter treatment: Working with family members.* New York, NY: Guilford Press.

Stuart, R. B. (1969). Operant-interpersonal treatment of marital discord. *Journal of Consulting and Clinical Psychology, 33,* 675–682.

About the Authors

Brad Donohue is a licensed clinical psychologist and professor in the Department of Psychology at the University of Nevada, Las Vegas (UNLV). He directs UNLV's Family Research and Services program, which is focused on development, evaluation, and dissemination/training of family-assisted assessment methods and behavioral intervention protocols targeting goal achievement. He is currently coeditor of the *Journal of Child & Adolescent Substance Abuse*, and editorial board member for seven other scientific journals. He has directed research projects funded by the National Institute on Drug Abuse, Substance Abuse and Mental Health Services Administration, and National Institute of Mental Health. He has published more than 120 scientific manuscripts, primarily in the areas of substance abuse, conduct disorders, child maltreatment, and mental health disorders affecting athletes. He is one of the developers of the Family Behavior Therapy that is reviewed in this book, as well as other evidence-based protocols. He has co-authored five books, including *Treatment of Adult Substance Abuse Using Family Behavior Therapy: A Step-by-Step Approach*. Dr. Donohue has received awards for his research, including UNLV's Outstanding Faculty Award, Student Focused Award, Barrick Scholar Award, Western Psychological Association's Research Award, and Winn Dixie's Good Citizen Award.

Nathan H. Azrin recently retired from Nova Southeastern University's Center for Psychological Studies where he was professor for 30 years. He received his PhD from Harvard University in 1956, where he worked with B. F. Skinner to establish principles underlying reinforcement and punishment in laboratory experiments. Considered a pioneer in the application of behavior therapy to humans, his scientific work includes development of the Community Reinforcement Approach for alcoholism, Family Behavior Therapy for substance abuse and conduct disorder, the Token Economy for behavior problems, Reciprocity Counseling for marital discord, Regulated Breathing for stuttering, and Habit Reversal for Tourette's disorder. He has published approximately 200 scientific manuscripts in peer-reviewed journals and 10 books, including *The Token Economy: A Motivational System for Therapy and Rehabilitation*, and best-selling *Toilet Training in Less Than a Day*. Dr. Azrin was editor or editorial board member for 17 scientific journals, including the *Journal of Applied Behavior Analysis*, which he founded. He has received numerous awards from psychology organizations, including the Distinguished Contributions for Applications to Psychology Award from the American Psychological Association (APA), the Edgar Doll Award for Outstanding Contributions to Intellectual and Developmental Disabilities from APA's Division 33, the Outstanding Contributions to Applied Behavior Analysis Award from APA's Division 25, the Raymond Cattell Award for Scientific Applications of Psychology from the American Psychological Society (APS), the Impact for Science Award from the Association for Behavioral Analysis (ABA), and the Lifetime Achievement Award from the Association for Behavioral and Cognitive Therapies (ABCT). He has been recognized by *American Psychologist* as one of the top-cited psychologists in the world.

Author Index

Subject Index

About the CD-ROM

Introduction

This appendix provides you with information on the contents of the CD that accompanies this book. For the latest information, please refer to the ReadMe file located at the root of the CD.

System Requirements

➤ A computer with a processor running at 120 Mhz or faster

➤ At least 32 MB of total RAM installed on your computer; for best performance, we recommend at least 64 MB

➤ A CD-ROM drive

Using the CD With Windows

To install the items from the CD to your hard drive, follow these steps:

1. Insert the CD into your computer's CD-ROM drive. The license agreement appears (for Windows 7, select Start.exe from the AutoPlay window or follow the same steps for Windows Vista).

   The interface won't launch if you have autorun disabled. In that case, click Start➤Run (for Windows Vista and Windows 7, click Start➤All Programs➤Accessories➤Run). In the dialog box that appears, type D:\Start.exe. (Replace D with the proper letter if your CD drive uses a different letter. If you don't know the letter of your CD drive, see how it is listed under My Computer.) Click OK.

2. Read through the license agreement, and then click the Accept button if you want to use the CD.

3. The CD interface displays. Select the lesson video you want to view.

Using the CD With Macintosh

To install the items from the CD to your hard drive, follow these steps:

1. Insert the CD into your computer's CD-ROM drive.

2. The CD icon will appear on your desktop; double-click to open.

3. Double-click the Start button.

4. Read the license agreement and click the Accept button to use the CD.

5. The CD interface will appear. Here you can install the programs and run the demos.

What's on the CD

The following sections provide a summary of the software and other materials you'll find on the CD.

Content

Any material from the book, including forms, slides, and lesson plans if available, are in the folder named "Content."

This companion CD-Rom contains worksheets, handouts, and checklists intended to provide resources for practitioners and clients within therapy sessions. These practical materials will help practitioners throughout the therapeutic process: from organizing a client's file to treatment checklists, implementing strategies, and client assignments. Included on the CD-Rom in an easy-to-use and reproducible format, these worksheets are organized to correspond to the book's chapters and follow the evolution of the FBT treatment process. Some of the forms are intended to assist in the maintenance of client record keeping procedures. Therefore, it is recommended that appropriate administrative staff review and potentially customize these forms to be consistent with the agency's culture and relevant state and federal laws, if applicable.

Applications

The following applications are on the CD:

OpenOffice.org OpenOffice.org is a free multi-platform office productivity suite. It is similar to Microsoft Office or Lotus SmartSuite, but OpenOffice.org is absolutely free. It includes word processing, spreadsheet, presentation, and drawing applications that enable you to create professional documents, newsletters, reports, and presentations. It supports most file formats of other office software. You should be able to edit and view any files created with other office solutions.

Notes *Shareware programs* are fully functional, trial versions of copyrighted programs. If you like particular programs, register with their authors for a nominal fee and receive licenses, enhanced versions, and technical support.

Freeware programs are copyrighted games, applications, and utilities that are free for personal use. Unlike shareware, these programs do not require a fee or provide technical support.

GNU software is governed by its own license, which is included inside the folder of the GNU product. See the GNU license for more details.

Trial, demo, or evaluation versions are usually limited either by time or functionality (such as being unable to save projects). Some trial versions are very sensitive to system date changes. If you alter your computer's date, the programs will "time out" and no longer be functional.

Customer Care If you have trouble with the CD-ROM, please call the Wiley Product Technical Support phone number at (800) 762-2974. Outside the United States, call 1(317) 572-3994. You can also contact Wiley Product Technical Support at http://support.wiley.com. John Wiley & Sons will provide technical support only for installation and other general quality control items. For technical support on the applications themselves, consult the program's vendor or author.

To place additional orders or to request information about other Wiley products, please call (877) 762-2974.